ASSOCIATION FOR SCOTTISH LITERATURE

NUMBER FIFTY-ONE

JACOBEAN
PARNASSUS

Scottish Poetry from the Reign of James I

*

The ASSOCIATION FOR SCOTTISH LITERATURE aims to promote the study, teaching and writing of Scottish literature, and to further the study of the languages of Scotland.

To these ends, ASL publishes works of Scottish literature (of which this volume is an example); literary criticism and in-depth reviews of Scottish books in *Scottish Literary Review*; and scholarly studies of language in *Scottish Language*. It also publishes *New Writing Scotland*, an annual anthology of new poetry, drama and short fiction, in Scots, English and Gaelic. ASL has also prepared a range of teaching materials covering Scottish language and literature for use in schools.

All the above publications are available as a single 'package' in return for an annual subscription. Enquiries should be sent to:

ASL, Scottish Literature, 7 University Gardens, University of Glasgow, Glasgow G12 8QH. Telephone +44 (0)141 330 5309 or visit our website at **www.asls.org.uk**.

ASSOCIATION FOR SCOTTISH LITERATURE

NUMBER FIFTY-ONE

JACOBEAN PARNASSUS

SCOTTISH POETRY FROM THE REIGN OF JAMES I

Edited by Alasdair A. MacDonald

GLASGOW

2022

Published in Great Britain, 2022
by the Association for Scottish Literature
Scottish Literature
University of Glasgow
7 University Gardens
Glasgow G12 8QH

ASL is a registered charity no. SC006535
www.asls.org.uk

ISBN: 978-1-906841-45-4

A catalogue record for this book
is available from the British Library.

Set in Minion Pro

Typeset by ASL, Glasgow
Printed and bound by Bell & Bain Ltd, Glasgow

CONTENTS

ACKNOWLEDGEMENTS

I am grateful to the Publications Committee of the Association for Scottish Literature for accepting the present volume, thereby creating the opportunity to bring a highly interesting but unfamiliar corpus of early modern Scottish poetry to the attention of a wide readership. I am deeply obliged to the expert reader of the files as at first submitted, and for many valuable suggestions and corrections. Duncan Jones, the ASL Director, gave much useful practical advice, and Mark Blackadder designed the attractive book-cover.

Essential and efficient assistance was given by the following institutions: Edinburgh, National Library of Scotland; Edinburgh, University Library; Glasgow, University Library; Groningen, University Library; San Marino, Henry Huntington Library. The Council of the Scottish Text Society kindly granted permission to re-edit five poems by Ayton from the edition by Charles B. Gullans (1963).

On certain points of detail I have benefited from advice given by the following friends and colleagues: Professor Wout van Bekkum; Mr Ian Cunningham; Professor Jane Dawson; Dr John Flood; Dr Theo van Heijnsbergen; Professor Michael Lynch; Professor David Parkinson; Dr Jamie Reid-Baxter. Errors are solely attributable to the editor.

Edinburgh, 31 March 2021.

ABBREVIATIONS

BL	British Library
CUL	Cambridge University Library
EEBO	Early English Books Online
ES	*English Studies*
DSL	*Dictionary of the Scots Language*
EUL	Edinburgh University Library
Fasti	*Fasti Ecclesiæ Scoticanæ*, ed. Hew Scott, 11 vols. (Edinburgh, 1915–)
IR	*Innes Review*
JEBS	*Journal of the Edinburgh Bibliographical Society*
JNR	*Journal of the Northern Renaissance* [online]
MLR	*Modern Language Review*
NLS	National Library of Scotland
ODNB	*Oxford Dictionary of National Biography* [online]
OED	*Oxford English Dictionary* [online]
SHR	*Scottish Historical Review*
SLJ	*Scottish Literary Journal*
STS	Scottish Text Society

ABOUT THIS ANTHOLOGY

This anthology aims to promote awareness of a neglected corpus of early modern Scottish poetry. The present selection of texts demonstrates that the poetry of the first quarter of the seventeenth century comprises a rich and vigorous literary culture and is by no means the pale derivative that has often been alleged. A subsidiary aim is to show that this body of writing, despite its preference for the use of the English language, constitutes a genuine and worthy achievement within the history of Scottish literature. Poems by a few reasonably well-known figures (e.g. William Drummond, Sir Robert Ayton) are included, but most of the authors featured are probably unfamiliar.

The volume is conceived as a reader-friendly selection from the work of a constellation of poetic contemporaries. After the general introduction, the poems are allowed to speak for themselves. For efficiency of cross-referencing, poets are identified by codes formed of the initials of their names, and specific poems by the numbers following such codes, with a forward slash preceding any line-numbers. Where difficult words occur, on-page lexical glosses are provided; where explanatory information is required, that is provided in the separate section of notes. The latter also include any marginal annotations made by the poets themselves, and are reproduced between the symbols † and †. The poems have been chosen on the basis of several criteria: their literary quality, their representation of the work of the individual authors, their illustration of particular genres, and their relevance to social, cultural and historical issues. Each poet is introduced with a concise sketch giving details and dates of their life and writing. Poems are given complete, the only exceptions consisting of passages extracted from long works by Patrick Gordon and William Mure. In most cases, the copy-texts have been seventeenth-century prints, inspected either directly or via photographs; only in a few cases were manuscripts involved. Five poems by Ayton (RAY1–5) have been edited from Gullans (1963), with the kind permission of the Scottish Text Society.

Early modern texts in their original and raw state (even as printed) can present real challenges for the modern reader: facsimile reproduction would therefore have been inappropriate, and the style of editing adopted has rather aimed at facilitating access to the texts. Punctuation, capitalisation and italicisation have been adjusted to modern norms. Obvious errors in the texts of the early printers are silently corrected, but emendations (signalled by asterisks) are recorded in the notes. Printers' ornaments are disregarded, as are differences in letter-forms, with obsolete letters replaced by their modern equivalents. Inverted letters are silently corrected, as are letters in the wrong sequence. Necessary but missing letters are supplied in square brackets, and standard abbreviations (often involving superscript letters) are expanded. Numbering of stanzas, which is occasionally found, has been replaced by numbering of lines. The word 'Finis' at the end of some poems has been omitted. The letters i/j and u/v/w/uu/vv are rendered as appropriate, with i/u normally for vowels and j/v/w for consonants. Abstract nouns are capitalised where personification may have been intended. In a few cases, the hyphens which, following the fashion of the age, sometimes link strings of adjectives and nouns, have been reduced in the interest of clarity. The use of the apostrophe as a marker of omitted letters is retained, but where possession is at issue the apostrophe has been adjusted to follow modern practice (for both singular and plural nouns). Poem-titles in square brackets are, unless otherwise noted, supplied by the editor.

The spelling of the original texts has, however, not been modernised, and it is hoped that the edition steers an acceptable compromise course between respect for the original texts and respect for the modern reader. The poems present few difficulties of comprehension, although two features very common in older Scots usage deserve notice: (a) absence of the relative pronoun in adjectival clauses – e.g. 'This is the right \which\ inricheth his renowne' (sG2/125); 'You \who\ all the world with tragike volumes fill' (sG2/129); (b) present-tense verb-endings with -s, in combination with plural subjects – e.g. 'The Muses scarse in circuit is sat downe, / When laureat troopes comes kneeling mee before' (sG2/7–8). If these points are borne in mind, much that at first sight may seem crooked will be made straight.

INTRODUCTION: STEPS TO PARNASSUS

Not only in the affairs of men do tides operate, but also in the affairs of literary history and criticism. The poets sampled in the present volume have suffered greatly from such contingency, though they deserve rather to be appreciated for the high quality and interest of their writings and for their innovative and collective contribution within the larger history of Scottish literature.

While the poetry produced in Scotland under James VI has been well studied (e.g. Shire 1969; Jack 1988; Dunnigan 2002; Lyall 2005), that which was composed in Scotland after the Union of the Crowns, under the King's newly acquired identity as James I of England, Ireland and (in nostalgic fantasy) France has mostly been neglected (valuable exceptions being Jack 1972; Spiller 1988; Parkinson 2013). In fact, neglect might be said to have been the lot of most Scottish poetry written in the seventeenth century, a period which, despite its enormous historical, political, religious and constitutional interest, has long been regarded as a cultural no-man's-land, lying indeterminately between the work of the medieval *makaris* and the renewal of Scots vernacular literature in the eighteenth century. Kurt Wittig, in the structural organisation of his influential book, *The Scottish Tradition in Literature* (1958), invoked the tidal imagery of ebb and flow: unfortunately, between as it were two periods of cultural high-water, little trace of the seventeenth century was left, beyond some faint ripples in the drying sand. Since Wittig, not much has changed, and the latest multi-volume history of Scottish literature passes over the century with barely a mention (Brown et al. 2007).

This curious state of affairs is the result of a combination of factors, of which the practical difficulty of accessing texts is the most straightforward. The works of William Drummond of Hawthornden, Sir Robert Ayton, Sir William Alexander and Sir William Mure have, it is true, been edited for the Scottish Text Society, but in limited print-runs prepared by, and principally for, scholar-specialists. In the nineteenth century the poetry of Alexander Craig of Rosecraig and a few of his contemporaries was edited by the indefatigable David Laing, but in publications that, until very recently, have been even harder to locate. The consequence is that the poetry of seventeenth-century Scotland remains to a large extent unexplored, whereas – ironically – many medieval works have in the meantime acquired canonical status in the received account of Scottish literature.

Happily, photocopying and digitisation are now able to remedy the situation by facilitating access to the originals. In particular, the Early English Books Online database has opened the door to a huge number of early printed publications, irrespective of where the rare surviving copies may physically be preserved. The advantages are obvious and great, and are readily illustrated. For example, in 1890 the authors of what is still the standard history of early printing in Scotland were unable to locate the works of James Cockburne, even though fifty years earlier these had been known to Thomas McCrie (Dickson and Edmond 1890: 503; McCrie 1856: 394): these 'lost' poems are again available, and specimens figure in the present anthology. Likewise, a distinguished critic was once puzzled by a poet named simply 'Gordon', who at that point was no more than a known unknown (Shire 1969: 229). Today Patrick Gordon, whose major works were printed (1615) not in Scotland but at Dort (Dordrecht) in the Netherlands, can be brought in from the cold, revealing *inter alia* his fascinating presentation of King Robert the Bruce and the Battle of Bannockburn – iconic topics, memorably treated by the fourteenth-century proto-poet of Older Scots, John Barbour. Students of the literature of the seventeenth century now have at their disposal a number of first-ever text-editions (Reid-Baxter 2010; Flood 2014; MacDonald 2018), in addition to several important literary and analytical studies by historically-minded critics (Spiller 1988; Parkinson, ed. 2013; Verweij 2016). The time has therefore come for the investigation of what is actually an extensive corpus of interesting early modern texts.

Another rediscovered area of Scottish literary culture is that of writing in non-native languages. A selection (with translations) of neo-Latin poems pertaining to the pre-1603 reign of King James has recently been published, though the remarkable quantity and quality of the Latin verse produced in Scotland between the mid-sixteenth and the mid-seventeenth centuries would have justified the filling of several further volumes (Reid and McOmish 2017; Petrina and Johnson 2018; Reid and McOmish 2020). The present anthology contains only vernacular poetry, but some of the authors included (e.g. Ayton, Quin, Gordon) also composed verses in Latin. When James made his return visit to his kingdom in 1617, he was welcomed wherever he went with propines of verses in Latin and Greek. These were quickly collected and printed as *Nostodia in serenissimi, potentissimi, et invictissimi monarchae, Jacobi* [etc.] [Poems of return, to the most serene, mighty and unconquered monarch, James]. The collection was reissued the following year under the title of *The Muses' Welcome*, with the addition of several works in English by Alexander Craig, William Drummond and William Mure (Green 2017; Stevenson 2013). However, the Classical and native tongues were not the only languages cultivated at that time: William Drummond composed verse in English, Latin and French; Walter Quin did likewise, with the addition of Italian; and David Echlin, physician to Queens Anne of Denmark and Henrietta Maria, published two whole volumes of poetry in French (1627, 1628). Books in Latin, Greek, French, Italian and English were all present in the personal libraries of both William Drummond and George Lauder, and beside those languages Drummond also read in Spanish and Hebrew, and Lauder in Dutch. Such literary and linguistic proficiency might today seem remarkable, but it was typical of the Renaissance, and in this respect Scotland marched perfectly in step with other countries of western Europe (MacDonald 2014).

Since those days, however, patterns of culture have changed, in Scotland as elsewhere. Literary fashions once dominant or important have long ago vanished (e.g. Petrarchism, Platonism). Ancient pastoral and its Renaissance imitation (cf. Sir Philip Sidney's *Arcadia*) can now for many readers seem unattractively modish and artificial. The large-scale abandonment of the Classical languages in public education has turned what was formerly a routine dimension of European culture into *terra incognita*, and allusions to Ancient history and mythology, once effortlessly understood, have been reduced to riddles requiring elucidation. Moreover, Christian content in literature is today at a discount, and the very art of rhetoric is regarded with diffidence.

In addition to such general trends, a number of more particular sociolog-
ical, political, religious and linguistic factors have conspired to impede the
appreciation of much of the literature of early modern Scotland. Presbyterians
have often been wary of anything emanating from Episcopalian or Catholic
writers. The memory of persecuted Covenanters may still colour reactions
to any literature imbued with Stuart royalism. The widespread espousal –
beginning with the vernacular Scots poetry of the eighteenth century – of
an aesthetic privileging the native, the natural and the demotic can hinder
sympathy for the cosmopolitan and elitist styles cultivated by the *literati* of
the seventeenth century. Perhaps most importantly, the increasing assimila-
tion of Scottish to English literary manners, and the concomitant cultivation
of the English language, have been regarded as unpatriotic developments
(Henderson 1898: 387; Wittig 1958: 129). A measure of such changes in taste
is the striking decline in the reputation of William Drummond. David
Masson's Victorian biography (1873) marked the apogee in the fame of this
greatest poet of seventeenth-century Scotland, but thereafter Drummond's
star dipped as that of Lallans rose. Happily, there are some signs that the
scales of critical consensus may once again be coming into better balance
(MacDonald 1976; Kerrigan 2008: 141–68), though there is perhaps now the
risk that Drummond may be supposed to be the only Scottish poet of interest
and merit in the period.

The common critical opinion which developed in the twentieth century
as a result of such factors, and which has been characteristically negative,
is unfortunate and to a large extent misguided. First of all, it is scarcely fair
that the use of English on the part of early modern Scottish poets should be
singled out for disparagement, seeing that the Kirk was ready and willing
to accept English as its official language. In any event, English and Scots, as
languages descending from closely related varieties of Anglo-Saxon, were
in large measure mutually comprehensible. Moreover, as the poetry in the
present anthology shows, the Scoto-British poets who tried their best to write
in English often found that features of their native Scots proved resistant
to eradication. Modern egalitarian unease – to the extent that it may exist –
at a 'mob of gentlemen that wrote with ease' can only seem incongruous,
given the simultaneous approbation of the works of aristocrat-poets of the
Middle Ages (e.g. King James I, Walter Kennedy, Gavin Douglas), to say
nothing of the literary moths that fluttered round the royal candles (e.g.

William Dunbar, William Stewart, Sir David Lyndsay, Alexander Scott, Patrick Hume of Polwarth, Alexander Montgomerie). Several shibboleths, clearly, are ripe for reconsideration.

Although some may suppose that the departure of James VI to London in 1603 left Scotland as a kind of cultural desert (cf. Henderson 1898: 386–87), the reality as far as poetry is concerned is otherwise. Not every poet moved south in the King's wake, and those who did were quite likely to return. The King's relocation was regretted, but that did not mean that those who held fast to the idea of a royal head of state were deprived of subject-matter, since events at the London Court were keenly followed. The passing of Queen Elizabeth was discussed; James was appropriately greeted on arriving in his new capital; his escape from the Gunpowder Plot was mentioned with relief; the marriage of his daughter Elizabeth to the Elector Palatine was enthusiastically celebrated; and the deaths of Prince Henry, of Anne of Denmark, and eventually of James himself, were suitably lamented. The latter's 1617 return visit to Scotland in fact gave rise to a veritable outpouring of poetry, in which pæans of joy went not untempered with practical and realistic advice. Indeed, the Jacobean poets, though royalist, maintained a healthy independence of viewpoint, and mere proximity to power was never sufficient to compel political and moral assent. Such an attitude of reserve is apparent, for example, in the neo-Stoic sonnet of Sir Robert Kerr, composed, according to the author, in the royal Bedchamber itself (RK2).

There were also poets who avoided the contaminations of the Court and its ways. Before 1600, Alexander Hume had forsworn the secular verse of his youth (none of which survives) and had become the minister of the parish of Logie, north of Stirling (Lawson 1902). Like-minded figures are John Dykes, his brother-in-law James Melville, and Francis Hamilton of Silvertonhill (Reid-Baxter 2005, 2012, 2013). The deeply pious Elizabeth Melville, herself the daughter of a courtier and the first female Scottish poet to see her verse in print, was a friend of Hume's and also kept aloof from Court culture, though she composed religious *contrafacta* on the basis of the secular songs popular among the high and mighty (Reid-Baxter 2013; 2017). Alexander Gardyne was another who expressed regret at having written profane verses (AG9). On the other hand, Sir William Mure, whose reputation is that of a serious and solemn poet in the reign of Charles I, commenced under James by penning amatory lyrics (Tough 1898). The speech which he puts into the mouth of the Carthaginian Queen Dido (WM3) is vibrant with erotic passion – though that youthful effusion did not appear in the very public medium of print (Brammall 2015: 110).

For yet other poets, the anticipated blaze of royal favour could turn out to be the light that failed. Simion Grahame, after experiencing unspecified early disappointments, seems to have set his hopes on compensatory patronage. He dedicated his first printed collection to the King (London, 1604), in a volume distinguished visually on each page by elaborate ornamental framing round the text of the poems. Alas, Grahame's expectations seem not to have been realised and the enlarged reissue (Edinburgh, 1609) was instead, and with more modest visual decoration, offered to the perhaps more tractable John Graham, 4th earl of Montrose. In the process, the original prose dedication and a complimentary poem to King James were suppressed, and a new poem containing a virulent attack on the ways of the Court was introduced (SG8).

King James and William Fowler, who wrote by far the greater part of their poetry before 1600, are on that very account not represented in the present volume; on the other hand, some poets who are included (e.g. Ayton, Craig, Murray) can be presumed to have been active before 1600, though the texts may not have survived. The present selection restricts its purview to the new century, while recognising that in the area of culture no absolute dividing-line can be drawn at any single year, and that a degree of continuity is inevitable. Personal and family relationships, after all, establish connections through time. William Drummond was the nephew of William Fowler, who, an important literary figure in the circle around James at Edinburgh, became secretary (1589) to Anne of Denmark, and, in London after 1603, addressed poems to Arabella Stuart, James's cousin. For his part, Sir William Mure was proud to be the nephew of Alexander Montgomerie (d. 1598), memorialised by the King as the 'master poet'. Moreover, a classmate of George Lauder's at Edinburgh University was the son and nephew respectively of the poet-brothers Patrick and Alexander Hume (MacDonald 2018: 30).

A different kind of cultural bridge is furnished by the large anthologies of poetry first assembled within the Edinburgh households of legal professionals of the sixteenth century. In such collections was preserved most of the lyric poetry known from medieval and Renaissance Scotland (van Heijnsbergen

1994; MacDonald 2003; Bawcutt 2005). As a result of career-promotions and advantageous marriages, the descendants of those legal professionals not infrequently attained to yet higher status in society, as members of the Jacobean and Caroline gentry. In their libraries, the pages of their ancestors' manuscripts continued to be turned, and in this way acquaintance with older literary styles, genres and traditions was transmitted to the later age (MacDonald 2018: 107). Printed books could have a similar effect. Gavin Douglas's *Eneados* was, from the 1553 London edition, commended by David Hume of Godscroft in his history (Edinburgh, 1644) of the House of Angus (Bawcutt 2019: 77). Alexander Montgomerie's *The Cherrie and the Slae* (printed 1597) had been a significant work at the Edinburgh Court, where a specimen stanza was quoted by the King in his 1584 *Reulis and Cautelis* (Craigie 1955–58: I, 82; Parkinson 2000: I, 176–274; Shire 1969: 117–38; Lyall 2005: 107–12). That stanza-form reappears in Patrick Hannay's *Philomena* (1622), though it is unclear whether the choice was motivated purely by the intrinsic merits of Montgomerie's masterpiece, or partly also by the prestige deriving from the royal endorsement. In any event, *The Cherrie and the Slae* remained popular into the new century, and was reprinted in 1636, 1645 and 1668. After the year 1625, as before 1600, no sharp cultural cæsura can be drawn, and several Jacobean poets (e.g. Craig, Drummond, Gardyne, Lauder, Lithgow, Mure) continued active in the reign of the successor monarch.

Despite the prolonged absence of the monarch from Scotland after 1603, there occurred – at least in the first third of the century – no hiatus or diminution in the practice of poetry north of the Border: *pace* Wittig, Scotland had actually never seen such a swelling flood-tide of literary production. The Scottish Jacobeans, moreover, had a strong sense of belonging to a textual community (for this term see Verweij 2016: 12–19), and evidence thereof can be found in the eulogistic and liminary verses with which they introduced the volumes of their fellows. Several poets touch on the topic of the relation of matter to art (e.g. Cockburne, JC2; Craig, AC1; Gardyne, AG1, AG9), and although this is to some extent a traditional expression of modesty – for example, leading Sir Robert Kerr, in a tone of superior irony, to deprecate his own sonnet (RK2) as 'this starved rhime' – it also presupposes an appreciable degree of literary self-awareness.

❧

In earlier days, poems had mostly been published by being copied out and circulated in manuscript, a procedure which catered sufficiently well for smallish numbers of readers, many of whom would have known the original authors in person: in the compact burghs of Edinburgh and the neighbouring Canongate many such potential readers lived close to the royal or law courts, where lay their common social or professional connections. After the turn of the century, however, and although the copying and circulating of manuscripts did not cease (cf. the poems of Ayton and Kerr), publication of verse became increasingly an affair of print culture. For most of the poems in the present anthology no anterior manuscript versions exist. In the new dispensation, the location and nature of the receiving audience would perforce have been less predictable, although the size of that audience would without doubt be greater than that of the family and coterie groups of the previous century. After James's removal to London, the possibility of physical access to the ruler was greatly reduced and therefore could no longer be so significant an inspiration. Many poems ostensibly addressing the King must therefore in reality have been mainly intended to be appreciated from the printed page by readers with no direct engagement with royalty. Liminary verse – quintessentially a phenomenon of the age of print (cf. Reid-Baxter 2008) – provides a guide to the respective social and cultural audiences envisaged by the Jacobean poets, and its very existence shows that prince-pleasing had ceased to be the authors' main motivation. Literature, in other words, had become a more open and public affair. The changed situation is reflected in the dramatic increase in the output of Scottish printer-publishers, where the number of titles appearing between 1600 and 1625 is double that of the previous quarter-century (cf. Aldis 1970).

Yet this statistic does not tell the whole story, since Scottish poets (e.g. Robert Allen, William Alexander, Robert Ayton, Alexander Craig, Patrick Gordon, Simion Grahame, Patrick Hannay, George Lauder, William Lithgow, David Murray) were now free to look also to London for the printed publication of their writings. This new opportunity was not without consequences. Perhaps unsurprisingly, references to English locations and topics begin to appear in the writings of the Scots. Craig, who was familiar with Whitehall, animadverts to the beauties of Farnham, Salisbury Plain and Woodstock (AC5), and Hannay pointedly contrasts the idyllic meads along the Thames with the hell of life at Croydon (PH4). Allen evidently knew not only the

Court, but also the Strand, Cheapside, Ratcliffe, and the Royal Exchange, where Thomas Archer, printer of Allen's 1613 *Teares of Joy*, had his shop (RAL5). The names of English notables begin to be found among the dedicatees, patrons and admirers claimed by the Scottish poets (whether writing in the vernacular or in Latin). Thus Craig, among the epigrams in his *Poetical Recreations* (Edinburgh, 1609), included some to Robert Cecil, 1st earl of Salisbury, and to Frances Howard, countess of Hertford. Where the names of members of the Scottish nobility likewise appear, this provided a good opportunity for poets to mention the additional titles granted within the peerages of England or Ireland. In 1611 Murray addressed his sonnet sequence *Cælia* to Richard Preston, a favourite of James, who had become Lord Dingwall in 1609 and ten years later would become earl of Desmond; for his part, Hannay in 1622 dedicated *The Nightingale* [etc.] to Craig's former muse Frances Howard, who by then had become duchess of Lennox.

English writers, for their part, begin to supply liminary addresses to the works of those Scots who had made a breakthrough in London. For example, David Murray, knighted in 1605, was in his *Sophonisba* (1611) honoured with a sonnet by Michael Drayton, and Patrick Hannay received complimentary verses from a veritable clutch of English friends, who admired not only his *A happy Husband* (1619) but also the works collected in his *The Nightingale* [etc.]. Drayton had been quick off the mark in hailing James's accession with *A gratulatorie Poem* (1603), and he dedicated his *Poly-Olbion* (1612) to Prince Henry. Though he himself never made the journey to Scotland, he despatched from London 'Familiar Epistles' to William Drummond (Drummond 1711: 153–54). The same period also saw Scottish writers reacting to specific works of English literature. One such case is Sir William Alexander's filling of a *lacuna* in the narrative of Sidney's *Arcadia* (1621); another is Patrick Hannay's *A happy Husband*, which, though not exactly a sequel to the murdered Sir Thomas Overbury's popular and frequently reprinted poem on the character of the perfect *Wife, now the Widow* (1614), was a witty and overgoing riposte by an ambitious poet-about-town, willing to latch on to a metropolitan *cause célèbre*. In all this there is clear evidence of a cultural and social inter-traffic, and in such a perspective the journeys to Scotland made in 1617 by King James himself, and in the following year by Ben Jonson (Loxley et al. 2015) and by John Taylor, the ever impecunious so-called 'Water Poet', seem less extraordinary than might be thought.

The widening of literary horizons inevitably had an impact on the language-use found in the printed texts of the Scottish Jacobean poets – even if such printed publications cannot be taken as a reliable guide to the poets' personal language habits within their own domestic and social circles. In 1603, William Alexander had published at Edinburgh his *Tragedie of Darius*, using an experimental combination of Scots and English suited (as he hoped) to the newly united kingdom (Kastner and Charlton 1921–29: I, cxcvi). As an alternative procedure, already existing works in Scots might on reissue be anglicised, or more thoroughly anglicised, to trick them out for the taste of the times. Comparison of the 1622 and 1623 texts of George Lauder's first collection of verse, printed respectively at St Andrews and London, shows this clearly. The same treatment was applied to texts connected with religious culture – as seen, for example, in the differences between the 1603 and c. 1604 texts (from the same Edinburgh printer) of Elizabeth Melville's masterpiece, *Ane Godlie Dreme*, as also in the sixth print (1621) of the *Gude and Godlie Ballatis* (MacDonald 2015: 74–81).

Despite the notional target of perfect English, Jacobean poets on occasion fell back on the convenient extra resource of Scots language forms if metre or rhyme might thereby be facilitated – a practice explicitly acknowledged by Patrick Gordon (Spiller 1988: 140). At the same time, the Scots sometimes allowed usages which, though seemingly employing English lexis, would hardly be expected from a writer born south of the Tweed: examples are *hath* for *have* (cf. Scots plural *has*), as in SG2/127; the plural verb-forms *distelleth* for *distill*, and *trips* for *trip*, as in PG3/215, 217; and *thou's*, contracted from *thou shalt*, as in PG3/264. Not all Scottish poets were as consistently successful in writing English as was William Drummond. A somewhat different strategy was adopted by Alexander Gardyne in his *A Garden of Grave and Godlie Flowres* (1609), and was predicated on the background of the anticipated readers: many of the poems in this volume are entirely in English, but those addressed to specifically Scottish figures are more tolerant of orthographical, morphological and stylistic features from Scots. The attitude of the Jacobeans towards the use of English cannot adequately be explained in the simplistic and unidimensional terms of a supposed decline in the poets' sense of patriotism, but must be considered in the light of the normativising dynamic stemming from the political reality of a united kingdom, the linguistic practice of the Kirk, and the potential commercial advantage offered by an enlarged market.

Despite the (self-) imposed anglicisation of their language and style, the Scottish Jacobeans did maintain a strong sense of patriotism, and this emerges in tributes to their home localities. An emotional attachment to place – always a prominent feature of the Gaelic poetry of the Highlands – had never before been much in evidence in the literature of the Lowlands (MacDonald 1991). At the same time, and as a new phenomenon, a number of different, and geographically distinct, centres of culture can be discerned. These might take various forms, as for example: (a) a single poet catering to a specific individual in the provinces; (b) groups of intellectuals and professionals keeping in touch with their fellows through meetings and correspondence; (c) associations of poetry-loving worthies living in a particular town. The first sort would be exemplified by James Cockburne and his religious poetry, written for Jean Hamilton, Lady Skirling (in Peeblesshire); the second, by the network of literary-minded Calvinists in the East Neuk of Fife and beyond, centred on James Melville (Reid-Baxter 2017; 2008: 84); the third, by the cluster of civic, clerical and university notables in Aberdeen, whom Alexander Gardyne addressed in many poems of his *Garden of Grave and Godlie Flowres*. In addition, there was a group of poets connected with Lanarkshire and the south-west of Scotland, including William Lithgow, Robert Allen and Patrick Hannay. Before 1600, the Court at Edinburgh had exercised a centripetal and well-nigh monopolistic influence within Lowland vernacular literary culture. However, after the Union of the Crowns, in the absence of King and Court, and with different patterns of patronage, Scottish literary culture became variegated, diffuse and fissiparous; it also gained in London a new dimension with plenteous possibilities. Although the 1617 cornucopia of gratulatory poems written by local dignitaries, academics, schoolmasters and town officials to welcome the ruler of the three kingdoms on his grand progress through his native country might still seem only to illustrate the essential and stimulating power deriving from the status and figure of the monarch, such exuberance actually bears witness to an impressive level of literary talent present in the land (cf. Green 2017). The royal visit, so to speak, was the spark that caused a mighty literary engine to spring into action.

At the same time, Scottish topography comes to feature in the poetry of the Jacobeans: Kinnaird, Perth and the Tay for Alexander Craig; Edinburgh, Glasgow, Lanark, Dumbarton Rock, Loch Lomond and the Clyde valley for William Lithgow; Aberdeen for Alexander Gardyne; Glasgow, Hamilton and the Clyde for William Mure; Haltoun and Lothian for George Lauder. William Drummond, lamenting Prince Henry, invokes the Forth, Clyde and Tweed in his *Teares, on the Death of Mœliades*. Even more imposing is his *Forth Feasting*. In this tribute of welcome to King James, Drummond alludes to the Grampian Mountains and the Ochil hills, and makes much of a catalogue of Scottish rivers as part of the speech made by the personified Forth. At Drummond's hands, the Forth, which from its source west of Stirling to its estuary east of Edinburgh flows through a region rich in patriotic and historical associations, is endued with a shimmering aura of mythology, and the resulting artistic creation becomes the perfect vehicle for the poet's royalist adulation.

Other manifestations of Scottish patriotism are also encountered. One such is Walter Quin's account of the late-medieval military commander, Bernard (Bérault) Stewart, who in 1508 died at Corstorphine, near Edinburgh. This renowned soldier, a distant relation of James IV, had led the French army of Charles VIII in its conquest of Florence and Naples, and the hero's triumphal (albeit fatal) visit to Scotland had been commemorated by William Dunbar (Flood 2014: 146–206; Bawcutt 1992: 82–87). The revival of interest in Bernard Stewart bespeaks an early modern attempt to recall and to capitalise upon a glorious episode at the late-medieval Scottish Court. It probably also catered to the interests of James's heir, Prince Henry, by all accounts a virtuous and upright young man, with strong interests in matters military and chivalric (MacLeod et al. 2012). Quin's work is said to have been originally written in French, and the English version may actually have been prepared for Prince Charles. Humanist scholars were likewise affected by the prevailing sense of patriotism. One was the strong Protestant John Johnston (d. 1611), who celebrated in Latin verse the sequence of Scottish kings from Fergus I to James VI (*Inscriptiones historicae regum Scotorum* [Historical notes of Scottish kings] (Amsterdam, 1602)), and also a list of non-regal figures (*Heroes ex omni historia Scotica* [Heroes from the entire history of Scotland] (Leiden, 1603)). Yet another was the Catholic antiquarian Thomas Dempster (d. 1625), who in Bologna compiled a catalogue of the lives of Scottish authors. In this first-ever work of Scottish literary history, written in Latin, Classical and vernacular perspectives are blended – resulting, for example, in the labelling of Alexander Montgomerie as the 'Scottish Pindar' (Irving 1829: II, 496; Morét 2000).

The poets represented in the present anthology lost no time in scanning the new horizons opened up by the Union of the Crowns. While tears were shed at the departure of the King (cf. Craig AC3), more energy was invested in hailing the achievement of political amalgamation, which was seen as resolving ancient antipathies and ending centuries of conflict between north and south (cf. Ayton RAY4; Craig AC2). A somewhat overworked trope involved wordplay on Albion and All-be-one (cf. Craig AC3; Mure WM4; Gardyne AG2, AG3), and in response to the spirit of the age Scottish poets such as Craig and Murray were proud to proclaim their Scoto-Britishness on the title-pages of their volumes. The fact that no corresponding 'Anglo-Britane' is recorded in the *OED*, however, suggests that the notion of the United Kingdom appealed disproportionally to those from north of the Tweed: indeed, historians have noted that the English and Scottish views of the union differed in many respects (cf. Wormald 1994), but one is concerned here with the Scots. The voluntary and jubilant merging of a Scottish within a Great British identity elicited allusions to England and English history, and it enabled such flights of fancy as the watery co-operation between the Forth and Thames on the occasion of the transportation by river of the corpse of Queen Anne (Hannay PH1). Some poets had a still wider perspective, and tell of their physical presence on the continent of Europe, even when thinking thoughts of home. For example, Simion Grahame reveals his nostalgic longing for Scotland while languishing by an Alpine torrent (SG4), and William Lithgow, a sturdy Clydesdaler, tells of shivering at Negroponte and sweating his way up Etna (WL2, WL6). In earlier periods, mere naming of localities famous in literature and mythology had been the norm: the Jacobean novelty is the connection of poet and place with actual lived experience – as expressed by Simion Grahame: 'So what I have, I have it not by showe, / But by experience, which I truly knowe' (SG4/119–20).

An inevitable result of the expanded horizons was that the leading Scottish poets of the early seventeenth century became as keen to import new literary influences as they were to discard superannuated models and fashions. As far as the latter are concerned, the vetust authority of the greatest medieval English poets – which the so-called 'Scottish Chaucerians' had been happy to acknowledge – was by 1600 played out. Thus, in the Preface to *The famous historie of … Bruce* (1615), Patrick Gordon looked down on 'old ryme like to Chaucer', and proclaimed his modern respect for recent and Protestant poets such as the Frenchman Guillaume Salluste Du Bartas and Sir Philip Sidney, and revealed his enthusiasm for the aesthetic theory contained in the rediscovered *Poetics* of Aristotle. The venerable technique of systematic alliteration in poetry had its last fling in *The Pilgrime and Heremite*, attributed to Alexander Craig in a print of 1631: this was a literary curiosity, couched in a stanza-form unknown to any medieval master, and in a style pithily described as 'Langland crossed with Petrarch' (Spiller 1988: 148). On the other hand, influence from England remained strong, though it flowed along new channels. For example, the idiom of Classical and Renaissance pastoral leaves a deep mark on Drummond's *Forth Feasting*; the deliberately rough satirical manner of John Donne is imitated in Craig's *Satyra Volans*; 'metaphysical' wit gives colour to the works of several poets in this anthology (e.g. Grahame, Hannay, Kerr); the concise lyric style of Ben Jonson, his associates, and their witty Caroline successors, is encountered in the poetry of Robert Ayton and the young George Lauder.

A powerful factor promoting convergence between the literature of England and Scotland was that in both countries early modern poets spent long years at school and university in the study of the Latin and Greek texts which comprised the common educational syllabus of the Renaissance. Accordingly, those lines of Alexander Craig and William Drummond which most pullulate with Classical allusions should not be dismissed as individualistic or exaggerated, but rather viewed in the light of, and as parallels to, the assiduously learned manner cultivated by Jonson and like-minded European contemporaries. In addition, the humanist preoccupation with the interpretation and translation of the Bible impacted with comparable effects across frontiers. King James, as a school-boy, had had George Buchanan as his teacher, and the latter's hugely admired neo-Latin renderings of the Psalms would surely have provided the King with something to emulate in the vernacular. The appeal of psalms was ubiquitous in the age of Reformation, and many versions were composed in the indubitably good and godly, but all too frequently plain and plodding, ballad-stanza style associated with Sternhold and Hopkins and favoured by the Kirk. An alternative path was taken by those poets who cast their versifications in elegant and varied stanzas, such as had in many countries been employed in secular lyrics – as in the psalms of Clément Marot, and of Sir Philip Sidney and his sister Mary. In the present volume, the versions of Psalm 104 by Sir David Murray and of Psalm 1 by Sir Robert Kerr are instances of this more ambitious kind of paraphrase, in which literary quality trumps slavish fidelity to the original, and where the result is free from the constricting responsibility of liturgical application. In tackling Psalm 104 Murray may conceivably have intended a deferential acknowledgement of the King's own version, printed in 1584 (Craigie 1955–58: I, 85–88, 314–15). However, where James might have sought *kudos* by taking as his starting-point not the eloquent Buchanan but the notably accurate Latin prose rendering of the Christian convert and Hebrew scholar Immanuel Tremellius (d. 1580), Murray and Kerr ranked felicity of execution above precise correspondence to the Biblical original; tellingly, several of Kerr's psalms are done not directly from the plain text of Scripture but from Buchanan's artistic and sophisticated recreations.

A third major literary influence on the Scottish Jacobeans (as on their English *confrères*) derives from the works of European poets writing in Italian, French and Spanish. This emerges most clearly in the sonnet, but also in other stanza-forms and lyrical genres typical of the Renaissance, such as the *sestina, ottava rima, canzone* and madrigal. Of several Scottish examples of the madrigal, two which are here included proceed from the same apian conceit: one (SG1) by Simion Grahame, based on Giovanni Battista Guarini (d. 1612), the other (WD6) by William Drummond, based on Torquato Tasso (d. 1595). The works of European poets of the Renaissance were prized by Scottish readers, and, as already mentioned, figure prominently in the libraries of William Drummond and George Lauder (MacDonald 1971; MacDonald 2018: 150–67).

The cultural influences bearing upon the Scoto-British poets were thus manifold – with elements drawn from native-Scottish, English, Classical, neo-Latin and European-vernacular models – and the end-result was a thoroughgoing *aggiornamento* of literary style and subject-matter. As far as the practice of poetry in Scotland is concerned, the early seventeenth century is a period of expansion, innovation, diversity and inclusiveness, and those critics of earlier generations who in relation to this period speak slightingly of 'purely English imitation work' are poorly informed (e.g. Speirs 1962: 94). Verse in the 'sweet new style' may subsequently have been a casualty of the political upheavals of the mid-seventeenth century, but it would be anachronistic to import such a proleptic view in any appraisal of the poetry of the age of the first British Stuart.

In the late twentieth century critics came to use the term 'Castalian' in designation of (especially) the poets at the Edinburgh Court of James VI (Shire 1969: 93–99; Jack 1988: 125–32). A line in the King's epitaph-sonnet on Alexander Montgomerie – 'Ye sacred brethren of Castalian band' (Craigie 1955–8: II, 107–08, 236) – was interpreted as implying the existence of an actual band of poets, brothers of the Muses, and organised somewhat in the manner of a close-knit literary *puy*, as known in the Middle Ages. Dominating the sacred brethren would be the god Apollo, a suitably flattering avatar for James himself. As a consequence of this interpretation, one critic dubbed Sir Robert Ayton 'the last Castalian', with the latter term understood as standing in contrastive relation to its better-known successor, 'Cavalier' (Shire 1969: 215–23).

Although the whole notion of a 'Castalian Band' has itself since been impugned (Bawcutt 2001; Lyall 2005: 5–6), that need not imply that the adjective has lost all its meaning, since 'Castalian' remains useful in relation to the Scottish literature produced during the quarter-century before 1600. On the other hand, for the following quarter-century it is desirable to use a different label. Since 'Cavalier' would scarcely be appropriate, given its customary association with the later and very different circumstances of the Civil Wars, the solution pragmatically adopted for the present anthology is 'Jacobean'. Although initially one might have supposed the latter term to apply to the entirety of James's long reign, in the foregoing discussion it has deliberately been reserved for the years after 1600; the advantage is that in this way a Scottish pair of 'Castalian' and 'Jacobean' emerges as a parallel and counterpart to 'Elizabethan' and 'Jacobean' in the historiography of English literature.

The primary reference of 'Castalian' is to Greek mythology and to the nymph whom Apollo metamorphosed into a fountain on Mount Parnassus, the sacred haunt of the Muses; there is thus an overlap in the connotations of 'Castalian' and 'Parnassian'. The relevance of the latter term to King James is already apparent in a poem by Walter Quin, published in 1600, in which he congratulated the King on his Visitation of St Andrews University in 1597:

> Haec cano pauco tamen non hac spe lusus inani,
> Sed quia iusserunt te compellare Camenae
> Dignatum subiisse suum, rex optime, fanum,
> Teque insigne suis monstrare exemplar alumnis,
> Ad iuga Parnassi quem contendendo sequantur;
> A quo nec dubitent Musarum dotibus aucti
> Praemia se meritis, et digna labore laturos.

I sing these few things, however, not because I am deluded by this somewhat idle hope [i.e., of being able to honour James], but because the Camenae [Muses] ordered you to condescend to bring yourself into their shrine, most excellent king, and to show yourself as an outstanding example to their disciples, so that they may follow you in climbing the heights of Parnassus; and having been augmented by you with the gifts of the Muses they should not doubt that they will win prizes worthy of their merits and toil. (Flood 2014: 86, 88)

Quin's poem was published in his *Sertum poeticum in honorem Jacobi sexti* [Poetic flower-garland in honour of James VI]. It ushers in the new century by portraying the King as the accomplished and leading poet deigning to give himself as an example to his literary apprentices, who are simultaneously the future intelligentsia of the country. In such a vision, the twin peaks of Parnassus may perhaps, by way of metaphor, be allowed to signify the colloca-tion of poetic skill and political service. The Scottish Jacobean poets seized on the image, and in their lines 'Parnassian' resonates both within the triumphal context of the Union of the Crowns and also in relation to the elevated poetical style demanded by such a subject. Thus Alexander Craig, had he been a king, would have resigned all his dominions to James in exchange for Parnassus (AC6); Simion Grahame opens his celebration of 'Glorious Britannie' by situating himself on Parnassus in order to sing of 'stately joy' (SG2); William Drummond wants the Muses to make Parnassus ring, in lamenting the death of Prince Henry (wD1); William Mure sees the climbing of Parnassus as the natural objective of all gallant and ambitious youths (wM1); William Lithgow, hoping to obtain poetic inspiration from the Parnassian Muses, offers them the modest propine of his 'Epistle Dedicatorie' (wL3), and, in his patriotic 'Elegie' to the 'never conquered Kingdome of Scotland', he pays tribute to a cohort of fellow Jacobeans, several of whom, in his opinion, write in the 'Pernassian veine' (wL8). 'Parnassian' functions as an indicator of both poetic style and poetic avocation, and is luckily free of the encumbering implication of any hypothetical 'Band'.

'Jacobean Parnassus' may therefore be used as a collective term to denote a post-1600 Scottish textual community of poets who participated in a common cultural context and who, with many attitudes and manners in common, wrote in chosen genres and on selected topics in an appropriately middle-to-high stylistic register. Many of these poets shared political and religious ideals, and their literary creativity was stimulated by, and found expression within, the exciting reality of a Great Britain ruled by a humanist-educated, poetry-loving, theologically informed, eirenically minded and Europe-focused Scottish king. The poetry of the Scoto-Britons reflects a significant, new, successful and self-conscious turn in Scottish culture, and requires appreciation on its own terms. It is the primary purpose of this anthology to provide an illustrative and representative sampling of this fascinating body of literature.

POETS AND POEMS

Simion Grahame (c. 1570–1614)

Almost all of Grahame's poetry is in his two collections: *The Passionate Sparke of a Relenting Minde* (London, 1604) and *The Anatomie of Humors* (Edinburgh, 1609). Two liminary poems by him are known: a sonnet in David Murray's *The Tragicall Death of Sophonisba* (London, 1611), and a poem prefixed to William Lithgow's *A most delectable, and true discourse* (Edinburgh, 1614). The *Passionate Sparke* contains eight poems and a prose dedication to 'James, King of England, Scotland, Fraunce and Ireland, etc'. The title-page declares that it has been 'Seene and allowed by authority', and the motto is *Quo fata vocant* [Whither the fates call]. The *Anatomie of Humors* reproduces several poems from the *Passionate Sparke*, though in changed order. However, it omits the earlier prose dedication and opening poem (addressed to the King), as well as 'To the famous Ile of Glorious Britannie', and instead supplies a new dedication to John Graham, 4th earl of Montrose and a 'To the Reader' (both of these in prose), four wholly new poems, and an expanded and reworked version of one poem from 1604. It also adds the substantial prose work *The Anatomie of Humors*, which, as well as incorporating some thirteen additional poems, is equipped with many scattered single lines and phrases (e.g. quotations, proverbs and idioms) in Latin, French, Spanish and Italian. The new title-page motto is from Proverbs 21:2 ('Every way of a man, is right in his owne eyes: but the Lord God pondreth their hearts') and the book was printed 'With Licence'. In *Sophonisba*, Grahame's Christian name appears as 'Simon'.

Simion was the son of Archibald Grahame, a merchant-burgess of Edinburgh and a prominent and staunch Protestant in the post-Reformation burgh (Lynch 1981). That would explain how Simion in 1580 came to be awarded the prebend of Brodderstanis (Brotherstones, Roxburghshire) for seven years, to defray the expenses of his schooling, and why the prebend was in 1587 renewed for his lifetime. The royal generosity doubtless led the poet, in the dedication which he prefixed to the *Passionate Sparke*, to hope for a continuation. The almost total absence of James from the 1609 volume suggests that Grahame's hopes were not fulfilled. Instead, the new dedicatee was the earl of Montrose, who in 1618 would receive two poems from William Lithgow.

The Catholic scholar Thomas Dempster, whose statements merit both respect and caution, wrote in 1625 that Grahame, after the tedium of a life spent in dissolution, was eventually called by the Holy Spirit to become a friar of the Order of St Francis of Paola (Irving 1829: I, 328). It is unclear when such a profession would have been made, but it would be intriguing if it had taken place before the dedication of the *Passionate Sparke* to King James. A religious conversion around that time might already have occurred or been underway; however, even if Grahame did join the Order he would not necessarily be a priest, since he could have been a lay-brother. A possible indication of his religious position may be seen in the final item of his two collections, 'His Dying Song'. In the 1609 volume, this poem bears a Latin psalm-text motto which is used liturgically as an antiphon in the Office of the Dead, where it expresses apprehension regarding the pains of death and the dangers of hell.

Dempster credits the poet with two untraced works – *Vale foeminis* [Farewell to Womankind] and *De contemptu mundi* [On contempt for the world] – and says that Grahame died at Carpentras, France, while on the way back to Scotland. The only other early comment on the poet is that by Sir Thomas Urquhart (1652): 'a great traveler and very good scholar, as doth appear by many books of his emission. But being otherwayes too licentious and given over to all maner of debordings [excesses], the most of the praise I will give him wil be to excuse him in these terms of Aristotle – *Nullum magnum ingenium sine mixtura dementiae.*' [No great mind without a dash of madness] (Jack and Lyall 1983: 162): this remark may therefore perhaps count as a tribute to Grahame's greatness of mind. In the dedication of the *Anatomie* the poet writes: 'My peregrinations enlarged my curiositie, my souldier's estate promised to preferre mee, and the smiles of Court stuffed my braines with manie idle suppositions.' He also complains of 'the inconstant wavering of [his] ever-changing Fortune', but does not go into details.

Such comments suggest a man with a wide experience (as student, soldier, courtier and traveller) of the ways of the world, and one indeed willing to go wherever fate should call. This experience may ultimately have induced a sense of disgust at the vanity of human wishes, with a spiritual conversion as result. In his 'Passionado' [Sufferings] Grahame writes of finding himself in the Alps, and his formal religious profession, assuming there was one, may have been made in Italy. His father was brother-in-law to Peter Douglas, who was a Catholic in Calvinist Edinburgh (Lynch 1981: 194), and there may have been a strain of recusancy in Grahame's family. John Graham, 3rd earl of Montrose, whom the poet commemorated in the 1609 *Anatomie*, was known for his tolerant attitude towards Catholics – as, for example, in 1584 to David Graham, the laird of Fintry (Graham 1996: 277). However, in view of the fact that Simion Grahame's name is encountered in works by David Murray and William Lithgow, he would have had greatly to dissemble, had he indeed opted for life as a Minim.

The use of the word 'pilgrimage' in the 'Passionado' need not necessarily imply a journey undertaken for the sake of visiting the shrine of any saint – the strongly Protestant William Lithgow also applied the term to himself – but, if religion were indeed Grahame's motivation, his winter and summer of wandering as a pilgrim would probably have been before 1604 and the dedication to the King. In the original version of SG3 he says farewell to Scotland, and sets out as a mournful pilgrim: in the drastically revised 1609 version (SG3B) of this poem he writes from Italy, wishing his country well, but revealing constant mindfulness of his Scottish homeland. It would therefore seem that he must have indulged in more than one period of wandering. The motto on the 1609 title-page is from the Geneva Bible, but whether that is a reliable indicator of Grahame's own religious affiliations, as opposed to those of Thomas Finlason, his printer-publisher, is unclear. Grahame's association with Murray and Lithgow would normally suggest a meeting of Protestant minds; however, the text quoted on the 1609 title-page is potentially ambiguous, merely saying that God's judging of the soul is independent of the individual's own choice (of life? of religion?). The licence for publication recorded on the title-pages of both Grahame's collections may be the printer's assurance that the volumes were free of dangerous religious doctrine. The poet's religious position remains uncertain.

Grahame has been described as 'a gloomy and stridently bitter figure' (Spiller 1988: 159), but it might be better to see him as a supporter of King and Union, albeit one whose course of life made him into an acutely observant moralist and satirist; the 'malcontent' was a fashionable figure of the decade. His lines show considerable skill in versification and there is no lack of rhetorical energy: he is a master of the brief and telling phrase, often expressed with effective alliteration. The autobiographical trace-elements in his poetry, gloomy or not, have the ring of being grounded in reality, even though the detail is obscure. The 'Passionado' may be the first Scottish poem on the theme of alienation (in the social, geographical, intellectual and possibly religious senses), and Grahame almost anticipates the Romantics in displaying an emotional response to the Alps.

Madrigall: Of a Bee.   [SG1]

Once did I see
A sounding bee,
Amongst her sweetned swarme;
Still would shee flee   *always; fly*
5   And favour me,
Then did I dreade no harme.

Now, whilst in nectred-glorie of her gaines
She sitts and suckes the fayre well-florisht flower,   *fully ripe*
My sugred hopes are turn'd to bitter paines,
10   And lookt-for-sweete is nothing elles but sower.
      Ah, cruel sweet, bee sweet and cure my smart;
      Honny my mouth, but doe not stinge my hart.

To the famous Ile of Glorious Britannie.   [SG2]

On Parnasse hill, whilst as I sit to sing
Of stately joy, the streames that by me slides
Sweet consort yeelds from the Castalean spring,   *harmony*
Whose murmure still in silver veines devides;   *rivulets*
5   Then, intricate with courses to and fro,   *interlinking*
      They seeme to turne whil'st as with speed they go.

The Muses scarse in circuit is sat downe,   *circle*
When laureat troopes comes kneeling mee before;
In humble show ech takes his lawrell crowne,
10 And sweares they shall this subject all adore:
      So am I forc'd by thee, O wondrous worth,
      In warbling notes sweete consorts to send forth.

With nine-voyc'd mouth, my Delphin song I sound: *prophetic*
Of all the world blest bee thou, Brittaine's ile,
15 Thou, onely thou within this mortall round,
On whom the heav'ns have lov'de so long to smile,
      For Phœnix-like thou hast renewde by kinde,   *nature*
      In getting that which lay for thee inshrinde.   *begetting*

Thy present time doth winter-blast dispaire,   *countervail*
20 At force of joy the barren branch decayes:
Long flourish'd hope now fruitfull is and faire,
Whose lod'ned birth with burthen bowes the bayes;   *heavy; bay-trees*
      So downeward tops, inclining still below,   *bending*
      Such homage to their owner do they show.

25 Then, soyle, in this most happie, harv'st your right,   *country*
Ripe sweete desire, in spight of wilde envie;   *reap; hostile*
So shall you with your monarches-matching-might
Make earthly kings to feare your conqu'ring crie.
      The circuit of this spatious ball at length   *world*
30   Shall yeeld unto your armie-potent-strength.

As sounds below relents the ayer above,   *mollify*
That hideous noyse of thunderclaps may swage;   *appease*
So proud usurping minds shall stoope, to moove   *bow down*
The lion redd to stay his roring rage –   *mitigate*
35   Their honors high when he hath made them thrall,
      Since with his force their forcelesse force must fall.   *submit*

Hee threatens th'earth with such triumphant might
That makes his foes afraid to heare his name,
On vertue's wings, oreshinde with honor's light,   *illuminated*
40 Borne through the world with ever flying fame,
    Which still the echo of his might resounds,   *ever; repeats*
    A terror threatning these terrestriall bounds.

His scepter proud and his great conqu'ring hand
Will erect troph's of high triumphes on all;   *monuments*
45 Earth-ruling minds, stooping at his commaund,
Adorn'd they are by him to bee made thrall.   *honoured*
    So, monarch, hee must caule ech potent king,   *summon*
    For him and his rich tributes for to bring.   *and his descendants*

No treason's gilt, such threatninges can abide,   *guilt*
50 Nor vipers wilde, who eates their tongues to barke,   *fierce*
With feares confus'd must needs their selves goe hide
And lye obscure in the Cemerian darke,
    From light debar'd, to presage* Pluto'es place,   *foreshadow*
    Where monstrous spirits such monsters shal imbrace.

55 Swel'd with envie, and poys'ned great with griefe,
Most serpent-like spewes vennome on their owne,   *each other*
Damn'd harts abhord, whose mutins breeds mischief,   *rebellions*
They with their selfe their selfe shall bee orethrowne;
    So div'llish braynes brings restlesse murther still;   *incessant*
    They, filthie frogs, ech one shal other kill.
60

Then, subjects true, on honor's throne set forth,
No death your eternized life can end,
For famous feates ad's wonders to such worth,   *deeds; add*
And truth doth still a shining light out-send,
65   Whose glancing beames, reflexing heere and there, *brilliant; reflecting*
    By flowing quilles of poets are made rare.   *exquisite*

Now, happie ile, sequestred live* no more,   *remote*
Since joyn'de, expell the excrements of wrath,   *now united; traces*
And let their foule ambitious factes implore   *deeds; ask for*
70 Their owne orethrow and well-deserving death.
     Rase downe, tread on their turrets of envie,
     Whose pride would mount above the valted skie.

The register of memorie beholde,   *record*
How God of wonders wondrous works hath wrought,   *miracles*
75 When, life past hope, to treason he was solde,
Till threatning-death in danger's mouth him brought;
     In such extremes deathe's ambush was in vaine,
     For heav'ns strong hand did save him stil unslaine.

All high attempts of div'llish foes was foyld,   *bold schemes*
80 All hideous noise of horrors did asswage;   *abate*
All tragike troopes of hellish thoughts was spoylde,   *defeated*
And rigor's selfe gave rigor to their rage,
     Ensignes displaid, whose terror them confounds,
     Whilst conqu'ring joy victorious trumpet sounds.

85 The ship, which death with tempests grief did threat'n,
And gulfes of seas was readie to devoure,
When restlesse-mercy-wanting-stormes had beat'n,   *merciless*
At last came safe unto her long-sought shore:
     So heav'n now brings him to his hav'ning place   *destined*
90   Still to succeed to him and all his race.   *descendants*

The upright in each true externall thing   *virtuous person*
Bewrayes the force hart-burning-love doth yeald,   *reveals*
For smiling lookes of such a gratious king
Shall make your love with life and blood be seald:
95   Unworthie to enjoy this mortall breath,
     Who for this king or countrie feares their death.

The altar is a spotlesse minde, whereon
You sacrifice and offer up good-will;
Love yeelds the fuell from the hart alone   *provides*
100 Which, once inflam'd, is quenchlesse, burning still;
    Then martiall feates shall breed couragious strife,
    In battels brave to trye a carelesse life.   *test; fearless*

Though the idea of your long desire   *ideal*
Unsetled time obscures him for a space,   *hides*
105 Yet shall this time with comming time expire,   *die out*
And then receive fruition of his face;   *enjoyment*
    Who justice seekes, his wisdome's eyes shall see,
    With reasons right each may contented bee.

Lo, spring-time comes, long darkned sun com's out,
110 All to renew that winter blastes had spoil'd,   *what*
When, sending forth his gorgeous beames about,
Hope's harv'st expel's which high dispaire had foil'd;   *that which*
    So hope triumphes, dispaire lies quite o'rethrowne;
    Sweet soyle, thou hast which God hath made thine own.

115 Misconster not his well-inclining-minde,   *misconstrue*
Doo not mistrust, for triall lurkes in time   *inheres*
Why to his kingdomes shall he proove unkinde
And glorie stayne of his adorning prime?   *good beginning*
    No counsaile can make him become so strange   *remote*
120   Nor earthly pompe his burning love to change.

Murmour no more, nor bee not discontent,   *complain*
When constant love and spotlesse justice stands
With eager piercing lookes for to prevent
All kind of foule oppression in his lands.
125   This is the right inricheth his renowne
    This is the oath made to his royall crowne.

And you, whose long tormented hearts hath still   *have ever*
With cloudie mistes and darknesse been obscur'd,
You, all the world with tragike volumes fill,
130   What woe's devis'd that you have not indur'd;
    Your register this rigor may recall,   *account*
    Shame, bloodshed, death, still captives led in thrall.

In guiltlesse-him no crueltie doth dwell,
Nor from his mercie never sprang mischief;
135   Your conscience read, and it shall surely tell   *examine*
His hands are wash'd as causelesse of your griefe;
    Then let the blood, the banishment and death
    Bee on their heads, the authors of your wrath.

What though a king? Yet kings are sometime forc'd   *even*
140   To yield consent with unconsenting hart,
As from his will unwillingly divorc'd,
That no uprore should rise [on] any part: *dissent*
    Such is the onelie prudence in a prince   *particular*
    That 'gainst a murm'ring Momus makes defence.   *threatening*

145   Why, doe not then degorge satyrike words;   *spew out*
Usurping right, thou shall usurpe thy braine: *in disturbing*
For lo, nought else such foolish feates affordes   *tricks; yield*
But div'lish guerdon for thy greatest gaine;   *devilish; reward*
    And still thou shalt make infamous thy name   *forever*
150   When as thy end's to end in endlesse shame.

If Christian thou, then Christian-like abide,
Till flowing favour from his kingly love
By stately rule thy fredome shall provide,
When minde's remorse and mercy shall him move;
155   So conscience thral'd made free, and griefe is gone,   *enslaved*
    Then shall his soyle contented live in one.   *land; united*

And dark'ned clouds, that lowers upon you[r] heads,   *lour*
Gives place unto the glori'us shining sun,
Whose burning beames with radiant splendor spreads   *extend*
160 A restlesse race not ending, still begun,   *always beginning*
      To show the ods 'twixt heav[n]'s cælestiall light   *contrast*
      And gloomy mist of helle's eternall night.

From treasure rich of God's immortall store
Let fervent love in firy flames descend,
165 And fill your hearts with pittie to implore
That heav'n's preventing hand may him defend;
      Let highest curse breath forth consuming woes   *divine*
      For to convert or else confound his foes.

A gratious king, whose mercie still abounds,   *always*
170 A gallant queene, by Nature made none such,   *incomparable*
A prince, whose worth Fame's restles trumpet sounds,
And princesse, she, I cannot prayse too much:
      A king, a queene, a prince, a princesse rare,
      O soyle, what soyle can with this soyle compare?   *country*

175 Then, happie ile, in this thy happie day,   *fortunate*
God's thundring voyce with harts relenting heare;
Whil'st heav'n's high troopes, theatred in array,   *angelic; drawn up*
With sounding joy before Christ's throne compeare,   *appear*
      In consort sweet melodious songs to sing:
180   Live, live, great James, most blest and potent king.   *powerful*

(a) To Scotland, his soyle. [SG3]   *country*

To thee, my soyle, where first
    I did receive my breath,
These obsequies I sing
    Before my swan-like death.
5 My love, by Nature bound,   *obliged*
    Which spotlesse love I spend   *give*
From treasure of my hart,
    To thee I recommend.
I care not Fortune's frowne,
10   Nor her unconstant Fate:
Let her, dissembling, smile
    And tryumph in deceate.   *deceit*
Curs'd be that man which hoords
    His hopes up in her lap,
15 And curs'd be he that builds
    Upon her haplesse hap.   *unlucky chance*
I tread on that blinde bawd,   *whore*
    And scorne hir sowre-mixt-sweet;
In spite of all her spite,
20   I spurne her with my feet.
Now let her spet more wrath,   *spit out*
    If any more yet bee;
Let horror of her hart
    Thunder at carelesse-mee.
25 Then all the flatt'ring showes
    Of Fortune I disdaine,
So fare-well, soyle and friends,
    A pilgrime once againe.

(b) From Italy to Scotland, his Soyle.

To thee, my soyle, where first
    I did receave my breath,
These mournefull obsequies I sing
    Before my swan-like death.
5 My love, by Nature bound,
    Which spotles love as dew,   *appropriate*
Even on the altar of my heart
    I sacrifice to yow.
Thy endlesse worth, through worlds   *fame*
10   Beginning still, begunne,
Long may it shine with beames most bright
    Of uneclipsed sunne.
And long may thou triumph,
    With thy unconquer'd hand,
15 And with the kingdomes of thy king
    Both sea and earth command.
At thy great triple-force
    This trimbling world still stoup's;   *defers*
The martiall arme shall over-match
20   The Macedonian trup's.   *troops*
And thou the trophees great
    Of glory shall erect,
The confeins of this spatious glob,   *limits*
    Thy courage shall detect.
25 O happie soyle, unyt,   *united*
    Let thy emperiall breath
Expell seditious muteners,   *rebels*
    The excraments of wrath.   *outgrowths*
With honor, trueth and love,
30   Maintaine thy thre-fold-crowne;
Then so shalt thou with wondrous worth
    Inritch thy ritch renowne.
In spyght of envye's pride,
    Still may thy florish'd fame

35 Confound thy foes, defend thy right,
    And spurne at cowards' shame.
    Amidst my sorrowing greefe,
      My wandring in exyle,
    Oft look I to that arth and saies: *direction*
40   Far-well, sweete Britain's iyle.

His Passionado, when he was in Pilgrimage. [sg4]   *[Poem of suffering]*

Quo fata vocant.   *[Whither the fates call]*

Thou Phaëton, thy firy course do'st end,
And Cinthia, thou with borrow'd light do'st shine,
These woods their silent horrors doo out-send
And vallies lowe their mistie vapors shrine;   *enshrine*
5   Each lively thing by Nature's course doth goe
    To rest, save I, that wander now in woe.

My plaints impart these soli'd partes to fill,   *contribute; solitary*
Whil'st roaring rivers send their sounds among;
Each dreadfull deen appeares to helpe me still,   *cavern*
10 And yeelds sad consorts to my sorr'wing song: *harmonies*
    How oft I breath this wofull word 'alace',
    From Eccho I sad accents backe imbrace.   *receive*

I wil' advance, what feares can me affray?
Since dreades are all debar'd by high dispaire;   *banished*
15 Like darke-nigh[t]'s ghost, I vagabond astraye,   *wander*
With troubled spri't transported here and there;
    None like my selfe, but this my selfe alone,
    I, martir'd man, bewaile my matchlesse mone.   *martyred*

You flintie stones, take eares and eyes to see
20 This thundering greif, with earthquake of my hart;
That you may sigh and weep with miser-mee,   *wretched*
Melt at the tragick commentes of my smart.   *account*
    Let these my teares that fall on you so oft,
    Make your obdurate hardnesse to be soft.

25 You liquid droppes, distilling from mine eyes,
In christall you my second selfe appeares;
Patterne of paine, how do'st thou sympathize   *correspond*
In visage wan, and pilgrim's weede thou beares?
    And on those signes of miscontent attire   *unhappy garb*
30   Still doe I read, debar'd from my desire.   *continually; study*

This hairie roabe, which doth my corps contain,   *sack-cloth; body*
This burden, and my rough unrased heade,   *unshaven*
A winter and a sommer have I bin
In dangers great, still wandring in this weede;   *always*
35   Loe, thus the force of my disasters strange
    Hath made me use this unacquainted change.   *unfamiliar*

I am dri'd up with dolors I endure,
My hollowe eyes bewray my restles night;   *reveal*
My visage pale selfe pittie doth procure,   *generate*
40 I see my sores deciph'red in my sight,   *revealed; looks*
    A pilgrime still, my oracle was so,   *prognostic*
    And made my name AH MISER MAN I GO.

Now doe I goe, and wander any way:
No strange estate, no kinde of trav'ling toyles,   *foreign power*
45 No threatning crosse nor sorrow can me stay   *obstacle; deter*
To search and seeke through all the sorts of soyles.   *countries*
    So round about this round still have I run,   *sphere; ever*
    Where I began, againe I have begun.

In strangest parts, where stranger I may bee,   *most foreign*
50   An outcast, lost, and voyed of all releife,
     When saddest sights of sorrow I can see,
     They to my grave shall helpe to feede my greife:
         If wonder's selfe can wofull wonders showe,
         That sight, that part, that wonder I will knowe.   *place*

55   Thus doe I walke on forreigne fields forlorne,
     To carelesse-mee all cares doe prove unkinde;   *unnatural*
     I doe the Fates of fickle Fortune scorne,
     Each crosse now bredes contentment to my minde;   *obstacle*
         Astonish of stupendious things by day,   *amazement*
60   Nor howling sounds by night can me affray.   *terrify*

     You stately Alpes, surmounting in the skyes,   *towering*
     The force of floods that from your heights doun falles,
     There mightie clamors, with my carefull cries,   *their*
     The eccho'es voice from hollow caves recalles:
65   The snow-froz'n clowds down from your tops do thunder,
         Their voyce with mine doth teare the ayre a sunder.

     And Neptune, thou, when thy proud swelling wrath,
     From gulphes to mountaines mov'd with winter's blast,   *depths; raised*
     In anger great, when thou didst threaten death
70   Oft in thy rage, thy raging stormes I past,
         And my salt teares increast thy saltnes more,
         My sighes with windes made all thy bowells rore.

     The spatious earth and groundlesse deep shall beare   *bottomless*
     A true record of this my mart'ring mone;   *tortured moan*
75   And if there were a world of worlds to heare,
     When from this mortall chaos I am gone,
         I dare approve my sorrow hath bin such,   *attest*
         That all their witts cannot admire too much.   *wisdoms*

On the colde grounde my caytife-carcasse lyes,   *poor body*
80 The leaveles-trees my winter-blasted-bed:
Noe architecture but the vap'rous skyes,   *shelter; heavy*
Blacke foggie mist my weari'd corpes hath cled;   *bedeckt*
    This loathsome laire, on which I restles tourne,
    Doth best befit Mee-Miser-Man to mourne.

85 With open eyes night's darknes I disdaine,   *contemn*
On my cros'd-brest I crosse my crossed armes,   *folded*
And when repose seekes to prevent my paine,
Squadrons of cares doe sound their fresh alarmes;
    So in my sleep, the image of pale death,
90   These sighing words with burthen, brus'd, I breath: *refrain*

"I ever row'd my barge against the streame,   *vessel*
I scal'd those steppes that Fortune did me frame,   *hurdles; set*
I conquer'd, which impossible did seeme,
I, haples I, once happie I became.   *for a while*
95   Now sweetest joy is turn'd to bitter gall,
    The higher up, the greater was my fall.

What passing follies are in high estates,   *egregious*
Whose foolish hopes give promise to aspire;
Self-flatt'rie still doth maske the feare of Fates,
100 Till unawars deceiv'd in sought desire.
    This breeds dispaire, then force of Fortune's change
    Setts high estates in dread and perrill strange.

There secret grudge, envie and treason dwelles,
There justice lies, in dole-bewraying weede: *grief-revealing*
105 There sliding Time with alt'ring feates still tells   *deceiving tricks*
The great attempts ambitious mindes doe breed: *schemes*
    They who have most stil hunt for more and more,
    They most desire that most ar choak'd with store.   *abundance*

Henceforth will I forsake terrestiall toyes,
110   Which are nought els but shawdowes of deceat;
    What cover'd danger is in earthly joyes,   *hidden*
    When wilde Envie triumphes on each estate.   *hostile*
        Thou, traytour Time, thy treason doth betray,
        And makes youthe's spring in florish fayre decay.   *bloom*

115 What's in experience which I have not sought?
    All, in that All, my will I did advaunce;
    At highest rate all these my witts are bought;
    In Fortune's lottrie, I have try'd my chaunce:
        So what I have, I have it not by showe,
120   But by experience, which I truly knowe.

    Long have I searcht, and now at last I finde
    Eye-pleasing-calmes the tempest doth obscure,
    When I in glory of my prosperous winde,
    With white-sweld-sayles on gentle seas secure;   *billowing*
125   And when I thought my loadstarre shin'd most faire
        Ev'n then my hopes made shipwracke on dispaire.

    My light is dark, whil'st I am overthrowne,
    Poore silly barke, that did pure love possesse: *vessel*
    With great ungratefull stormes thus am I blowne
130 On ruthlesse rockes, still deafe at my distresse.
        So long-sought-conquest doth in ruins bost,
        And saies: Behold, thy love and labor's lost.

    Since all my love and labor's lost, let Fame
    Spit forth her hate, and with that hatefull scorne
135 In darke oblivion sepulchrize my name,   *entomb*
    And tell the world that I was never borne;
        In me all earthly dream'd-of-joy shall ende,
        As Indian herbes, which in blacke smok I spende.   *consume*

All-doting pleasure, that all-tempting-devill,   *indulgent*
140 I shall abhor as a contag'ous pest;   *plague*
I'le purge and clense my sences of that evill,
I sweare, and vow still in this vow to rest.
        In sable-habit of the mourning blacke,
        I'le solemnize this oath and vow I make.   *observe*

145 Then goe, wilde world, confused masse of nought,
Thy bitternesse hath now abus'd my brayne;
Avoid thy dev'llish fancy from my thought,   *remove*
With idle toyes torment me not agayne:
        My time, which thy alluring folly spent,   *wasted*
150   With heart contrite and teares I doe repent."

Against Time: Sonnet.   [SG5]

Goe, traytour Time, and authorize my wrong,   *record*
My wrack, my wo, my wayting-on bewray;   *servitude; reveal*
Looke on my heart, which by thy shifts so long   *tricks*
Thou tyranniz'd with treason to betray.
5 My hopes are fled, my thoughts are gone astray,
And sencelesse I have sorrow in such store   *abundance*
That paine it selfe, to whom I am a pray,
Of mee hath made a mart'red-man and more.   *martyr*
Go, go then, Time, I, hatefull thee, implore
10 To memorize my sad and matchlesse mone;   *lament*
Whilst thy deceipts by death I shall decore,   *honour*
My losse of life shall make them known each one.
        So I, poore I, I sing with swan-like song,
        Go, traytour Time, and authorize my wrong.

The Estate of Worldly Estates. [SG6]   *condition; distinctions*

Tempora mutantur et nos mutamur in illis.   *[Times change, and we in them.]*

Each hath his time, whom Fortune will advance,
Whose fickle wheel runs restlesse round about;
Some flatt'ring lye oft changeth other's chance,
Danger's deceipt in guiltie hearts breeds doubt.
5   It's seene
       What yet hath beene
    With tract of time to passe,
        And change
       Of Fortune strange
10   At last hath turn'd their glasse.   *hour-glass*

Envie triumph's on tops of high estate,   *position*
All over-hung with veiles of feigned show;
Man climbes above the course of such conceate,   *vain thought*
That, loftie-like, they loath to looke below.   *once above*
15   And what   *how*
       All's haszard that
    Wee seeke on dice to set:
        For some
       To height's doe come
20   Then falls in danger's net.

The gallant man, if poore, hee's thought a wretch,   *worthy*
His virtue rare is held in high disdayne;   *outstanding*
The greatest foole is wise, if he be rich,
And wisedome flowes from his lunatique brayne.
25   Thus see
       Rare sprit's to bee   *noble spirits*
    Of no account at all;
        Disgrace   *ruination*
       Hath got such place,
30   Each joyes at other's fall.

The brib'rous minde, who makes a god of gould,   *venal*
He scornes to plead, without he have reward;   *act in court; unless*
Then poore men's suites at highest rat's are sould,   *pleas; rates*
Whil'st av'rice damn'd, nor ruth hath no regard.   *pity*
35   For heere
     He hath no feare
Of God's consuming curse:
     His gaines   *profits*
     Doth pull with paines   *draw*
40   Plagues from the poore man's purse.

The furious flames of Sodom's sodaine fier
With fervent force consume vain pride to nought;   *burning*
With wings of wax let soaring him aspire
Above the starres of his ambitious thought.
45   And so,
     When hee doth go
On top of pride's high glory,
     Then shall
     His sodaine fall
50   Become the world's sad story.

Ingratitude that ill, ill-favour'd ill,
In noble brestes hath builded castles strong;
Oblivion setts-up the troph's that still   *triumphal displays*
Bewrayes the filthy wildnesse of that wrong.   *reveal; madness*
55   Ah, minde!
     Where, dev'llish kinde,   *nature*
Ingratitude doth dwell!
     That ill
     Coequals still
60   The greatest ill in hell.

On poyson's filth contagious error spreeds,
Heav'n's spotlesse eyes looks as amaz'd with wonder;
Their vipr'ous mindes such raging horror breeds
To teare religion's virgin-roabes asunder.
65   What then,
                O wicked men,
            And hel's eternall pray?
                Go mourne,
                    And in time turne
70   From your erroneous way.

What course wants crosse? What kind of state wants strife?   *lacks resistance*
What worldling yet could ever seem content?
What have we heere in this our thwartring life?   *frustrating*
Joy, beautie, honour, love, like smoak are spent.
75   I say,
                Time goe's away
            Without returne againe;
                How wise,
                    Who can despise
80   These worldly vapours vaine!

His Dying Song.   [sg7]

Now, haplesse heart, what can thy soars asswage,   *unfortunate; mitigate*
Since thou art gript with horror of Death's hand?
Thou, baleful thou, becomes the tragick stage,   *decorate*
Where all my tort'ring thoughts theatred stand: *torturing; lined up*
5   Griefe, feare, death, thought, each in a monstrous kinde,
        Like ugly monsters muster in my minde.   *gather*

Thou loathsome bed to restlesse-martred-mee,   *tormented*
Voyd of repose, fill'd with consuming cares,
I will breath forth my wretched life on thee.
10 For quenchlesse wo and paine my grave prepares.   *make ready*
     Unto pale-agonizing-Death am thrall,
     Then must I go and answere to his call.

O memorie, most bitter to that man
Whose god is golde, and hoords it up in store;
15 But O, that blind-deceiving-wealth, what can
It save a life, or add one minute more?
     When hee at rest, rich-treasures in his sight,
     His soule, poore foole, is tane away that night.

And strangers gets the substance of his gaine,
20 Which he long sought with endlesse toyles to finde;
This vilde-world's-filth, and excraments most vaine,   *outgrowths*
Hee needs must dye, and leave it all behinde.
     O man, in minde remember this, and mourne:
     Naked thou cam'st, and naked must retourne.

25 I naked came, and naked must retourne,
Earth's flatt'ring pleasure is an idle toy;
For now, I sweare, my very soule doth spurne
That breath, that froth, that moment fleeting joy.
     Then fare-well world, let him betray'd still bost
30   Of all mischiefe, that in thee trusteth most.

Burnt candle, all thy store consum'd, thou ends,
Thy lightning splendor threats for to be gone.   *flashy*
O how dost thou resemble mee, that spends   *consumes*
And sighs forth life in sighing forth my mone?
35   Thy light thee lothes, I loth this lothed life,   *abhors*
     Full of deceipt, false-envie, grudge and strife.

I call on Time, Tim's alt'red by the change,
I call on friendes, friendes have clos'd up their eares;
I call on earthly pow'rs, and they are strange,   *unresponsive*
40 I call in vaine, when pittie none appeares.
    Both Time and friends, both earthly-powers and al,
    All in disdaine are deafe at my hoarse call.

Then prayer, flowe from my heart-humbling knees,
To the supreame celestiall throane aspire;
45 And shew my griefe to heav'n's all seing eyes,
Who never yet deny'd my just desire:
    Man's help is nought, O God, thy helpe I crave,
    Whose spotlesse bloud my spotted soule did save.

Then take my soule, which, bought by thee, is thine;
50 Earth harb'ring worms, take you my corps of clay.   *dwelling*
O Christ, on mee eternall mercy shine,
Thy bleeding woundes wash all my sinnes away.
    Now, now, I come to thee, O Jesu sweet,
    Into thy hands I recommend my spreet.

[On the Court.] [SG8]

How blest is he, whose happy dayes are spent
Far from the Court, and lives at home in ease:
It's onely he who'se ritche with sweet content
And builds no nest on top of cædar trees:
5   No storming strife, nor yet no viprich kinde   *viperish nature*
    Of treason's gilt, doth harbor in his minde.   *guilt*

He eats that bread which sweating labor yeelds,
With open doores secure in his repose;
He walks alone, abroad on spatious fields,
10 Goe where he please, he needs not feare his foes:
  He trades on that, which proud ambition brings,   *tramples*
  And scornes the threatning terror of great kings.

I grudge to see when manie a scurvie clowne,   *poltroon*
Of no desert, triumphs in their desire,   *merit*
15 And from the top of honor doth throwe downe
Heroyk spirits, presuming to aspire.
  Shame wher's thy blush? Can heavens content with this, *be happy*
  To see good kings deceaved with Judas' kis.

Thou hellish Court, where cut-throate flattrie dwels,
20 Where simple trueth no kind of shailter finds,   *protection*
Where baser mindes, with pride and envy swels
Where rueling hearts are like inconstont winds,
  Where Fortun blinde playes to a poultron's chance *promotes; luck*
  And maks deceat in glittering robs to dance.

25 You painted snakes, whose bitter poysning gall   *disguised*
With want of pittie plagues the poore man's purse,
Gasping damnation doth attend you all,   *yawning; await*
Ther's no relax for your eternall curse.   *remission*
  Then curst be Court, thou monstrous map of hell,
30   Where envy, pryde, and treason loves to dwell.

[Anti-love.]   [SG9]

Some martiall men bewitch'd with beautie rare,
Are intricate in laborinths of love,   *trapped*
And forc'd to trie in fancie's flattring snare,   *undergo*
What sweet-mixt-sowre or pleasing paines can prove.   *perform*

5 Then Nymph-like-shee, with strange inticing looke,
Doth so enchant the gallant minded men,   *virtuous*
The bayte still hides the poyson of the hooke,
Till they be fast; and thus betray'd, what then?   *secured*

Poore captive slaves in bondage prostrate lies,
10 Yeelding unto her mercie-wanting-will:
She in disdaine scornes all their carefull cries,
And Circes-like triumphes in learned skill.

With ambling trips of beautie's gorgeous grace,   *leisurely steps*
Aurora-like in firie colours clad,
15 And with bright reflex of her fairest face,
She tempting goes with brainsick humors lad.   *foolish; led*

Fearing that if she should but looke below,
Then beames would from her burning eyes descend
On ivorie brest proud swelling hils of snow
20 Would melt, consume, and all their beauty spend.   *lose*

And so she lets her curled lockes downe fall,
Which doe allure the gentle cooling winde
To come and play, still wrapping up in thrall
Chaines of her haire, fond lovers' hearts to binde.

25 Beautie in prime adorn'd doth feede the sight,   *youth*
From crimson lips sweet nectar's gust forth flowes,   *taste*
Odours perfumes the breath, not Nature's right,
White ivorie hands a sacred touch bestowes.

[27]

And when those pearle of orientall-rankes
30   With treasure rich of tempting sound devides,
From two bright daintie moving-corall-bankes
In cirkled eares calme smoothing speeches slides.   *attentive; glide*

Each sencelesse sence, on doting pleasure fast,   *trapped*
Doth in a carelesse register inroule: *foolish; enlist*
35   Wishing that course of swift-wing'd time to last,
Which spots the spotlesse substance of the soule.   *stains*

But oh, behold, Nature in mourning weede
Weepes to be wrong'd with superstitious art:
For what can braines of rare invention breede,   *devise*
40   Or what's unsought, which pleasure may impart?

The sharpest wit, whose quicke deceaving still
Makes restlessse, musing of their minde to trie
Vaine trifling snares, mixtur'd with magick's skill:
So art adds that which Nature doth denie.

45   And thus much more, sweet Syrens' songs she sounds,
To charme, conjure, and tempt his list'ning eare:
Oh, then the poore captived wretch abounds
In perverse vowes, and monstrous oaths to sweare.

By furious force of Fancie more than mad,
50   With fond desire in restlessse course he hunts: *chase*
Blinde love can not discerne the good from bad,
When on the eye-plum'd tayle of pride it mounts.

The curious minde makes choise of good or ill,   *inquisitive*
Then scales the fort of his engine to clym   *intelligence*
55   Above, the top of art exceeding skill,
Perfect in that predominates in him.   *that which*

Drunke with the wonders of a worthlesse worth,
From prospect of a looking-glasse he takes
Strange apish trickes to set his folly forth
60 Mock'd with the gesture that his shadow makes.

When foolish feates no waies will serve his turne,   *tricks*
All hope is drown'd in despaire's groundlessse deepe: *bottomless*
In restlesse bed he, martir'd man, must mourne,
Thoughts, sighs, and teares admit no kinde of sleepe.

65 Thus layes the conquest conquerour of fieldes,   *brings down*
On his hurt heart he carries Cupid's skarre;   *wound*
The skurvie fainting coward basely yieldes   *wretched*
To idle love, the enemie of warre.

Now trumpets sound, brave martiall musick turnes
70 To fidling noise, or else some am'rous song;
That glorious Fame her wings of worth now burnes,
When golden youth in prime must suffer wrong.   *at its peak*

Thus gallant sprights doe quintesence their wits,   *distill*
Spending the rare invention of their braines   *wasting*
75 On idle toyes, at which high honor spits,   *contemns*
Nor memoriz'd memorials remaines.   *famous*

James Cockburne (fl. 1605)

The only known literary works by Cockburne are both on religious subjects, surviving bound together in a unique volume in the National Library of Scotland. Each has its own title-page, and was printed and published at Edinburgh by Robert Charteris in 1605. The first, *Gabriel's salutation to Marie*, is a versification of the Biblical account of the Annunciation; the second, *Judas' kisse to the sonne of Marie*, tells of the betrayal of Jesus in the Garden of Gethsemane, with the subsequent trial and Passion. Prefatory short poems introduce both main works.

The poet was probably the younger brother of Sir William Cockburn of Skirling. In February 1604, the latter married his first cousin Jean Hamilton, daughter of James Hamilton of Libberton (Carnwath parish, Lanarkshire); the marriage produced one son and two daughters. In the dedication of *Gabriel's salutation* to the eighteen-year-old Lady Skirling, dated at Christmas, Cockburne gives his location as Cambusnethan. His presence in that part of Lanarkshire can be explained by the fact that for almost a century, the Cockburns of Skirling had made a practice of marrying with the family of the Somervilles of Cambusnethan (*Fasti*, I, 257; Cockburn & Cockburn 1913: 139–43). In a liminary sonnet to Lady Skirling in *Judas' kisse*, Cockburne records his pleasure that she, with her great personal beauty, should be the mother to 'our famous race', and such a remark is compatible with avuncular joy at the birth of an heir. Unfortunately, the impecunious Sir William was reduced to selling Skirling, a burgh of barony, in 1621.

The extended Cockburn family is known for its connection with literature (van Heijnsbergen 2013: 55–59). For example, John Cockburn of Clerkington in 1560 married Helen Maitland, daughter of the poet Sir Richard Maitland (d. 1586), and at one time the keeper of the important Maitland Folio MS of Scottish verse (Craigie 1919–27: II, 5); moreover, several of Helen's siblings were also poets. The quality and subject-matter of James Cockburne's writing indicates that he was a man of education and faith. However, though a connection with the Church would be typical for a younger son, there is no record of his being a clergyman, and Cockburne and his sister-in-law are perhaps rather examples of lay piety. The two title-pages are furnished with Biblical quotations in Latin, and *Gabriel's salutation* contains a few phrases in that language. As the author of poems of spiritual direction intended for a lady, Cockburne's role may be compared with that of Alexander Hume, who addressed his *Hymnes, or Sacred Songs* (1599) to Elizabeth Melville. The presence in *Gabriel's salutation* of a liminary stanza by William Alexander of Menstrie, together with the very fact that Cockburne's work appeared in print at all, indicates that the poet must have been appreciated beyond the immediate Cockburn-Hamilton-Somerville coterie. It is striking that in the poem the Virgin Mary displays acquaintance with the fashionable female lifestyle pleasures of the seventeenth-century gentry (e.g. going to dances, singing carols, decorating her hair, using perfume and make-up), even while indignantly repudiating such vanities.

Cockburne expresses some diffidence about his talents as a poet. In a preface to *Gabriel's salutation* he affects to dismiss his creation as 'these few disordered lynes', and, in introductory verses 'To the Reader' of *Judas' kisse*, he describes that work as a 'naughtie [worthless] pamphlet'. Such deprecation is probably not merely modesty, but implies the poet's awareness that his writing, as a human creation, can never compare with the perfect handiwork of God. While he invites the reader 'with sober judgement [to] censure every lyne', he nonetheless hopes that respect for its content will protect his poem from being scorned. *Judas' kisse* contains a prefatory sonnet directed to the Nine Muses, in which Cockburne declares that he contemns what is 'fantastick', and reveals that his motivation is essentially moral and spiritual: 'Trueth bids me try my skill, trueth to compyle' – an aesthetic that fits both his works. He hopes to be stirred up to compose some work of true significance, since on the Day of Judgement he will have to give an account of every 'ydle word'. Such an apocalyptic perspective is typical of the religious outlook of the times, and, on the following page, the poet declares that he in fact acknowledges only one muse, the Holy Spirit. In strictly ideological terms, therefore, Cockburne might almost have to be reckoned as an anti-Parnassian, but there is no doubting his poetic ability and technical skill. Paradoxically, his art requires him to disavow his artistry. It is interesting that the Calvinist clergyman and historian Thomas McCrie (1772–1835), perhaps the only person to comment on Cockburne's verse, should have detected in him a 'bold but unchastened imagination' (McCrie 1856: 394).

Invocation. [JC1]

What tyme the cock, with wyde displayed wing,
Did beate his breast and then proclame the day,
His peirsing note unto my thoughts did bring
My dewties all, and first how I should pray.
5 Then on my knees I turnde me where I lay,
With mourning speech even thus I did begin:
"O Lord, I thee beseech, thy justice stay,   *hold back*
Call not to mynde the lyfe I lived in.
Grant me thy spirite that I may rightlie rin
10 Unto that Lambe that did thine rigor mease,   *placate*
To offer thee by him, for highest sin,
A broken heart for burning sacrifyce."
      Then I besought that all the Three in one,
      The worke would blesse my pen had undergone.   *undertaken*

**To the honoured ladie of highest hope, Mistresse Jeane Hammiltone,
Ladie Skirling.** [JC2]

Not to the worldling, waltering in his wealth,   *rolling*
Nor to the usurer recounts his gaine,
Not to the sicke, whose thoght is on his health,
Nor to the insolent, of lyfe prophane,   *immoderate*
5 Not to the ignorant, of brutish braine,
Nor to the stupide Stoick, will I send thee,   *insensible*
Not to the learnde, whose knowledge, with disdaine,
Will scorne the poet that so lowrdlie pend thee,   *clumsily wrote*
Not unto babes, whose age cannot defend thee,
10 Nor silver-seeking minstrels, for to sing,
Not unto careles men, who when they end thee,
Unclosde will thee within some window sling,   *throw*

[32]

But to a ladie sweet I will thee offer,
Who, having reade thee, closlie will thee coffer.   *lock away*

15 Then, fairest faire, whose matchles maners mylde
And haughtie thoghts dimerites high affection,   *lofty; deserve*
Who might have beene the mother of that Childe,
If any Gentile had beene in election,   *chosen*
But since it is – I speake it with correction –
20 Thou art no Jew, but in the Jew indented,   *in contract*
By grace, love, mercie and by free adoption
Of that great God our miserie prevented,
Then praise his name the way so well invented.   *devised*
Praise thou the Spirite that sanctified the birth,
25 Praise Jesus Christ, so freelie that consented
To cloath his God-hoode with the filthie earth.   *divinity*
    Praise all the Three; they only crave *Peccavi*,   *[I have sinned]*
    Changed hopeles *Eva* in an happie *Ave*.   *[Hail]*

Gabriell his Salutation to Marie. [JC3]

Out from the orders of the angels all
Sings holie hymnes about the throne of grace,
The Lord commands to come unto his call
The winged Gabriell, straight to embrace
5 An happie charge for Eve's unhappie race,   *commission*
    Who, since her husband's fall, had lyen within
    The foule alluring baytes of filthie sin.

Swiftlie he came, sweetlie the Lord did say:
"Thou that hes oft my message borne in yre
10 Kings to destroy, and countries did deny
My God-hoode great, with hote consuming fyre,

Go now in peace, let all thy rich attyre
    Be azure hew, bright starres therin thou fix;
    I will my justice with my mercie mix.

15 I will redeeme, recall, I will reclame,
    Not by desert, but by adoption;
    Not for their merites, but my glorie's name,
    No, not compelde, but at my option   *free choice*
    The house of Jacob, by my onelie Sonne,
20   Borne of a mayde, and the beleevers all
       That breathes beneath my ever-moving ball.   *sphere*

I will perfite my promise made indeede   *complete*
    To the first man, through facilnes that fell,   *tempting words*
    That his begot should bruse the serpent's head,   *offspring*
25 Whose birth in bewtie should the rest excell;
    Then where that virgine rests I will thee tell,
       Of all the Tribes that I have taine for chose,   *chosen*
       The famous Nazareth doth her enclose.

Pure are her thoughts, chaste are her actions all,
30 Firme is her faith, and ferventlie doth pray;
    Divine in spirite, devote on me to call,
    Resolv'd in heart at every houre to pay
    The death her dew, or yet content to stay: *due*
       So are her vertues knowne, so flyes her fame;
35   Betrothde she is, blest Marie heght her name.   *is called*

Salute the mayde with humble dewties dew,
    Discharge my charge with reverence and feare,
    Seene shall it be, although it seeme untrew,
    That of my Sonne she is the mother deare:
40 For, when with glorie great thou drawes neare
       And warbles forth thy voice, thou shall perceave
       The holie Spirite the Saviour conceave."

Thus said the Lord, when Eole's windie fanne
The weeping dew from tender trees had rent,
45 And when the horned-Moone with visage wane
Her borrowed light had back to Tytan sent,
That all the night before he had her lent,
    And this he said, while all the hoste of heaven
    Proclaimde his glore, for such commission given.

50 And having said, his armes abroad he threw,   *wide*
And blest the messinger before him lay,
Then silent sat. Away the angell flew,
And in the aire his wings did wyde display;
He clave the cloudes and cut the vapors gray,   *split*
55   He made the heavens admire, the waters wonder,   *marvel*
    To see his glore, and heare his thuds of thunder.   *peals*

With holie canticles and hymnes he sings
The joyfull newes of man's salvation;
In flames of fyre were graven between his wings
60 The Birth, the Buriall, and the Passion,
The Death, the Rysing, and Conception
    Of Jesus Christ, yea and the totall summe
    Of all his wondrous works that were to come.

Dronke with delights, sweet Nazareth he soght,
65 That place he compast thrice arou[n]d and over;   *surveyed*
In Marie's presence shortlie is he broght,
Grave was his grace, when he on wing did hover;
At last his heaven-borne sight he did uncover,   *appearance*
    And with a shudder all the house he spangled   *made glitter*
70   With twinkling dew, unto his plumes were tangled.   *attached*

Amazde at first, but not greatlie agast   *horrified*
To see his glorie great, she changed hew;
A blushing rednes swiftlie came and past

And dayntilie her whitenes did subdew;   *delicately*
75 The lightning rayes that from her eye-lids flew,
    When sodaine joy made tumbling teares overflow,
    Would soone have set an heape of hearts on low.   *in a blaze*

    The first seene signe of her trew chastitie
    Round fleeting flew, and cannopyed her skinne;   *veiled*
80 Two frothie globes of equall quantitie
    Playde on her breast, with vaynes blew, blushing, thin;
    Her tempting mouth above her dimpled chin,
        Her rankes of pearle her halfe up-spreading roses   *teeth; lips*
        Still other kist, while still each other closes.

85 Between the branches of her bodie lay   *arms*
    Great Egypt's wonders in the holie print,   *book*
    Whereon she reade, and, having reade, would stay
    To meditate, how Moses meeke was sent
    To that proud prince, who never would repent
90   Till all his chariotes, wheeles and assle trees   *axletrees*
        Indented were with sandes amidst the seyes.   *swallowed*

    Whiles would she turne, and over-turne the leafe,
    Whiles gravelie gather up some sentence darke;   *deep meaning*
    Whiles sadlie sit twixt doubting and beleefe,   *seriously*
95 How the first age was closed in an Arke;   *ended*
    Whiles with her foremost joynt she would remarke   *forefinger*
        The trimbling sacrifice that Abram olde
        Made of his tender sonne, with courage bold.

    At last her heart did kindle up her spirite;
100 Her spirite commanded both her knees to bow.
    On yeelding knees the Lord she did intreate,
    Her pithie prayers pure he would allow,   *sincere*
    Which in his presence there she did avow,
        Desyring that in heart he would resolve
105   The apprehensions high she did revolve:

[36]

"What meanes the brangle, so round about mee hang, *confusion; hung*
Whose glancing rayes shew opall changing hewes? *shining*
What meanes the winged spirite, so sweetlie sang
The second Adam's birth with joyfull newes?
110 What boy it is, my soired spirite renewes *youth; wounded*
 With Angel's eyes? What meanes these words of mirth,
 'Glorie to God and peace to man on earth'?"

At these her words, her faith her feare recalled. *restrained*
His beautie's blaze forbade her to admire, *aura; be fearful*
115 For loe, the sanct, his message to unfold, *holy one*
Proclamde these suggred words with smyling cheare: *sweet*
"Hayle Virgine pure, hayle David's daughter deare,
 Hayle well of wemen all, *a qua et unde* *[by and from whom]*
 The Lambe beis borne, *tollens peccata mundi.* *[removing the world's sins]*

120 Hayle Marie mylde, replenished with grace,
Beloved of God, dowed of all cheritee, *endowed with*
That, of the bleeting eires of Adam's race, *lamenting heirs*
This onelie blessing great belongs to thee.
Then, to discharge this message given to mee,
125 I blesse thy actions all, I blesse thy name,
 I blesse that blessed babe springs of thy wambe."

The holie happie salutation given,
New admirations through her senses ran, *senses of wonder*
With thoughts confused and steiked eyes to heaven, *painfully dazzled*
130 Unto the winged spirite, she thus began:
"Am I a mother, never knew a man?
 Or with the scornefull maydes shall I be loathed,
 Whose onlie fault is this, I was betrothed?

Free flees my thoughts, unspotted is my fame,
135 I loath all companie that may allure;
I ballance not my pleasures with my shame;
With Jephthe's girle I live a virgine pure, *like; daughter*

I scorne to be enrold as Sichem's hure;   *whore*
    Therefore the Lord in his appointed day
140   Will grant salvation to this tent of clay.   *body*

I never went to see nor to be seene,   *spectate*
To tymbrell sound I never caroll song;   *tambourine*
I never danced, in cabinet nor greene,   *hall; lawn*
Short passages, nor moving measures long;   *quick-steps; stately*
145 Earings of gold in treasses never hang
    Lyke twinkling stars; I never learnde to smyle
    With rolling eyes, nor merging minyearde style.   *sinking to; wanton*

I never shew my snow-white swelling globes,   *revealed*
To give the insolent the more delyte;   *immoderate*
150 I never walked in silken shyning robes,
The feeders of ourfacill appetyte: *over-keen*
Dittayes of love I never did indyte;   *lyrics*
    I never used perfumes nor paynted face,
    Nor treted courtlie beck with minsing pace."   *sought; nod; gait*

155 "No, Marie, no, thy spotles thoughtes are knowne,
Thy faith is seene to the al-seeing eye;
Through all the earth thy blessings shall be showne,
Then feare thou not reprochfull infamie.
The Spirite in God shall over-shadow thee;
160   By him thou shalt conceave that holie one,
    That sit for ever shall on David's throne.

Great shall he be, his kingdome shall not move,   *end*
Over all the house of Jacob shall he sway;
All power shall be granted him above,
165 The corners of the earth shall him obey.
The Gentile kings to him shall tribute pay
    Upon their knees, in honour of his birth,
    At Bethleem,* with gold, incense and mirth.

Heaven's soldiers shall scumme the toplesse skyes, *clear*
170 And sound the phamphere of his fame on hie, *fanfare*
Preists, propheits, patriarks, with holie cryes
That night about poore sheepherds' heads shall flie; *around*
The angels and archangels in degrie, *order*
    And winged cherebins, with warbling voice,
175   Round in a ring shall mightelie rejoyce.

With all the blessed troupe's hierarchies,
As powers, thrones, and dominations:
Blest seraphins and principalities,
Victorious martyres with immortall crownes,
180 Young innocents, pure virgine, whose renownes *reputations*
    Gainst all assaults have keept their chastetie,
    As myd-wyve skild that office shall supplie.

Now while these melodies shall mountaines move,
And every angell shall another leade;
185 This wonder, wondrous for to approve, *proclaim*
Each sheepherd shall tune on an oaten reade, *play; reed pipe*
With lylting lowde fast home-ward shall they speede, *singing*
    And cause the countrie people all conveene,
    To praise the Lord, for wonders by them seene.

190 Then shall the ocean tumble up her sand, *ruffle*
And prease her bounds to breake, thy Sonne to see; *strive; limits*
The wandring starres shall twinkling over him stand,
Which was the guyde to Herode's princes three;
The fyrie lampe of heaven's blew cannopie
195   Lest he be last his service to advance, *offer*
    Shall give thy babe good morrow with a glance. *radiance*

All flesh shall fold, all nations shall have peace, *give way*
Sybilla'es prophecies no faith shall have; *credence*
By him the Delphin oracle shall cease, *through*

200 The Gentiles' gods no longer shall deceave;
     And, if thou would of me this question crave,
          What name he heght, these errours shall expel: *is called*
          Manie they are, but first 'Immanuell'.

     The Gentiles' hope, and Jacob's morning starre,
205 The rocke of rayne, and the cornerstone,
     The flower of Jesse, that doth sent so farre,   *scent*
     The trew Messias, and that holie one,
     The Prince of Peace, the Resurrection,
          A Christ, a Jesus and a Salviour,
210   A Lambe, a Silo, and a great Pastour.   *shepherd*

     The furnisher of faith, the mercie-sait,
     The sanctuarie great of man's refuge,
     The Lord's annoynted and his rewler great,
     The word, the way, the prophete and the judge,
215 The ruther of the Arke in the deludge: *steersman*
          The bread of lyfe, the alpha and the end,
          The dove that Noe in his ambassage send.   *embassy*

     The well of lyfe, the bread sent down from heaven,
     His Father's image, bewtifull and faire,
220 Brightnes it selfe, to whom all glore is given,
     The first begotten, and his Father's aire,   *heir*
     The serpent strong, the helle's all-spulyier,   *harrower*
          The bishoppe of our soules, and brother deare:
          Blest be thy bellie such a babe doth beare."   *womb*

225 Now while this winged spirite had told this tale,
     The sweete alluring lookes and comelie grace,
     The mayde that at his entrie seemed pale,
     Shynde lyke the birneist beames of Tytan's face;   *burnished*
     Dread left her thoghts, feare gave high joy the place,
230   Her eyes, eares, heart, and tongue were all content,
          Unto his happie charge to give consent.   *message*

"Thou the Creator of all creature,
That formed the globe, the morning and the nights, *earth*
That set the seyes, and made the aire so pure, *placed*
235 That spangled all the heavens with fyrie lights, *decorated*
Confirme thy promise, made in all our sights;
    And let thy hand-mayde finde that happie blessing,
    Which Israel's dames could not obtain by wishing.

With hyssope purge and purifie my heart,
240 Direct thy Spirite to cloath me with his wings:
Thy graces great on me, pure me, impart,
Mount up my earthlie thoghts to heavenlie things: *raise*
And since that I even of the king of kings
    The mother am, Lord, lift my voice on high,
245   With some sweete song thy name to magnifie."

As this [s]he said, the sweete renewing Ghost,
Cled with a cloud, begouth to doe his dew; *began; duty*
With glorie great he fild the house almost,
Like to a turtle white his image grew. *dove*
250 Betwene the angell and the mayd he flew
    With soft, sweete, sober course, and then did light *motion*
    Betwene her lips, then vanisht out of sight.

O far-fetcht fainting breath, O chivering chin, *exquisite; trembling*
O flightring heart, and eyes entombe in teares, *fluttering; drowned*
255 O hollow warbling throte, now, now begin,
With never tyring tune, to fill the eares
Of everie creature my blessing heares.
    O happie soule, see thou these verses warpe, *proclaim*
    Lyke these sometimes were sung to David's harpe. *those which once*

Marie's song.

260 The heavens' eternall al-foreseeing king,
Our thoughts' deepe searcher, Nature's father great, *examiner*

The world's strong mover, founder of all thing
Within the round and the infernall pit: *earth*
    Strange graces hes he granted unto me,
265   That without sin I should sing lullabie.

From high he hes beheld my pure estate,
And made my flightring spirite his praise proclame; *fluttering*
His kindnes hes no periode nor date
To all him loves; all holie be his name;
270   The proud he hes despysed for love of me,
    And bids me sing on high sweete lullabie. *aloud*

He hes deject the mightie from their thrones,
And mounted humble hearts of poorest spirite; *raised*
Refresht he hes the hunger-sterving bones *dying of hunger*
275 Of simple soules lay begging by the streete;
    He hes sent downe his angell unto me,
    And bids me rock the babe with lullabie.

That happie promise now he will fulfill,
Made in sweete Eden's glauncing gardene gay, *radiant*
280 To Abram on the sacrificing hill,
To him whose harpe drave Saul's evill spirit away;
    He hes resolved, the mother I should be
    To his deare deare, and sing sweete lullabie.

For which sweete song such guerdone shall be given, *reward*
285 When hopelesse age hes poynted out my end, *indicated*
The fourth place in the diamantine heaven, *starry*
Where troupes of winged spirites shall me attend;
    And on the earth each age shall speake of me,
    For singing their sweete Saviour's lullabie.

Walter Quin (c. 1575–1640)

In the context of the poets in this anthology, Quin was an exotic outsider. He was born in Dublin, and for reasons unknown arrived in Scotland in the 1590s from the Jesuit university of Ingolstadt (Bavaria) to enrol as a student of theology at Andrew Melville's Protestant university of St Andrews. Quin's Latin writings on the subject of the English succession attracted the notice of the authorities, and they gained the favour of King James. In his multi-language collection *Sertum poeticum* [Poetic flower-garland] (Edinburgh, 1600) Quin hailed James as *inter alia* the darling of the Muses, the great peace-maker, the heir of King Arthur, the future ruler of all three British kingdoms, the sole commander between Norway and Spain, the descendant of Henry VII, and the obvious and legitimate successor of Elizabeth. He provided a commendatory stanza to William Alexander's verse-drama *Darius* (Edinburgh, 1603). Like David Murray, Quin was attached to the service of Prince Henry, to whom he acted as tutor, and he lost no time in following the Scottish Court to London. On the Prince's death (1612), he contributed poems to the London memorial volume assembled by Joshua Sylvester, *Lachrimae lachrimarum* [The distillation of tears]; in the 1613 reprint of this work, Sylvester added a supplement of *Sundry Funeral Elegies*, with contributions by John Donne and other prominent English poets.

Quin subsequently transferred to the household of Henry's brother Charles, proclaimed Prince of Wales in November 1616. For the latter he prepared – it would seem, from an earlier version in French – *The Memorie of the most worthie and renowmed Bernard Stewart, Lord D'Aubigni renewed* (London, 1619): this contained, first, a verse account of the heroic career of this relation of King James IV (supported by a string of references from historical sources), followed by poems in praise of Prince Charles. The many complimentary poems addressed to Quin by others (including one from Alexander) prefacing this work is an indication of the esteem in which he was held. When a few years later Charles married Henrietta Maria of France, Quin celebrated the event in his *In nuptiis principum incomparabilium* [On the nuptials of the incomparable princes] (London, 1625), with poems in English, Latin, French and Italian. Of all the poets who moved south after James's accession to the English throne, Quin probably had the briefest personal contact with Scotland itself. Nonetheless, his commitment to the ethos of the Jacobean Court was strong and unwavering, his social circle was well developed, and his remarkable facility in languages equipped him to make a valuable contribution to Scottish literature.

Elisabeth Stewart: A Sonnet.   [wQ1]

A BLIST SWEET HEART, O nymphe of noble kind,   *race*
Thou art, as sheweth thy name by presage cleere: *portent*
A blessing by the heavens to earth assignd,
As heart to bee accounted sweet and deere.
5   A BLIST SWEET HEART, thy nource, and such as neere   *nurse*
Were to thy craddle, gan the first to greet: *began; thee*
Thy royall parents oft with smiling cheere,
Have named the their HEART both BLIST, and SWEET.
This use they also for a greeting meet   *suitable*
10   Who now thy beautie though in blossom sie:
But when the same by growth shall be compleet,
And shall with vertues rare adorned bee.
      Then all, but one, a king, thine above all,   *except*
        A BLIST SWEET HEART shall thee account and call.

**Epithalamium by Walter Quin for the mariage
of W[illiam] A[lexander and] J[anet] E[r]sk[ine].** [WQ2]

Loe, heir a youth, of yong men paragone,
Loe, ther a nymphe, the honour of her sex,
By happye lot combind together soone   *quickly*
By love, which doth not them by crosses vex;   *impediments*
5 For with delay the flower of youth doth waste:
    O Hymen, come, and knit this couple fast.   *securely*

Yet never, Hymen, didst thou couple linke
That was more meet to be together bound:
What ever thing praiseworthie wee may thinke
10 Both in thar age and sex in them is found.
Therefore as they and wee thee call in haste:
    O* Hymen, [come, and knit this couple fast].

Most comelye shape and feature doth adorne
Both with proportion like and symmetrye,   *similar*
15 And under planets like they have beene borne
With manneres like and vertue's sympathie;
As hee, so she is gentle, wise and chast:
    O Hymen, [come, and knit this couple fast].

To them both Phebus and the sisters nine
20 Impart their hevnly giftes abundantlye;
To him their swetest dittyes they assigne,
To her their sweet and pleasant harmonie;
Then, that this double sweetnesse wee may taste,
    O Hymen, [come, and knit this couple fast].

25 With sweet and hevnlye muse allureth hee,   *words; attracts*
And doth contend and please the rarest witts,   *finest minds*
Her lute, with which his muse doth well agree,
Of passionate mindes doth ease the raging fitts,   *troubled moods*
And cheereth such as into dumpes are cast: *depressions*
30   O Hymen, [come, and knit this couple fast].

Therefore, since hee and shee so sympathise   *agree*
In outward parts and qualities of mind,
And in all points that may to love entise,
As shee alone is meet his hart to binde
35 And hee to louss her maiden belt from waste,   *girdle; waist*
    O Hymen, [come, and knit this couple fast].

Dame Juno, patronesse of wedlocke's band,
Delightfull Cupid, with thy mother cleer,   *beauteous*
Bright Phebus with the Muses be at hand,
40 To grace and honour those your darlings dear;
And when from hall to chamber they be past,   *bedroom*
    O Hymen, [come, and knit this couple fast].

Then lett not shame, nor mother's tender love,
Nor pittye fond of any maide, her mate,   *foolish; companion*
45 Hold backe the bride from field, where she shall prove   *battle*
Victorious, after but a small debate,   *contention*
And when with bridegroom's arms she shall be claspt,
    O Hymen, [come, and knit this couple fast].

With favour great of powers celestiall,
50 With parents' blissing and especiall joy,
With kind assent of friends and kinred all,
Without envious grudging or annoy,
With love and concord, that may ever last,
    O Hymen, [come, and knit this couple fast].

The Prince's Epitaph, written by his Highnes' servant, Walter Quin. [WQ3]

Lo, here intomb'd a peerelesse Prince doth lie,
In flowre and strength of age surpris'd by death,
On whom, when he on earth drew vitall breath,
The hope of many kingdoms did relie;
5   Not without cause: for heavens most liberally
To him all princely virtues did bequeath,
Which to the worthiest princes here beneath,
Before had been allotted severally.   *individually*
    But when the world of all his vertues rare
10 The wished fruit to gather did expect,
And that he should such glorious workes effect,
As with the worthiest Fame might him compare,
    Untimely death then from us did him take,
    Our losse and griefe, heaven's gaine and joy, to make.

Of his last retiring to Corstorfin. [WQ4]

Linternum, though obscure, the place became
Of famous Scipio's last abode, when, Spaine
And Carthage having conquer'd, with disdain
Ungratefull Rome he loth'd and left the same.   *scorned*
5   Corstorfin, as obscure in shew or name,   *appearance*
Did noble Bernard for her guest retaine,
From thankelesse France when he came home againe,
To Scipio like in fortune as in fame.   *alike*
    Linternum, whilest her venerable guest
10 Did her inhabit, greater worth possest,
Then great and worthy Rome in all her treasure.
    Corstorfin also may be said as well,
Whiles worthy Bernard deign'd in her to dwell,
Of worth to have possest, as great a measure.

Of his buriall in the same place. [wQ5]

Brave Bernard, of a noble linage borne
In Scotland, whom such vertures did adorne,   *achievements*
As did him more ennoble, and in France
Deservedly to honour high advance;
5   Who England's parted roses, and with them
The Scottish thistle, in their royall stemme
Help'd to unite; who of a ruler wise
And valiant warriour well deserv'd the prize,
In Italy, chiefe theater of his worth,
10   And victories; whose fame from south to north,
From east to west did through all Europe flye,
Interr'd doth in obscure Corstorfin lie.
But I mistake: his better part is past   *departed*
To heav'n, on earth his fame shall ever last.

Elizabeth Melville, Lady Culross (c. 1575–1631)

Melville had all the qualifications to be associated with the Jacobean-Parnassians. She was the daughter of the courtier Sir James Melville of Halhill (d. 1617), who as a diplomat served King James and had several interviews with Queen Elizabeth. His *Memoirs* show that he comported himself with confidence in high society, and several of Elizabeth Melville's uncles likewise occupied distinguished positions in royal, civic or legal service. However, his poet-daughter's deeply held religious convictions led her to turn away from the worldly allurements of Court life for the sake of a closer walk with God.

In this respect she recalls Alexander Hume, and both came from a similar social background in the upper gentry. Hume indeed greatly admired his fellow poet, and dedicated to her his *Hymnes, or Sacred Songs* (Edinburgh, 1599), speaking of himself therein as 'Your brother in the Lord Jesus'. For a long time, almost the only known poetic production by Melville was *Ane Godlie Dreame* (Edinburgh, 1603) – a meditation on sin and the chance of salvation, incorporating an account of a journey through an allegorical land-scape, of which the physical dangers and pains prefigure the tribulations of the Christian soul in the sinful land of the living. By virtue of this poem, which, being perfectly suited to the times, was frequently reissued, Melville has the distinction of being the first female Scottish poet to see her own work in print. The short poem included in the present anthology accompanied *Ane Godlie Dreame* in the same volume. In having recourse to the well-tried genre of dream-vision, Melville looks back to the Castalian world of Alexander Montgomerie and beyond (MacDonald 2009a), but in her convictions she connects with later and avowedly Presbyterian poets, such as James Anderson, James Melville and John Dykes (Reid-Baxter 2005, 2013; Ross 2019).

In recent times, a substantial corpus of religious poetry in manuscript has been discovered, and this can with confidence be attributed to Melville (Reid-Baxter 2010). This greatly adds to her status as poet and substantiates Hume's 1599 reference to 'your compositions so copious, so pregnant, so spirituall, that I doubt not but that it is the gift of God in you'. Though Melville's thematic range is not wide – all her poetry is profoundly occupied with the anguished awareness of sin and the anxious quest for the reassurance of justification – her command of verse technique is unerringly good. The intensely personal lyrical voice in such writings would have rendered them more suitable for circulation in manuscript among her spiritual kin, rather than for dissemination via the public medium of print.

Several of Melville's lyrics are *contrafacta* (religious reworkings) of worldly, amatory and popular songs, which they follow in their stanza-form, rhyme and, as far as possible, in their wording; such religious adaptations were propagated among the godly by being sung to the melodies of the existing models (Reid-Baxter 2005). Melville, like Sir William Mure, came from a house where such worldly songs were well known and appreciated. Like Alexander Craig (AC8), she made an imitation of Marlowe's famous lyric 'Come live with me and be my love' (Reid-Baxter 2010: 7–9), albeit that, unlike Craig, Melville transformed the original secular song into a religious poem. She was clearly well aware of the mainstream of Jacobean court culture, but deliberately turned her back upon it: for her, Parnassus meant metaphysics, not mythology.

A comfortabill song. [EM1]   *comforting*
   To the tune of 'Sall I let her go?'

Away, vaine warld, bewitcher of my heart,
My sorrow shawes, my sinnes maks me to smart:
Yit will I not dispair, bot to my God repair,
   He hes mercie ay, thairfoir will I pray;
5   He hes mercie ay, and loves me,
   Thouch be his troubling hand he proves me.   *by; tests*

Away, away, too lang thou hes mee snared,
I will not tyne more time, I am prepared: *lose*
Thy subtill slicht so slie, thou hes dissavit mee: *trick; deceived*
10   Though they sweitlie smyle, smoothlie they begyle,
   Thogh they sweetlie smyle, suspect them;
   The simpill sort they syle, reject them.   *folk; blind*

Once more away, showes, loth the world to leave,   *illusions*
Bids oft away with her that halds me slave;
15 Loth am I to forgo, that sweit alluring fo.
    Sence thy wayes are vaine, shall I them retaine?
    Sence thy wayes are vaine, I quyte thee,   *leave*
    Thy pleasure shall no more delyte mee.

A thousand tymes away, ah, stay no more.
20 Sweete Christ, me saif, lest subtill sin devore:
Without thy helping hand, I have no strenth to stand;
    Lest I turne asyde, let thy grace me guyde:
    Lest I turne asyde, draw neere me,
    And when I call for help, Lord, heir me.

25 Quhat shall I do? Ar all my pleasures past?
Shall worldlie lusts now take their leave at last?   *delights*
Yea, Christ, these earthlie toyes shall turne in heavenlie joys.   *vanities*
    Let the world be gone, I will love Christ alone,
    Let the world be gone, I cair not;
30   Christ is my love alone, I feare not.

Sir Robert Ayton (1569–1638)

Although there is a wealth of documentation pertaining to the later period of Ayton's life, that is not the case for the years before 1600. After his time at St Andrews, where he overlapped with Alexander Craig, he seems to have been abroad in the 1590s, and it is assumed that he studied in France: this period on the Continent, during which some of his early verse may have been written, is relatively obscure. Around 1603, however, he arrived in London, and his career thereafter was centred on the Court, where he became Gentleman of the Bedchamber and Groom of the Privy Chamber. In 1612 he – and not John Donne – succeeded William Fowler as secretary to Queen Anne, and, at a later date, he would act in the same capacity for Queen Henrietta Maria. In 1609, Ayton travelled in Germany, where he was entrusted to deliver to a selection of Protestant princes copies of James's reply to the Pope's reply to the King's *Apologie for the Oath of Allegiance* (1607): in recognition of this service, he was awarded a pension and in 1612 knighted. Ayton was independently wealthy, and he further benefited greatly from numerous pensions and appointments. He was a highly successful man of the establishment, and in 1615 was granted denization (naturalisation) in England. In 1623, on the death of the Provost of Eton, Thomas Murray of Tullibardine, he was a candidate (although without success) for that same position, against several very prominent and distinguished figures (e.g. Sir Francis Bacon, Sir Dudley Carleton). He moved mainly in the circles of English courtiers, officials, poets and authors, and was ultimately honoured with burial in Westminster Abbey, below a monument featuring his head in bronze.

Ayton's friendship with Craig led him to contribute a liminary sonnet in the latter's *Poeticall Essayes* (1604) and to a sonnet in the same poet's *Poetical Recreations* (1609). These two poems, together with another liminary sonnet in William Alexander's *Monarchick Tragedies* (1604), are the only vernacular works by Ayton to appear in print. His other vernacular works survive in manuscript, often in multiple copies: for example, his lyric 'Upon Love' (not included here) survives in no fewer than fourteen such versions (Gullans 1963: 183–4, 295–300). The poem was indubitably popular, and it may have served as an influence on George Lauder's lyric on the same theme (GL4). In their cultivation of a lightly cynical elegance, such poems anticipate what is generally considered typical of the Caroline style.

The only poem by Ayton appearing as an independent printed work was, significantly, in Latin: *Basia: sive Strena* [Affectionate greetings: or, a New Year's gift], dedicated to Sir James Hay (London, 1605). At a later date, however, he permitted his Latin poetry to be collected into Arthur Johnston's *Delitiae poetarum Scotorum* (Amsterdam, 1637) (Reid 2013, 2016; Reid and McOmish 2020). The difference in the manner of publication – manuscript *vis-à-vis* print – shows that for Ayton, who moved habitually in elevated and aristocratic circles, 'the stigma of print' – a concept originally proposed in relation to the English poetry of the sixteenth century (Saunders 1951) – was presumably still relevant, at least as far as vernacular verse was concerned. Scoto-British poets of lower social status suffered less from such inhibition.

[An Exhortation.]   [RAY1]

If high excess of irrelenting smart   *unyielding pain*
Inforce not words to fayle, and thoughts to faint,
My love would now convince both tongue and heart
To say farewell unto my sweetest saint;
5 But while affection would my woes reveale,
And say unto my sweetest heart farewell,
My senses are soe suffocat'd with care
They sigh, they grone, then sayes nothing but faire.

Then, fairest faire, read in my sighes and teares
10 The secrete anguish of they dyeing slave,   *thy*
Who, for the love unto thy worth he beares,
Hath consecrat'd his soule unto the grave,
And now is forc'd from thy dissdaines to goe
Where death may end his never ending woe,
15 Yet swearing still by all the lights above
Ten thousands deaths shall never end his love.

And, thus resolv'd, I only begg of the,
Amidds my sadd exile, this poore releife,
That, if thou cannot thinke with love on mee,
20 Thou would with pitty pause upon my grieffe,
Or, if perhapps this little seeme too much,
As, Ah!, I feare thy rigour shall be such,
That, when some friend my name to minde shall call,
Thou'll only sigh and wish mee well, that's all.

[To Mistress Margaret Lesly, Thereafter Lady of Madertie.]   [RAY2]

Religious relics of that ruinous place
Which sometimes gloried in the glore of saints,
Now hath noe glore but one whereof it wants.   *lacks*
That one saint's beauty makes it heaven of grace,
5 In balmie feildes, which fairds her flourie face   *adorns*
With sweet perfumes of cornes, of trees, of plants,   *crops*
While Neptune swells with pride, when there he hants,   *dwells*
And laughs for joy such beauty to embrace.
Beare me record, that while I passed by
10 I did my dut'ous homage to your Dame:
How thryce I sight, thrice on her name did cry,   *sighed*
Thrice kist the ground for honour of the same;
      Then left those lynes to tell her on a tree,
      That she made them to live and mee to dye.

[The Power of Love.]　[RAY3]

Can eagles' birds fly lower then there kinde,　　　　　　*young; nature*
Or can ambition stoope to servile gaine?　　　　　　　*descend*
Can free-borne breasts be forc'd against there minde
To put the maske of love upon disdaine?　　　　　　　*semblage*
5　Can love be bought, can avarice constraine
Greate Cupid to do homage unto gold?
Can he his wings, can he his flames restraine,
Or be induced to wishes worldlings would?　　　　　　*might desire*
Noe, noe, my fates are in the heavens inrold:　　　　　*written*
10　Men's lawes may force my life, but not my love;
Men may my eyes, but not my heart, behold;
My eyes may thers, my heart my owne shall prove.
　　And ere I change, by t'heavens I vow, to leave
　　A joyless bedd, and take a joyfull grave.

[On the River Tweed.]　[RAY4]

Faire famous flood, which sometyme did devyde,
But now conjoynes, two diadems in one,
Suspend thy pace, and some more softly slyde,　　　　*somewhat; flow*
Since wee have made the trinchman of our mone.　　　*spokesman: moan*
5　And since non's left but thy report alone
To show the world our captaine's last farewell,
That courtesye, I know, when wee are gon,
Perhapps your lord, the sea, will it reveale.
And you againe the same will not conceale,
10　But straight proclaim't through all his bremish bounds,　*salty*
Till his high tydes these flowing tydeings tell,　　　*watery greetings*
And soe will send them with his murmering sounds
　　To that religious place, whose stately walls
　　Does keepe the heart which all our hearts inthralls.　*captivates*

Upon the 5th of November.   [RAY5]

The mighty Mavors, jealous to behold	*Mars*
A Mars more mighty nor himself below,	*than; on earth*
Did once resolve his rivall to ore'throw	
By assassins, whome open force made bold.	*violence*
5 But finding there that open force did fold	*give way*
Under the princely valour of his foe,	
Hee then determin'd to assayle him soe	
As noe defence should his offence withhold.	*prevent*
Thus comes he downe to Pluto'es pale abode,	
10 And there for fyre and brimstone straight doth call,	
Wherewith he thinks to play the thundering god,	
And make the world admire his ryvall's fall.	*marvel at*
But sease, fond Mars, to make the world to wonder;	*foolish*
Ten thousand lawrells save's our Mars from thunder.	

Æthon Cragio suo.   [RAY6]

[Ayton, to his friend Craig]

Fane wold I sing, if songs my thoghts culd ease,	
Or calme the tempest of my troubled mynde:	
Faine would I force my silent Muse to please	
The gallant humor of thy wanton vane:	*talent*
5 But O, a miser mancipat to paine,	*in thrall*
Sould slave to sorrow, wedded to mischief,	*sold*
By mirth of songs, perhaps more greefe might gane,	*increase*
In vane of them I should expect relief:	
Then, sacred Craig, if thou wold ease my greefe,	
10 Invite me not to wantonize with thee:	*sport*
But tune thy notes unto my mourning cleif,	*key*
And when I weepe, weepe thou to echo me.	
Perhaps the teares that from a Craig shall floe,	*rock*
May prove a soveraigne balme to cure my woe.	

To his coy Mistres.   [RAY7]

What uthers doth discourage and dismay
Is unto me a pastime and a play.
I sport in her deneyalls and doe know
Weman love best that does love least in show.

5   Tuo sudden favors may abate delight,   *too*
When modest coynes sharpes the appetite.
I grow the hotter for hir cold neglect,
And more inflam'd when sho shows least respect.
Heat may aryse from rocks, from flints so fyre,

10   So from hir coldnes I doe strik desire.
Sho, knoweinge this, perhapes resolves to try   *test*
My faith and patience, offering to denay
What e're I aske of hir, that I may be
More taken with hir, for hir slightinge me.

15   When fishes play with baites, best, anglers say,   *the trick*
To mak them bite, is drawe the baite away.
So dallies sho with me till, to my smart,
Both baite and hooke stickes fastened in my hart.
And now I am become hir foolishe prey,

20   And, that sho knowes, I cannot break away.
Let hir resolve no longer to be free
From Cupid'es bondes, and bind hir self to me.
Nor let hir vex me longer, with despair
That they be crewell that be younge and fair:

25   It is the old, the creased, and the blake   *wrinkled*
That are unkynd, and for affectione lacke.
I'le ty hir eyes with lynes, hir eares with moanes,
Hir marble hart I'le pearce with hydious groanes,
That nather eyes, eares, hart sall be at rest

30   Till sho forsaike hir sier to love me best;   *guardian*
Nor will I raise my seige nor leave my feild,
Till I have mead my valiant mistres yeeld.   *made; stern*

[Song.] [RAY8]

O that my tongue had beene as dumbe,
    As now I finde
    My eyes were blinde,
When they did make my heart become
5 A vottary unto a saint
That hath noe eares to my complaint.

Had I but made my eyes my tongue,
    My very lookes
    Had serv'd for bookes,
10 Wherein she might have read her wrong;
But now my words as charmes she feares,   *spells*
And serpent-like doth shutt her eares.

Yet who would not have cry'd for ayd,
    Burnt to the quick?
15   A senseless stick,
To Vulcan's tyrranny betrai'd,
Will wast itself in moyst expence,
And keepe a noyse as if't had sense.

Speake then, must I, though to noe end,
20   For love doth say
    That silence may
Much more then freindly speech offend:
Love once profess'd, and then forborne,   *withheld*
Turns deafe neglect to spightfull scorne.

Upon Prince Henry his death, to Prince Charles.   [RAY9]

Admired Phœnix, springing up a pace
From th'ashes of another Phœnix' bones,
Which too, too courteous, yielded the his place,
Lest earth were burthen'd with two birds at once
5 Of that rare kinde which loves to live alone,
Whose only essence is to be but one.

Alexander Craig of Rosecraig (c. 1567–1627)

Craig, who described himself in 1606 as 'Scoto-Banfa', was born at Banff, on the Moray Firth, and there he probably died. He was a student at St Andrews from 1582 to 1586, where he was a contemporary of Robert Ayton. He went to London in the wake of King James in 1603, attached to the household of George, Lord Home (d. 1611), James's Lord Treasurer and from 1605 Earl of Dunbar. Craig was awarded a pension for life. He published two collections of poems in London (*The Poeticall Essayes of Alexander Craige Scotobritane*, 1604; *The Amorose Songes, Sonets and Elegies*, 1606), but did not remain there long. By 1609 he was back home, had married, and had bought Rosecraig (close by the ruined castle of Banff) as well as a house by Rothiemay, north of Huntly. In 1621 he represented Banff in the Scottish Parliament. His two collections after his London period were *The Poetical Recreations* (Edinburgh, 1609) and *The Poeticall Recreations* (Aberdeen, 1623). Despite the near-identity of their titles, these two volumes differ considerably in their contents – the first consisting of a wealth of short poems addressed to Craig's contemporary patrons and friends, and the second consisting of poems on generalised moral or Classical subjects. On the occasion of King James's visit to Kinnaird (Perthshire) in 1617, Craig delivered a poem which appeared in the *Muses' Welcome* of the following year. After his death, *The Pilgrime and Heremite* was published under Craig's name at Aberdeen (1631), though the poet may well have been working on it as early as 1623 (Spiller 2013: 379). However, this poem, both in genre and style, with its ostentatious use of alliteration, is an outlier in Craig's work, and its length excludes it from the present anthology.

Craig may have been a late-starter in poetry, for none seems to survive from before James's accession to the English throne. In his evident preference for the retired life on his own property, he may be compared to William Drummond. Craig's initial enthusiasm for James's move to England, and his subsequent apparent disillusion with life at Court, corresponds to the pattern noted for Simion Grahame, albeit with less overt sign of cooling in his attitude towards the King: indeed, his 1617 welcome poem shows him still as a patriotic royalist, urging the King to return to the land of his fathers.

Craig began as the writer of occasional and celebratory poems. He was a voracious reader of certain favourite authors (e.g. Herodotus, Plutarch), whose works he mined for a host of recondite references: this has led him to be accused of having a 'stuffed head' (Spiller 1988: 147), and it is undeniable that in some of his best poems Craig makes large demands on the general knowledge of his reader. On occasion his far-fetched allusions seem to be less than perfectly appropriate, and to be mainly designed to please those readers delighting in curious knowledge. In the sonnets of *Amorose Songes*, his largest single work, he addresses no fewer than eight ladies: Idea, Cynthia, Lithocardia, Kala, Erantina, Lais, Pandora and Penelope. Drummond criticised Craig's love-sonnets as those of a 'Poore braine-sicke man', and noted that 'Such sillie rime can not make women love.' (Kastner 1913: II, 247). However, it has been suggested that Craig is not celebrating actual mistresses but rather responding to the potential variety in the rhetoric of love poetry, with his bevy of ladies standing for poetry that is, respectively, Platonic, seriously virtuous, intellectual, bucolic, Petrarchan, sensual, noble and modest, and richly endowed (Jack 1969: 378). In his two volumes of *Recreations* Craig found himself on perhaps firmer ground – with epigrams on contemporary public figures, on personal friends, and on traditional topics of public morality. These are written from a neo-Stoical, and ultimately anti-aulic, standpoint, by one who has opted to distance himself from the political and social centre. From such a position, it was but a small step to the genre of advice to princes and to the cultivation of a brusque and quasi-imperative manner (AC16) reminiscent of the satires of John Donne and of the famous lyric 'The Lie', attributed to Sir Walter Ralegh.

The Author to his Booke. [AC1]

When Dedal taught his tender sonne to flee,
Out through the subtile watrie vaults of aire.   *vaporous*
"Goe not too high, nor yet too low", sayd hee,
"Of floodes beneath, of fire above beware";
5   So, home-bred rimes, you Icare-like must rise,
Mid-way betwixt the vulgar and the wise.

For you shall be unto the vulgar sort,
No fit propine, because not understood;   *gift*
And with the wise you must have small resort,   *association*
10 Since they can reape, in reading you, no good;
Like Dedalus I then direct, thus flie,
Goe neither low nor yet, I pray, too hie.

And though you be directed to a king,
By any meanes approach not Court, I pray,
15 For some will say my precepts pricke and sting,
And some shall scorne, some carpe, some caste away;
But, as you must, if that to Court thou goe,
Since freindes are few, I pray you breed no foe.

Aerii montes et mollia prata, nemusque,
20   *et vos carminibus flumina nota meis,*
Quod me tam gracilem voluistis ferre poetam,
indignor, magnæ laudis amore calens.

[O you lofty mountains, lush meadows and groves, and you rivers
recorded in my poems, I, though burning with the love of great praise,
am disappointed that you have wished to make me a poet so slender.]
—Pontanus

To the Kinge's most excellent Majestie. [AC2]

Epistle Congratulatorie and Parænetic. *full of advice*

Scarse had my Muse respir'd the smallest space, *recovered breath*
From paynting prayses of our civill pace, *peace*
Pack'd up by thee, most gratious King, of late *concluded*
In Calidon's disturb'd unquiet state,
5 When loe, the kalendes of this pleasent spring, *beginning*
Unto my eares did joyfull tydinges bring
That bles'd Eliza had resignd her breath,
And payde the last and hindmost debt to death.
O fatall death, the fatall end of all,
10 With equall mace thou chops both great and small, *degree; cut down*
And thou design'd her diadems to weyre, *designated; wear*
Of royall blood her nyest agnat heyre. *closest male-line*
   Thou, like a Noah, long hast kep't thy Arke,
Thoyld manie storme by daye, and gloomie darke, *endured*
15 Yet would not breake thy ward till time thy God *bounds; until*
Hath lent thee leave, and bids thee walke abrode. *at liberty*
But his commaund since thou wouldst nothing do, *without*
Loe, he hath joynd his blessinges thereunto:
Come foorth with wife and children, sweete command,
20 The blessing brook* and multiply the land. *enjoy*
   Thus am I solv'd of all my wonted doubt: *cleared*
Nor wits nor weirdes thy fortunes bringes about, *humans; fates*
But that eternall providence above:
Which thou art bound to serve with feare and love.
25 Those newes of new, have wak'd my sleeping vaine, *recent; mind*
And makes me write unto your Grace againe
Most harty greetings of thy happy chaunce,
Since thou art king of England, Ireland, Fraunce,
Besides that famous and unmatch'd renowne
30 Of thy unconquered olde and Scottish crowne.
Long desuetude hath rusted so my quill,
My wits are weake, but great is my good will,

Though scoffing idiots will my paines deprave, *efforts vilify*
And Aristarchus all the credite have.
35 I am to thee, dread Leige, thy aerie elfe: *spirit-servant*
I borrow but thy words for to prayse thy selfe.

Let Muse-foe Mars elsewhere abroad go dwell,
Of warres and wounds let forraigne fachions smell: *factions*
Peace dwels with thee, where it hath dwelt so long,
40 Prone to propell, and to permit no wrong. *drive away*

Wise Periander wreates, that crownes of kings *writes*
On many fearefull fluctuations hings:
And that a monarch's suretie no way stood
In victories, in warrie broyles, and blood; *armed conflicts*
45 But in the love of subjects trust and true, *faithful*
Thence, said the saige, did setling sure ensue. *safe settlement*

Grave Xenophon thy registers records, *echoes*
That deeing Cyrus spoke these selfe same wordes. *dying*
Aratus rare said so to Philip great,
50 That love and peace confirm's a king's estate.
In speculation schoolemen beene divine,
But thou exceeds them, sov'raigne Syre, sensine, *of later date*
For thou has put their sacred gnom's in ure, *maxims; operation*
Perfection in thy practique makes thee sure.
55 Let forraine lands now looke with Envie's ee,
And who would rule, let him come learne at thee:
When ather Momus or Rhamnusia barkes, *while; either*
Thy wits are wondrous both in wreates and warkes. *wisdom; writings*

Oft times said Otho in a rage, that hee
60 Had rather chuse nor be a king to die;
And Diocletian said, to be a king
And well to rule, was most difficill thing.
When Dionise at Siracusa sweare
That Damocles some while his crowne should weare,
65 But, being crownd, he plainely did protest,
He never could be blithe to be so blest.
Were those on life for to behold thee now, *alive*

They could not raigne, nor could they rule as thou;
Thy match on mould nor was, nor yet shall bee: *earth*
70 Thus might they learne for to be kings at thee.
    Ariston's praise is thine, as I suppose,
Thou keeps thy friendes, and reconciles thy foes.
Vespasian-like, whom Rome obeyd with love,
A shepheard both, and carefull king thou prove:
75 Thy folde bene broke, and lo, thou has tane paine *has been*
To recollect thy errant flockes againe. *gather; straying*
Thy scepter and thy sheephooke both are one,
Thou, under heaven, their herd and lord alone.
    And now as Homer paynted Priam foorth,
80 Thou has beside thee men of wit and worth: *wisdom; virtue*
Can any harme or strange thing now betide thee,
Ucalegon, Antenor are beside thee?
Like Macedo the wondering world may doubt thee, *wonder at*
Parmenio and Philotas are about thee.
85 For all these kingdomes which thou doest command,
A part by hop's, a happy part in hand, *expectations; lucky*
Thou has a kingdome to thy selfe unknown;
Looke rightly too, and Cecil is thine owne.
    Were Plato now on life, then would he say
90 That thy republikes blessed are this day:
For thou art wise, and now wise counsell hants, *resorts to*
And with thy wisedome thou supplies their wants.
    Yet this much more I plainely must impart,
A friendly counsel from a faithfull heart:
95 Though farre from Jove and thunder-claps I dwell,
My lines of love, of truth, and zeale shall smell.
Read then my rymes, most wise and prudent Prince,
And let a hog teach Minerve but offence. *without*
Not that I thinke your Grace has any need,
100 Or know's not els what's here, before you reed;
No, I attest great sacred Jove above, *swear by*
I only write to manifest my love.

While in my tugure, such is my estate,   *hut; condition*
I take repast of poore unpeppered kate;   *unseasoned gruel*
105 I thanke my God for such as he doth give,
And pray's withall, that well, and long thou live,
And in seces at solitarie tymes,   *retirement*
Thou art remembred in my rusticke rymes.
Sinetas poore unto the Persian king
110 Cold water in his hollow palme did bring,
Which Artaxerxes lovingly out-dranke,
And gave Sinetas both reward and thanke.
Right so those rivols of my poore ingyne,   *trickles; brain*
I heere present, from out this palme of mine.
115 Read then, dread Leige, those travails of my love,   *labours*
Elaborate and done for thy behove.   *devised; benefit*

   1. Thus I begin. Since adulations vaine,
In courts, with kings and monarch must remaine.
To assentators thou must give some eare,   *connivers*
120 But be no prouder of their prayse a haire:
For Macedo would needs be cald a god,
And to this end his edicts blew abrod,   *trumpeted*
Which on his head did heape disgrace the rather,
Sith hee asham'd that Phillip was his father.   *because*
125   2. Give parasites enough, but not too much,
And be not lavish, least thy lucke be such
As Timon Colneus, who outspent
On Demtas and Gnatonides his rent.
Of that unthankfull numer live anew,   *crowd; plenty*
130 To promise much, and to performe but few:
Be thou the stone, precellent Prince, of tuch,   *touchstone*
For to secerne the honest mindes from such.   *distinguish*
   3. The faithfull man that once hath done thee good,
And for thy life hath ventered life and blood,
135 Be thankfull still to him, doe not despite him,   *always; neglect*
But with thy selfe thinke thou can nee're acquite him.   *fully reward*
Prove not unkinde to cause poore Phocian die,

That thus hath fought, and wun the field for thee;
But when such friends so nigh thy sides are seene,
140 Remember then but them thou had not beene.   *without*
    4. Serapion who is not taught to speike,
Let him not want, suppose he shame to seike;   *even if; beg*
He is thine owne, and loves thee as the leave,   *rest*
His speaking lookes will tell when he would have.   *eloquent*
145 Be, prudent Prince, a Pompey in this case:
A benefite unsought hath double grace.
    5. Change not too oft the rulers of thy state,
For that may breed intestine strange debate: *internal conflict*
The fleeis, els full, for sucking more will slake,   *if; further; refrain*
150 But hungry gnats will make thy woundes to ake.
I pray for them, as did Hymera old,
For Dionise, the tygrish tyran bold:
'Lord save', sayd shee, 'our king from death, disgrace,
For were he gone, a worse would get his place.'
155 Since in this point th'apodosis is plaine,   *conclusion*
I turne my stile unto your Grace againe.   *apply my pen*
    6. If any friend in loving forme reveale   *friendly manner*
Twixt you and him your o'ursights, love him well: *oversights*
Since Plato sayes, the bravest mindes bring foorth
160 Both hatefull vice, and virtue of most worth.
Wise Plutarch writes, in fertill Egipt grew
With medicable, envenomd hearbes anew.   *curative; aplenty*
Doe no rebuke, nor publique shame approve,
But friendly counsaile, which proceedes from love.
165 Be not a drunke Cambises, in despeire
For counsell kind, to kill Prexaspes' heire.   *in return for*
    7. Take Turinus, and smooke him to the death,
Who falsly sels for bribes thy royall breath.   *decree*
    8. Though Alexander in a raging ire,
170 For praysing Philip, his renowned sire,   *father*
Kind Clities kild, be thou more meeke in minde,
And to the praysers of thy parents' kinde.   *family*

9. Within thy heart let no injustice hant,   *dwell*
Let not the wrong'd man weepe for justice' want: *lack*
175 Pausanias' plaintes proud Philip did disdaine,
And cruelly for his contempt was slaine.

10. A woman olde fell downe upon her knee,
And cryed, 'Demetrius, heare my plaints and mee.'
'I have no leasure', answerd he againe:
180 'Hee takes no leasure', sayd the wife, 'to reigne.'
Doe not thine eares, Demetrius-like, obdure,   *shut hard*
With patience heare the sad and plaintive poore.

11. Proud Leo spoyld Justinian his croune,
Deform'd his face, and cut his nose quite doune.
185 But when he got his diadems againe,
He punisht those that erst procur'd his paine: *first*
Each gut of rheume that from his nose did floe,   *drop*
Gave argument for to cut off a foe.   *reason*
O do not thou, great Prince, delight in blood:
190 Of crueltie thow know's can come no good.
Be thow Licurgus, though thow lackes ane ee,
Forgive Alcander, make him man to thee.   *follower*

12.* Vitellius-like, have not a facill will,   *fickle*
Now to graunt grace, and straight commaund to kill.
195 13. Great are thy fortunes, farre beyond beleife,
Thou needs no realmes, nor foraine rents by reife;   *income; plunder*
Thy minde may well luxuriat in thy wealth,
Thy crown's are thine but blood or strife or stealth: *without*
And since thy fortunes are so rare, O than,   *then*
200 Each day with Philip thinke thou art a man.

14. Thogh Agathocles Sicil did enjoy,
Yet was hee sometime but a potter's boy:
And that his pride should not become too great,
In vessels but of loame he tooke his meate.   *earthenware; food*
205 Thy witts the Weird's with great promotion tryes,   *wisdom; Fates; test*
For woonder few are happy both and wise.
Though thou be free from blast's of any storme,
Bee humill still, and keepe thy wonted forme.   *humble; usual*

15. Wreat not thy law's with blood as Draco did,   *write*
210 The God of heav'n such crueltie forbid:
A happie life makes ay a happie end,
Be thou a Solon, Draco'is law's to mend.

   16. Herodotus the histor, and right so   *similarly*
The poet Pindars, wreats with many mo,   *many others*
215 That monarchs great, examples good should give,
Since from their lords the laiks learne to live.   *people*
Kinges* be the glas, the verie scoole, the booke,   *mirror*
Where private men do learne, and read, and looke:
Be thou th'attractive adamant to all,   *magnetic stone*
220 And let no wicked wrest thy wits to fall.   *villain; force*
   Goe not to Delphos where Apollo stands,
Licurgus-like, with off'rings in thy hands,
By hellish votes and oracles to see   *pagan rites*
What to thy law should paird or eiked bee.   *subtracted; added*
225 From great Jehovah counsaile seeke, and hee
Shall give both gnom's and oracles to thee,   *maxims; prophecies*
And shall thy spir't with prudence so inspire,
As all the world shall wonder and admire.

   17. From countries farre, great king, behold and see,
230 With rich oblations legates come to thee;   *tributes*
With Vexores and Tanais be glaide
Of fame and honour; let it not be saide,
Thou art a greedie Ninus. Fie, for shame,
That were a staine unto thy noble name.

235   18. Last, since thou art the child of peace, I see
Thy works and writes, are witnes both with mee: *writings*
(Thy works I have no leasure to unfold,
And though I had, are tedious to be told.)   *too many to count*
Thy writes are wond'rous both in prose and ryme;
240 Let virtue wax and flourish in thy tyme.
Though thou be best and greatest, both, of kinges,
Mongst poets all, is none so sweetely singes.
Thou art the sweet Musæus of our dayes;
And I thy prentice, and must give thee prayse:

245 Some other writer must thy woorth proclaime,
Thou shalt not sing upon thy selfe, for shame.
Thou hast transalpine poets of thine owne,
Whose tragique cothurns through the world are knowne:
Thou has likwise of home-bred Homers store,
250 Poore Craige shall be thy cheryl, and no more.   *churl*
Since all my life suppose I poetize,   *even if*
I see seavin Philippeans must suffize:
Not that thou art not liberall at will;
No, no, wise prince, but caus my verse are ill;
255 Yet since this furie is but lent to few,   *inspiration; given*
Let us not want, thow shall have verse anew.   *skimp; sufficient*
If these seeme pleasant, I shall singe againe,
If not, I will from being bold abstaine,
And cease to write; but never cease to pray,
260 The God of heav'n preserve thee night and day.

Scotland's Teares. [AC3]

When fabling Æsop was at fatall Delphos tane,
And there by doome condem'd to be precipitat and slane,   *cast down*
He like a woman weep't, and tooke delight in teaires,
Cause they alleviat and made lesse the conscience of his caires;   *awareness*
5 But Solon, when he spi'd his deerest sonne was dead,
He weepd the more, because his teaires to grief gave no remead: *relief*
Yet neither he nor he by teaires could salve his ill,   *heal*
Though of those salt and fruitles flouds impetuus spaits they spil.   *torrents; shed*
Then, maymed Scotland, thou made orphane from delight,   *wounded; deprived of*
10 Whom all the hosts of heavens abhor with undeserved despight,
With deeing Aesop mourne, or wofull Solon weepe,
And tho, as they, thou weepe in vaine let not thy sorrow sleepe:
With frustrat Æsau shout, curse life and wish to dee,   *cheated*
Since Jacob with his mother's helpe thy blessing steals from thee.

15 Now, rivall England, brag, for now, and not till now,
Thou hast compeld unconquered harts and sturdy necks to bow.
What neither wits, nor wars, nor force afore could frame,   *minds; achieve*
Is now accomplisht by the death of thy imperiall dame.
Eliza faire is gone, into the land of rest,
20 To that Elisium predecried and promis'd to the blest: *destined*
And England for her sake now weaires the sabill weede,
But, Scotland, if thou rightly looke, thou has more cause indeede.
They for a Dian dead, Apollo'es beames enjoy,   *in place of*
And all their straying steps, allace, our Titan dooth tonnoy.   *delays; annoy*
25 Now dawn's their glorious day with Phœbus' rayes bespred,
And we are but Cymmerian slaves with gloomy clouds ou'rcled.   *bedeckt*
Rich neighbour nation then, from thy complaining cease,
Not thou but we should sigh, and so to our complaints give place.   *room*
Our garland lacks the rose, our chatton tins the stone,   *collet; loses*
30 Our volier wants the philomel, we left, allace, alone.   *aviary; nightingale*
What art thou, Scotland, then? No monarchie, allace,
A[n] oligarchie desolate, with straying and onkow face,   *dismal; unnatural*
A maymed bodie now, but shaip, some monstrous thing,   *wounded; without*
A reconfused chaos now, a countrey but a king.   *disordered; without*
35 When Paris fed his flockes among the Phrigian plaines,
Ænone's love was his delights, his death were her disdaynes.
But when, allace, he knew that Priam was his sire,
He left Ænone sweet, and syne for Helene would aspire.   *then*
Proud pellex, England, so thou art the adulterat brid,   *concubine*
40 Who for Ænone thinks no shame to lye by Paris' sid.
Who knowes ere it be long, but our (your) happie king,
With Belgic, Celtic, Aquitan, to his empire may bring?
And he – why should he not? – your Troynavant shall leave,
And unto Parise spurre the post, his right for to receave?   *ride hastily*
45 Then, then shall England weepe, and shed abounding teaires,
And we shall to our comfort find companions in our caires.
And till it so befall, with pitie, not with scorne,
Upon this confinde kingdom looke, as on a land forlorne.   *deprived*
Wise Plato would not once admit it in his minde,
50 He lov'd Xenocrates so well, he could become unkinde;

And no more can we thinke, dread Leige, though thou be gone,
Thou will ungratly leave us thus disconsolate alone.
By contrars contrars plac'd, no dout most clearely kith, *reveal*
And now thy absence breedes our bale, whose biding *sorrow; residence*
        made us blith.
55 O were thou not both wise and good, we should not mourne,
We would not for thy absence weepe, nor wish for thy returne.
Long sleepe made Rufus loose the use of both his eene. *lose*
O do not thou, sweet Prince, make stay, lest thou forget us cleene,
Like Epimenidas when thou returns againe:
60 The shapp of al things shall be chaing't; thine owne sheepe shall be slaine.
Democrit rather choose, no king at all to bee,
Then over wicked men to rule, and such, allace, are wee:
Our jewell England joyes, and yet no way dooth wrong us; *enjoys*
The world may see we were not worth, that thou shuld be among us.
65 But since it must be thus, and thou art forc'd to flitt, *depart*
Now, like a heart, in to the mids of thy great body sitt:
And from thy Troynavant, which pleasure's store impairts,
Behold thy kingdom's round about thy hand, in all the airts; *directions*
Examples old thou taks, and layis before thy face.
70 The famous Numids thought the midst to be most honoured place;
Thus, by Hyempsal's side, Adherbal Salust sets,
And so Jugurtha in the midst, wee reed, no intrance gets;
Grave Maro makes likway, the queene of Cartage brave, *similarly*
Betwix Ascanius and the wise Æneas place to have;
75 Dooth not Apollo too in proudest pompe appere,
With bright and day-adorning beames in his meridian sphere? *midday*
So thou has choos'd the midst of all thy kingdom's knowne,
For looke about thee where thou list, thou looks but on thine owne. *please*
And since the gods decree, great King, that so shall bee,
80 Since peace must florish in thy time, and wars must cease and die,
But competition too, since thou has England's crowne, *without*
Which was a heptarchie of old, of uncontrould renowne. *limitless fame*
Let us and Al-bi-on, that wee with one consent,
    One God, one King, one Law may be, t'adore, serve, keepe content.
85 In Rome the Sabins grew, with Tyrians Trojans mixt,

And Juda joyn'd with Israel; but, least wee seeme prolixt,
And that our loving plaint's and teares may now take end,   *laments*
Thee to thy crowns, thy crowns to thee, the great good God defend.

Eliazabeth, Late Queene of England, her Ghost. [AC4]

Cease, loving subjects, cease my death for to deplore,   *bewail*
And do no more with drirrie cryes my dolful hearse decore.   *dreary; adorn*
Though, like Cynegirus, when both the hands are gone,
Yee would detaine mee with your teeth in my emperiall throne;   *hold*
5 Bee Thracians now I pray, and hence-foorth cease to mone,
Ere it bee long in quiet peace ye shall finde five for one.
For, if ye can beleeve my prophetizing ghost,
Æneas gave Anchises trust, you shall not thinke me lost.
The death of one, some say, the birth of one should bee:
10 Three mails and femels two you have, most famous five for mee.   *males; females*
For, as I seald my will, my designation dew,   *proper intention*
And did concredit by the rest to my Achates trew,   *entrust*
So now my ghost is glad, that by my care, his paine,
My countries have their lawfull king, the king his crowns againe. *in return*
15 Then bransh, imbellis'd soyle, most pleasant, most perfite: *put out shoots*
The onely earthly Eden now for pleasure and delighte.
Rich England now rejoice, heave up to heaven thy hands,
The blessed Lorde hath blest thy bounds beyond all other lands:
Since no Sardanapal is now become thy king,
20 No Dionise nor Nero proud, my death to thee doth bring.
A king unwoont to give, or yet to take, offence,   *unaccustomed*
A godly David ruleth now, a prophet and a prince.
The pupill now is blith, the widow weepes not now,
No depredations in thy boundes, the rushbush keeps the kow,
25 The lyons now agree, and do in peace delight;
The thirsel now defends and guards the red rose and the white.   *thistle*
The British saints shake hands, with crosses joynd and spred,

Whose cullours on the glassie salt no terror small have bred: *flags; ocean*
Those now conjoynd in one through Neptun's bounded roares,   *restricted*
30 Shal make the ventring mercheand sail secure to forane shoares.   *enterprising*
Flee, swift-wingd Fame, and tell the best and rarest news,   *fly*
That time hath yet brought foorth by night or day'es delightfull hew's.
For ships and swans most rich, most faire, and famous Thamis,
Tell Neptune, Thetis, Triton too, the haps of great King James.   *fortunes*
35 Thou murdring galliglas, who long my laws withstood,   *cateran*
Learne to obey, and bath no more thy blade in British blood.   *bathe*
All you, my subjects deire, do homage dew to him,
And that shal make my blessed ghost in boundles joyes to swim.

To his Calidonian Mistris.   [AC5]

*Themistocles, after a great victorie by navall battell, came to visite the
slaughtered bodyes of his enemies, and found by the seaside many jewels and
chaynes scattered. Then said he to his freind, who then by chaunce followed
him: 'Gather these spoyles, for thou art not Themistocles.'*

   *This worthles epistle, like a loose or neglected jewell, though the wise
and woorthy Themistocles overpas, I pray thee, sweete mistres, peruse and
preserve, least it perish; sence too, and for thee, it is done: when I am absent, or
dead, it may breed thy delight, and make thee haplie remember thou once had*

     A loving and kind man,
     Craige.

When I remember on that time, that place,
Where first I fix'd my fansie on thy face,
The circumstances how, why, where, and whan
My mistres thou, and I became thy man;
5 Whilst I repeat that proces full of paine,
How first we met, and how we twind againe,   *separated*
Our sweete acquaintance, and our sad depart,   *parting*
It breedes a sea of sorrowes at my heart.

And yet for all these sorrowes I susteine,
10 With sigh-swolne heart, and teares-bedewed eyne,
As I have lov'd, so shall I love thee still   *always*
Unto the death, hap either good or ill.   *happen*
And now I sweare by that true love I owe thee,
By all the sighs which day by day I blow thee,
15 By all the verse and charming words I told thee,
By all the hopes I have for to beholde thee,
By all the kisses sweete that I have reft thee,   *stolen from*
And all the teares I spent since last I left thee,
That absence helps, not hinders, my desire
20 And sets new force and fagots to my fire.   *brands*
Each thing that chance presents, and lets me see,
Brings arguments, and makes me thinke on thee.   *reasons*
For, when they told me of that wrathfull flame,
Which from the high and holie heav'n downe came
25 On Paul's faire church, and that cloud-threatning steeple,
And how it flam'd in presence of the people,
Then with my selfe thought I, this fire was quensht,
But mine endures, and by no tears is drensht;
And were not hope accrestis with desire,   *increases*
30 I had long since consum'd amid this fire.
     And when I viewd those walles of Farnhame fayre,
Where Lamuel with his lady made repaire,
I layd me downe beside the ditch profound,
Where Guinever, dispairing dame, was drownd,
35 And fell on sleepe upon that fatall brinke,
And still on thee, sweete hart, I dreame, I thinke.
And were it not, that by the tract of time
The well was full with earth, with stone, and lime,
There had I drownd, and by my fatall fall
40 Made end with her of love, and life, and all.
Yet halfe asham'd least curious eyes should finde me,
I went away, and left huge teaires behind me.
     And when I spide those stones on Sarum plaine,
Which Merlin by his magicke brought, some faine,   *pretend*

45 By night, from farr I-erne to this land,   *Ireland*
    Where yet as oldest monuments they stand,
    And though they be but few for to behold,
    Yet can they not, it is well knowne, be told.   *counted*
    Those I compard unto my plaints and cryes,
50 Whose totall summe no numers can comprise.   *numbers*
         Olde Woodstock's wrackes to view I was despos'd,   *ruins*
    Where Rosamond by Henrie was inclos'd.
    The circuits all and wildesome wayes I view,   *enclosures; sad*
    The laberinth, and Clifford's fatall clew,   *trap*
55 And where those time-worne monuments had beene,
    Where nought remaines but ruines to be seene,
    Yet in my hart moe wracks, moe wayes I fand,
    Then can be made by any humane hand.
    And all these wondrous wonders which I see,
60 Makes me but wonder more and more on thee.
    That thou be well, both night and day I pray,
    And for thy health once I carrouse each day;   *toast*
    From pype of loame, and for thy saike, I souke   *pottery; suck*
    The flegm-attractive far-fett Indian smouke,   *drawing; exotic*
65 Which with my braine and stomacke beares debate,   *conflict*
    And like the lethall aconite I hate:
    That poysning potion pleasant seems to mee,
    When I determe it must be drunke for thee.   *decide*
         From Venus' sports I doo indeed abstaine,
70 Nor am I now as I was woont so vaine:
    Chaste Dian's laws I do adore for good,
    Who kild her love Orion in the flood.
         Drunke Bacchus' maits I holde for none of mine,   *fellows*
    I taste no Celtic nor Iberian wine:
75 Looke on my lyns' Lyceum, none they smell,   *lines' temple*
    But Helicon's poore streams, where Muses dwell.
         For all those rare delights which England yeilds,   *fine*
    Of faces faire, of brave and fertill feilds,
    For all the pleasures which our Court frequent,
80 Such as man's hart would wish, or witt invent,   *brain*

Yet I protest, I rather beg with thee,
Then be sole king, where seav'n were wont to bee.

  But when my freend, thy berar, spurd with pane   *messenger*
The poist, to see this chalkie shoare againe,   *post-horse*
85 And brought thy symboll, discolor of hew   *letter; stained*
With commendations kind, but not anew,   *regards; many*
I ask'd him how thou was? Hee shooke his head.
'What, man', quoth I, 'and is my mistres dead?'   *lady*
'No', answerd hee, 'but seik, deir freend.' Quoth I,   *indisposed*
90 'Thou know's I love; I pray thee make no lye.'
'In faith, but seik.' 'And is no doubt err now?'   *only; suspicion*
'As weell', sayd hee, 'as ather I or yow.'
This hee affirmd with solem oaths anew;   *asserted*
And yet, allace, I doubt if they be trew.

95   Here where the pest approacheth us so narr,   *plague; near*
To smoother breath before wee be aware;   *smother*
For, at the gates of our most royall king,
Corrupted carions lie. O fearefull thing!   *rotting corpses*
Yet feare I still for thee, my love is such,
100 And for my selfe I feare not halfe so much.
And now I feare these fears, ere it be long,
Will turne to agues, and to fevers strong.   *diseases*
Long are my nights, and dolefull are my dayes,
Short sleeps, long waks, and wildsom are my wayes;   *vigils; dreary*
105 Sadd are my thoughts, sowr sighs, and salt my tearis: *bitter*
My body, thus els waik, both wayn's and wearis.   *weak; shrivels; tires*

  For losse of Calice, Mary, England's queene,   *Calais*
Had sighs at hart, and teares about her eyne,
'When I am dead, caus rype my hart', sayd she,   *cut open*
110 'And in the same shall Calice writen bee,
Die when I will, thy name shall well be knawne
Within my hart, in blood's characters drawne.'
But if, faire dame, as yet on liff thou bee,
This papyre then commends my love to thee,
115 And if thy life by wrathfull weirds be lost,   *Fates*
Chast Laura then, thy Petrarch loves thy ghost.

And yet my hopes assures mee thou art weell,
And in these hopes a comfort hidd I feell.
This for the time, sweet hart, that thou may kno,   *live*
120   I leave thy man, and love but thee; and so,
Till by thy wreat I know thy further will,   *writing*
I say no more, but sigh, and seals my bill.   *letter*

To the King's most Royall Majestie. [AC6]

Kind Attalus in annals old wee reid,
Was king of Pergame by the Romans' ayde;
Hee long time brookt the same but foraine feid,   *without; war*
Which made those noble Romans to be glad.
5 And yet becaus hee had no heyrs, 'tis sayd   *heirs*
Hee to those foresayd Romans did resigne
His diadem and crowne, and what he had
Hee gave to them, that erst made him a king.   *first*
Hade I beene made no poet, Sire, but prince
10 Of fertill bounds, for Parnase bare and dry,   *instead of*
Your Grace had got my crowne and all long since,
For I laik heyrs, and none more kind then I: *lack; related*
    To use thee sweet inchanting poet's vaine,   *talent*
    You gave mee reuls, I give you ryms againe.   *rules; rhymes*

Sonet. [AC7]

Anacreon two dayes two nights did watch,   *wake*
Till he return'd Policrates againe
These talents two which he receivd, fond wratch,   *poor wretch*
To wake for wealth, and pinch himself with paine.   *torment*
5 But contrare wayes, I saikles soull am slaine: *innocent*
I wake for want, and not for wealth, allace;
My voyce is hoarse with cryes, dry is my braine;
Yet get I not the smallest graine of grace.
A Cythared, thogh poore, did sweetly sing,
10 Caus Dionise did promise him reward:
And thus to thee I wreat, most gracious King,   *write*
In hope thy Grace will once my greiffs regard:
    And by my pen thy prayses shall be spred,
    From rysing sunn to his Hesperean bed.

Non omnis moriar.   *[May I not perish entirely.]*

Alexis to Lesbia. [AC8]

Come be my love, and live with mee,
And thou shalt all the solace see
That glassie gulfs or earth can bring,
From Vesta's wealth or Neptun's reigne.

5 For we shall on the mountains go,
In shaddie umbers too and fro: *groves*
In vallies low, and on the bray,   *slope*
And with thy feet the flowrs shall play.

And I shall make thee pleasant poses,
10   Of dasies, gilliflowrs and roses:
My armes shalbe a belt to thee:
Thine, if thou wilt, the like to mee.

Of Flora'es tapestrie thy gowne,
Thy cap shall be my lawrell crowne:
15   Which drest of Daphne's haire shall shine,   *arranged from*
Whyls on my head, and whyls on thine.

And thou upon thy rock shalt rest,   *spindle*
And heare the echoes from my brest,
For I shall sing in sonets shill   *sonorous*
20   The charming numbers of my quill.   *verses*

Yea, wee with woond'ring eyes shall gaze
On many sundrie curious maze,
And view the architecture fare,   *fair*
Of rich and statelie buildings* rare.

25   And we shall looke about and see,
The wrack of time before our ee,   *ruin*
The pendul stones, their builder's ban,   *hanging; curse*
Imploring help at hand of man.

And wee shall see the rivers rin,
30   With delicat and daintie din,
And how my Dovern night and day,
With sweet meanders slides away

To pay her debts unto the sea,
And like a wanton nimph doth flie   *run*
35   Through blooming banks, with smiling face,
Her lord the ocean to imbrace.

And wee shall see the towrs of tree,   *wooden ships*
Halfe seeme to swim, and halfe to flie:
Part in the sea, part in the aire,
40 And eag'l here, a dolphin there.

Wee shall behold Nereid nymphs,
Make waters welcome from their lymps: *springs*
And euery houre into the day,
Fresh floods and th'ocean billowes play.

45 And we shall heare the roches ring,   *rocks*
While storme-presageing mermayds sing,
And on the rocks the lav's shall roare,   *surges*
Salut and resalut the shoare.   *greet*

And when Apollo taks his rest,
50 With wearie horses in the west,
And Cynthia begins to shine,
Thy poet's tugur shall be thine.   *hut*

Then shalt thou see my homlie fare,
And what poore riches I have thare:
55 And if those things can move thy mind,
Come, come, and be no more unkind.   *unnatural*

Lesbia her answer to Alexis.

If all were thine that there I see
Thou paynts to breed content to mee,   *describe*
Then those delights might move my mind,
60 To yeeld, and be no more unkind.

Sith nought is thine that thou sets downe,   *since*
Save songs, thy selfe, thy belt, thy crowne,
Thy tugure, and thy homely fare,
And that poore wealth which thou hast thare,

65 I might be compted most accurst
    To dwell with thee, suppose I durst,   *were I to dare*
    And men might thinke me more then mad,
    To leave the better for the bad.

    Yet least I should be deemd ungrate,
70 To loath thee for thy poore estate,   *circumstances*
    Though Fortune be thy fremmit foe,   *hostile*
    No reason were, I should be so.

    Thy lines allure mee to be thine,   *draw*
    And thou shalt see it soone or sine: *later*
75 The christall streams shall backward move,
    Ere I forget thy faythfull love.

❧

To his dear friend, and fellow student, Mr. Robert Æton.   [AC9]

    Sing, swift-hoof'd Æthon, to thy matchless selfe,
    And be not silent in this pleasant spring;
    I am thy echo, and thy aerie elf,   *spirit-servant*
    The latter strains of thy sweet tunes I'll sing.   *echoes*
5 Ah, shall thy muse no further frutes forth-bring
    But *Basia* bare, and wilt thou write no more
    To higher notes? I pray the, tune thy string:
    Be still admir'd as thou hast bene of yore.
    Write, Æthon, writ, let not thy vain decay,   *talent*
10 Least we become Cymerians dark, or worse:
    If Æthon faill, the sun his course must stay,
    For, Phœbus' chariot laks the cheefest horse.
        Thogh Fortun frown, ah, why should vertue die?
        Sing, Æthon, sing, and I shall echo thee.

A Disswasion to his friend from his intended marriage.   [AC10]

Fair famous ile, where Zoroastres raign'd,
Where Bactrum once, the statelie cittie, stood,
Which, when th'ould name *Artaspe* was disdain'd,
Was *Bactria* cal'd, from fertill Bactrus flood,
5   Where some-time Ceter, Aram's sonne began
Of thousand citties the foundation sure,
In thee the wyves abuse the married man,
And both with slave and stranger play the whoore.
The dame with distaff beats her yeelding lord,
10   And for her pryde but punishment skaips free,   *without; escapes*
And poore Acteon dare not speak one word.
From Bactrian wyves the Lord deliver thee,
    Nor lead a life infamous, heart-brock, thrall.   *heartbroken*
    Far better were to wed no wife at all.

His regrate for the lose of time at Court.   [AC11]   *complaint*

O how time slips, and slelie slids away!   *imperceptibly*
God is forgot, and woe is mee therefore:
I waste the night, and weare away the day,
I sleep, dres, feed, talke, sport, and doe no more.
5   Far better were, with care to have redemed,   *bought back*
    Nor sell for noght the thing I most estemed.

His contents at his tugur.   [AC12]   *happiness; hut*

When lose of tyme at Court was all my gane,   *reward*
To take my leave I thoght it was my best,
And in some privat mansion to remaine,
Where I might, frie from envye's rage, take rest.   *free*
5   Now, blest be God, no portar bars my doore   *janitor*
By day, by night none keeps me but my kurre.   *guards; dog*

※

To John, Earle of Montrose, first Vice-Roy of Scotland: Epitaph.   [AC13]

If *Rhadamanthus* in th'Elisian field,
With *Æacus* and *Minos* judges bee,
And Gods over ghosts, they all of due must yield   *by right*
For piëtie, truth, justice, place to thee: *priority*
5   At least, *Montroes* for *Minos* must command,
And beare his scepter in the blessed land.

※

To His M[ajesty] at Kinaird.   [ac14]

Great man of God, whom God doeth call, and choose
On earth his great lieutennent's place to use,   *occupy*
Wee bless the tyme, wherein the threefold croun
And diademe, with peace and great renoun,
5   In that so long fore-told and fatal cheare,   *destined throne*
Thou on thy brave and royall brow didst beare;   *heroic*
As from that tym thy absence bred our bane,   *affliction*
Thy presence now restores our joy's againe:
Thou went away, to Scotland's deip displeasure,
10   But thy return brings mirth beyond all measure.

Astræa doth pronunce by thy sweit tong
What shuld of right to kings on earth belong:
Thy myld aspect doth realms and cities nurish,
And as thou frouns or faun's they fall and floorish.   *favours*
15 These swords the sherp and bloudie tools of warr,
Which peace hath sheath'd in rust, shall from a farr   *at a distance*
Bee drawn agane, and, when thou thinks it good,
Thy angrie brow shall bath the world in blood,
Thou canst dethrone, and give, the royall wreathe,
20 And hyd thy sword, and hold it in the sheath.
Yet now thou deign's to visit our cold north,
And with thy Court hath crost the sinuose Forth,   *winding*
Which, with meanders winding heer and there,
Great Britan's king upon her backe did beare,
25 Whois bouldin billoes, as they did of yore,   *swelling*
Shall set thee sure upon there yonder shore.   *safe; their*
And stately Tay, with stryving streams which marches   *competing; goes*
And skorns his course, shuld be controld with arches,   *overflows*
Who with his speats his spightfull raige hath dround   *torrents; violent*
30 The famose Perth's faire bridge, and brought to ground,
Shall straine the strenght of his strong streams, thou'll see,   *curb*
And be at peace with all the world for thee.
    Thow shall not loose thy labors, nor thy love,
Which in a Prince most rare, most rare dooth prove.
35 This bontie singular, which thou imparts,   *favour*
Encounters not with mis-conceiving hearts   *connects*
Nor with ingratefull subjects, for each one
Aknowledgeth the good which thou hast done.
Man never was more loved by ane other,
40 Nor David by kynd Jonathan his brother,
As thou by us; thou dwels in each man's heart;
Our joy, and our felicitie thou art.
    O had our breists of stuff transparent bene,   *material*
That all our thoughts might so to thee be sene,
45 Thy Scotland do'th (thy royall Grace wold tell)   *confirm*
For courage, truth, and love, the world excel;

And wee confesse, our joyes are perfect now,
Iff they could prove perpetuall; heavens allow
A longer stay than thou intends, that so
50 Our love-seik hopes might to the full tyd flo.
      To toyll and travell man is borne, wee see,   *labour*
As sparks of fire by nature upward flie:
Thy travell yet shalbe compenst with pleasure,   *rewarded*
Thou shalt have sports, and pairt of all our treasure.
55 Wee'll keep that custome with thy sacred Grace
Which, Athenæus writes, was kept in Thrace:
'The subjects gave their king when ever hee wanted;
When they wax'd poore, their suit's by him were granted.'   *petitions*
Thus each in love supplied an other's neid,
60 Both peace, and wealth, this kind commerce did breid;   *natural exchange*
And Persians, when they did present their king,
Some rare propyne they always us'd to bring.   *gift*
      But put the case, this forme which Persians used   *suppose; custom*
Wer by some base and wretched wormes refused,   *misers*
65 Thy faithfull quæstors, full of love and paine,   *treasurers; care*
(Whois betters have not bene, whose lyk againe
Thou canst not find) shall such aboundance bring,
As King nor Court shall want no kynd of thing.   *lack*
Not lyk those lowns, whom Athens old did trust,   *rascals*
70 They wer but theiv's unhonest and injust;
These Tamii the treasure stole by night,   *stewards*
And then they burnd the citadel by slight,   *trickery*
That by this fire their fraud shuld not be seene,
Nor they accus'd, that had so knavish beene.
75 Thy quæstors here are honest, wyse, and true;   *state-treasurers*
Thy treasure saiff, thy bastils built of new.   *fortresses*
      Stay then, dread Leige, O stay with us a while,
With pleasing sports the posting tyme begyle;   *hastening*
Thy fynest hawks and fleitest hounds shall find
80 Of fowls and beasts a pray of everie kynd.
For morning, both and evening, flight each day
Each hawk thou hast, shall have her proper pray;

Each fowl that flies shall meet thee in thy way,
And in their sorts shall *Ave Cæsar* say.   *manner*
85   Throgh forests, parks, and feilds hunt stag and haire,
It helps the health to have the native air.
Hee that taks pains and travell sleepeth best,   *hard work*
With greidines hee taks refreshing rest;
His meate to him seems savorie, sweet and fyne,   *food*
90 Hee glaidlie drinks the heart-comforting wyne.
Good blood, quick spirits, travel sweet do'th cherish,
And maks offensive humors for to perish.
And wyse-men write that colik, gout and gravel,   *the stone*
The woefull fruits of rest, ar cur'd by travel.
95 Let not thy horses fatt, for, standing idle,   *fatten*
They'll grow stiff neck'd and disobey the brydle.   *stubborn*
      Let faithfull Turbo menage thy affaires,   *look after*
And kill himself with care to ease thy caires.
Thou shalt not travel through hott barren bounds
100 Of Arabie, nor cold and snowie sounds   *channels*
Of Norwa, nor the Schythian savage montans,
Nor fenni Flanders, skant of healthfull fontans,   *marshy; poor in*
Nor through thy France, so full of fearfull jarrs,   *conflicts*
Where king and subjects waige intestine warrs,
105 But throgh brave Britan, of all realms the best,   *glorious*
With pleasures all, with peace and plenty blest,
Which God sejoyns from all the world, wee see,   *separates*
That none but Neptune shuld thy neighbour bee.
      Let not our love infer the least offence,   *bring*
110 Thou art our Lord, our kyndlie King, our Prence: *natural*
Our int'rest so is such, dreid Leige, in thee,   *involvement*
Thogh earth's great glob wer thyne, ours thou must bee.
From Jacob learne to love Canaan best,
The native soill: for, when his sonnes were blest,
115 Hee charged them to take him heame againe,
Him to interre in Ephron's flowrie plaine.
'Abraam there, and Sara sleep', said hee,
'There Isaak, and Rebecca both doe lye,

And there I buried Lea'. Joseph weiped.
120 In Ephron Jacob with his fathers sleiped.
    Joseph waxd chief in Pharao's court, and yet
Knowing the Tribs wold out of Egipt flitt,   *depart*
Hee took his brethren, and the people sworne,
His bones from thence shuld be to Ephron borne.
125 To keip their oath, his brethren and the rest
Imbalmed him and put him in a chest,
And when they fled from Egypt, as they sweare,
Moyses with him good Joseph's bones did beare.
    Live Nestor's dayes, King James, but live among us,
130 By blood and birth thou do'st alone belong us;
Stay then at home, to Thames make no returne,
Sleip with thy fathers in thy fathers' urn.
    But wee'r too bold to beg thy longer stay
Since God sets down thy jests and gyds thy way: *directs; deeds*
135 From death in famine God delivereth thee,
From sword in battell thou shall still be frie;
Destruction thou shall skorne and laugh at dearth,   *famine*
And shall not feare the cruell beasts on earth;
Ston's of the feild shall be in league with thee,
140 And beasts at peace with great King James shall be;
Yea, thou shall know peace dwells thy tents within,
In spight of Babell and that man of sin.
To thy great joy, O King, thou shall perceave,
Thy seed as grasse on earth; thou shall to grave
145 In fullest aige, lyk to a rig of corne   *field*
Broght to the barne in season due, be borne.
    And if the Lord hes said that thou must leave us,
If England must of this our joy bereave vs,   *rob*
If thou wilt goe, and leave us full of sorrow,
150 This prayer short from paynim pen wee borrow.   *non-Christian*
    Our sacred king, wyse James, the Lord defend
And royall seed, till all this all tak end;   *world*
Heavens grant to him his faire and vertuous wife,
In peace and plenty, long and happie lyfe;

155 Lord blesse, preserve, and keep him frie from ill,
Of happie kings let him be happiest still;
And, whilst he lives, let him not see nor heare
The death of one that to his Grace seems deare;
Let his dominions farr and long persever,
160 And, still adorned with justice, last for ever.   *always*
Tyme, stay thy hast, relent thy former furie,   *restrain*
And let King James our children's children burie;
O touch him not, proud Fortune, but in kyndnes,   *except*
Or if thou do'st, hee still defyes thy blindness.
165 Heavens grant this ile, with toyls tormoyled long,   *turmoiled*
May, be his meanes, be cur'd from sin and wrong;
God grant hee save religion from decay,
And reestablish such as runne astray.
Lord, let this starr in brightnes still abound,
170 To light the world so long in darknes dround,
And let each true and faithfull subject sing,
With heart and voyce conjoyn'd, *God save the King.*

To a rude and barbarous Boore, who wronged the Author. [AC15]

Some rude, unruelie, barbrous boores there bee,
Chiefe foes to Phœbus, and the Muses nine,
Will counterfeite Aurantius prowde: for hee
Wrong'd Sanazar, the poet most divine:
5   Both towne and towre destroyde in fearce despight,
Faire Mergellina, Sanazar's delight.

Th'ov'r-partied poet winked at the wrong,   *superior; forgave*
And his revenge remitted to the Lord,
The God of Hostes. Then newes were spread ere long,
10 Aurantius prowde was vanquisht, kilde, and goarde.
Heavens, grant all such a sudden, shamefull ende,
That dare presume a poet to offende.

[89]

And let their bodies bee embrewed still,   *steeped in blood*
Till earth drinke up their blood, and loathe their stinke:
15 At Stix let Charon grant them no good-will,
Till hundredth yeares they byde about that brinke. ·   *remain; shore*
    And when their friends their epitaph shall reade,
    Let it heape shame upon their children's head.

Satyra Volans. [AC16]   *[Swift-winged satire]*

Goe, swift-wing'd satyre, through all states, but feare,   *without*
Though thou a base and thanklesse errand beare;
Goe thou post-haste, and through all hazards hye thee;
Trueth is thy warrand; nip them that come nigh thee.   *bite*
5 Passe King and Prince, with praysing and with praying: *pass over*
And if to Court thou goe, make little staying;
Yet tell thus much to all, though it should wrong them,
There's but small trueth and honestie among them.
And hee that's helde in most respect by all,
10 His fellowes waite, and long to see him fall.   *look out*
Tell church, 'tis full of shisme, vaine pryde, and greede;   *schism*
They teach what's good, but doe no good in-deede.
Tell noble-men, they are prowde tyrants growne;
Ere they lacke practise, they'll oppresse their owne.
15 Tell some ignoble nobles in their faces,
They are not worthie of their fathers' places.
Tell to the best, they act but others' actions,
And vexe their neighbours to beare out their factions.   *support*
Tell rich men, riches would bee well employd;
20 Those that have much, have manie to destroy it.
Tell wretched Chremes, his example here,
Makes manie fast, where they have got good cheare: *provisions*
The traine retrainsh'd, the table curt and short,   *retinue reduced*
Sad solitude where I have seene resort:

25 The wrath of God consume that worthlesse worme,
   Who first began this lewde and pinching forme;   *vulgar; miserly*
   Hee lookes a man so hungrie in the face,
   As hee would eate him raw, and nere say grace.
   Tell subtill merchandes, they're perjured exporters   *wily*
30 Of needfull thinges; unprofitable importers
   Of needlesse thinges, which men buy head-longes, rash,   *impulsively*
   As scalerigs, wyne, tobacko and such trash.   *[obscure – see Note]*
   Tell those who still attende effaires of state,
   They keepe no place, nor greatnesse, without hate.   *position*
35 Tell, knowledge wanting zeale, is nothing worthe,   *lacking*
   And zeale but knowledge many shisme brings foorth.   *without*
   Pray judges have but two, not dowble, eares:
   Some say their hand, chiefe organe, sees, groapes, heares.
   Tell, lawyers are the children of horse-lieches,
40 Which crye 'Give, give', and make great gaine by speaches:
   Their chieffest sporte is but to sow dissention,
   And build their states by crooks, delayes, contention.   *tricks; deviousness*
   Tell clerkes and writers, they are farre from ill:
   Yet scrybes of olde expon'd the lawes at will.   *even; interpreted*
45 Tell physicke-mongers, drogs are growne unsure,   *mountebanks; drugs*
   And manie doctors rather kill, than cure.
   Tell th'usurer, his gaine for money lent,
   Is but maintained by actes of parliament,
   And parables, it cannot bee with-stood,
50 The talent dowbled, was helde service good.
   Tell zeal is blinde; tell love is turn'd to lust;
   Tell fainting age, it wastes; tell flesh 'tis dust.
   Tell youth it takes, in most excessive measure,
   In borthels lewde and taverns too much pleasure.   *whorehouses*
55 Tell beautie brave 'tis but admir'd a-while,   *gorgeous*
   And fondlie prays'd in poets' franticke stile.   *unrealistically*
   Tell great men that one parasite, one knave,
   Will make them lose the truest friende they have.
   Nip Fortune to the quicke; tell shee is blinde;
60 Tell Pithias too, to Damon hee's unkinde.

Tell, trueth hath left the citie in a grudge,
And in the countrey finds but small refuge.
Bid the satyricke find-fault poet take him   *hypercritical*
To some more lucrous trade; his vane will wracke him.   *gainful; talent; ruin*
Hee hath good wits, and yet a foole doth spende them: *brains; expend*
Fit to finde faults, but most unfit to mende them.
Thus having runne, and rayl'd, till all admire thee,   *upbraided*
Fall on thy face, beg pardon, and retire thee.

Sir David Murray of Gorthy (1567–1629)

David Murray's sonnet sequence *Cælia* was influenced by the manner of Sir Philip Sidney, and should probably be reckoned to the Castalian period; however, this early work first appeared in print in *The Tragicall Historie of Sophonisba* (London, 1611). The latter volume also contained other productions from Murray's 'unstay'd yeares', such as the pastoral 'Complaint of the Shepheard Harpalus' (the latter was several times reprinted independently, even into the 1620s). Murray's contemporaries must therefore initially have known his early poems on the theme of love from manuscript circulation. The present anthology includes only the final sonnet of the twenty-two comprising *Cælia*, since this item – which is untypical, in making no mention of the name of the beloved lady – may have been written later than the rest, and in the Jacobean age. The other three sonnets by Murray here reproduced are not from *Cælia*, but are independent compositions, mostly commemorating contemporaries from the poet's social or family circle. Murray's primary association was with the household of Prince Henry. In 1599 he had been appointed Gentleman of the Bedchamber, and he was retained in this function in 1603. He was knighted in September 1605, and when Henry's household was enlarged in 1610, Murray became Groom of the Stool. Given the Prince's somewhat serious character, it is not surprising that he should have been the dedicatee of *Sophonisba*, which is a tragic and edifying work, couched in the high heroic style and set in Ancient times, wherein the historical opposition of Rome and Carthage provides a stage on which are played out the clashing principles of public honour and private passion. Liminary sonnets by John Murray (David Murray's cousin), Michael Drayton and Simion Grahame commend the poem and the lofty ideals which it propounds.

Prince Henry died in November 1612, and his last words were breathed to David Murray, his trusted friend. Patrick Hannay addressed to Murray a prefatory poem (in Latin), in his own commemoration of the Prince, *Neptunus Britannicus* (1614). Murray's last independent publication (1615), an excellent paraphrase of Psalm 104, was dedicated to King James, who had published a version of his own in 1584. If a compliment was intended, the gesture does not seem to have had the effect of increasing Murray's favour with the King, and the poet chose to retire to his Perthshire estate of Gorthy. From there he contributed a liminary sonnet to *Poems by William Drummond* (Edinburgh, 1616).

On the misfortune of Bellizarius, great Lieutenant to the Emperour Justinian. [DM1]

Stay, passenger, and with relenting looke,   *sympathetic*
Behold heere Bellizarius, I pray,
Whom never-constant Fortune, changing aye,
Even at the top of greatnesse quite forsooke;
5 And, which is wondrous, in a moment tooke
Mee from the hight of an imperiall sway,   *command*
And plac'd me heere, blind begging by this way,   *road*
Whose greatnesse somtime scarce the world could brook.   *formerly*
And while thou daignes thy pitifull aspect,
10 Ah, sorrow not so much my fortunes past,   *lament*
As I beseech thee to bewaile this last!
That, from such honour abject-lie deject,   *cast off*
      I yet am forc'd a spectacle to live,
      Glad to receive the meanest almes thou't give.   *wilt*

To the right worthy Gentleman, and his loving cousin, Mr John Murray. [DM2]

While eagle-like, upon the lofty wings
Of thy aspiring Muse, thou flies on hie,   *aloft*
Making th'immortall sprites in love with thee,
And of those ditties thou so sweetly sings;
5 Where, quaffing boules of their ambrosian springs,   *goblets*
And sweetest nectar, thou divinely stayes,   *among the gods*
Low by the earth, poore I sings homely layes,
Till like desire of fame me upward brings;   *similar*
Then, borrowing from thy rich Muse some plumes,
10 Icarian-like beyond my skill I soare,
While comming where thy songs are heard before,
My lines are mockt, that thine to match presumes:
      And thus I perish in my high desire,
      While thou'rt more prais'd, the more thou dost aspire.

On the death of the Lady Cicily Weemes, Lady of Tillebarne.   [DM3]

Faire Cicil's losse, be thou my sable song,
Not that for which proud Rome and Carthage strave,   *competed*
But thine more famous, whom ago not long
Untimely death intomb'd so soone in grave.   *premature*
5 Deare sacred lady, let thy ghost receive
These dying accents of my mourning quill,
The sweetest-smelling incense that I have,
With sighes and teares upon thy hearse to spill.
To thee, deare saint, I consecrate ay still   *in perpetuity*
10 These sad oblations of my mirthlesse mind,   *offerings*
Who, while thou breath'd, this wondring world did fill
With thy perfections, Phœnix of thy kind:
    Frome out whose ashes hence I prophecie,
    Shall never such another Phœnix flie.

❧

On the death of his cousin, Adam Murray.   [DM4]

I know not whether discontent or love,
Deere friend, hath bred this thy abortive death,   *untimely*
Or if that both, united, shew'd their wrath,
To make thee this thy fatal last to prove;   *end*
5 But bee the motion what it list, did move   *produce*
This thy unlook'd for sad untimely fal,
Yet with the losse of breath thou los'd not al,
Thy better part still lives the heavens above,
And here thy pen immortaliz'd thy name,
10 From time, oblivion, envy, and the grave,
That to corruption now thy bones receive,
But can no way deface thy glorious fame,   *impair*
    Which still must sore on wings of endlesse praise,
    While yeers have months, months weekes, and weekes have dayes.

To his sacred Majestie.   [DM5]

That princely prophet, whose celestiall vaine   *talent*
In sweetest measures and soule-charming layes
To his deare harpe so fealingly bewrayes   *reveals*
Man's perfect way to pleasure and to paine,
5   Bequeath'd the skill of his skie-fostered braine   *heaven-inspired*
(Whilst he himselfe, crownd with immortall rayes
Of endlesse glory rests, not fading bayes)   *laurels*
Here, Phœnix like, to be renew'd againe.
And as from that Arabian bird's sweet ashe
10   One still proceedes, of like admired wing,   *continually*
The sacred furie of best Israel's king   *inspiration*
To Britane's monarch doth so fully passe,
    By which inflam'd, he sings that Heaven's decree,
    None worthy David's muse and harpe, but he.

A Paraphrase of the civ Psalme.   [DM6]

My soule, praise thou Jehovah's holie name,
For he is great, and of exceeding might,
Who, cloth'd with glorie, majestie and fame,
And covered with the garments of the light,
5   The azure heaven doth like a courtaine spred,
    And in the depths his chalmer beames hath layd.   *bed-frame*

The clouds he makes his chariot to be;
On them he wheeles the christall skies about,
And on the wings of Æolus, doth hee
10   At pleasour walke, and sends his angels out,
    Swift heraulds that doe execute his will;
    His words the heavens with firie lightnings fill.

The earth's foundation he did firmelie place,
And layd it so that it should never slyde;
15 He made the depths her round about embrace,
And like a robe her naked shores to hide,
  Whose waters would o'rflow the mountains high,
  But that they backe at his rebuke doe flie.

At the dread voice of his consuming thunder,
20 As these retire, the mountaines in the skie
Doe raise their tops, like pyramids of wonder,
And at their feet the pleasant valleys lie;
  And to the floods he doth prescribe a bound,   *limit*
  That they earth's beautie may no more confound.

25 The fertile plaines he doth refresh and cheare
With pleasant streames which from the mountaines fall,
To which, to quench their thirst, all beastes draw neare,
Even to the asse, whom never yoake did thrall:
  And on the trees by every chrystall spring,
30   Heaven's quiristers doe sweetly bill and sing.   *choristers*

The thirstie tops of skie-menacing hils
He from the clouds refresheth with his raine,
And with the goodnes of his grace he fills
The earth, with all that doth therein remaine;
35   He causeth her both man and beast to feede
  The wholesome herbes, and tender grasse to breede.

The fruitfull yvie, strict-embracing vine,   *ivy*
To glad man's heart he hath ordaind and made,
And gives him oyle to make his face to shine,
40 And to encrease his strength, and courage breede;
  The mighty trees are nourishd by his hand,
  The cedars tall in Lebanon that stand.

On whose wide-spreading, high and bushie tops
The flightering birds may build their nests in peace;   *fluttering*
45 And in the firre, that pitchie teares foorth drops,   *viscous*
He hath preparde the storke a dwelling-place;
        The mountaines are unto the goates refuge,
        And in the rockes the porcupines doe lodge.

He hath appointed seasons for the moone,
50 To fade, to grow, whiles faire to looke, whiles wane,   *dull*
And makes bright Phœbus, when the day is done,
In Thetis' lappe to dive his head againe:
        He clowdes the skies, and doth in darknes pight   *set up*
        Ou'r all the earth the courtaines of the night.

55 Then all the beastes from out the forrest creepe:
To seeke his pray the lyon loudlie roares,
The serpents hisse, the crocodile doth weepe,
As if she wold bewaile them she devoures;
        And when the sunne returnes they all retire,
60   And in their dennes doe couch themselves for feare.

And then doth man in safetie freelie goe,
To ply his worke with diligence till night.
Thy wondrous wonders, who, O Lord, can show?
The earth is filled with thy glory bright,
65   And thou hast stor'd the deepe-wyd ocean sea,
        With fish, beasts, monsters, nomberles that be.

There doe the winged wooden forts forth goe   *war-ships*
To climbe the glassie mountaines with their keeles;
There Liviathan wanders to and fro,
70 And through the waltring billows tumbling reeles,   *rolling*
        Who, in that liquid labyrinth enclos'd,
        Doth play and sport as thou him hast dispos'd.   *determined*

All living things, O Lord, doe wait on thee,
That in due season thou mayst give them food,
75 And thou unfolds thy liberall hands most free
And gives them everie thing may doe them good:
    Thy blessings thou so plenteouslie distills,
    That their aboundance all things breathing fills.

But if thy face thou doe withdraw in wrath,
80 Thy creatures all then languish, grieve and murne;
Or if thou, angrie, take away their breath,
They perish straight and into dust returne:
    But when thy Sprite thou sends, them to renew,
    All fresh doth flowrish, earth regaines her hue.

85 In his most glorious workes let God rejoyce,
Who makes the earth to tremble with a looke;
Let men admire, and angels with their voice   *marvel*
Extoll his name, whose touch makes mountaines smooke;
    To this thought-passing, speech-expreslesse Lord,   *ineffable*
90   While breath extends, will I still praise afford.   *lasts*

He will receive my humble sute in love,   *prayer*
And in his favour I shall ever joye;
The wicked from the earth he will remove,
And whollie heaven-dispising wormes destroy.
95   But whilst they buried lie in endlesse shame,
    My soule, praise thou Jehovah's holy name.

Sir William Alexander of Menstrie, Earl of Stirling (1567–1640)

William Alexander wrote competently and earnestly, if seldom memorably, in many genres, and his style, when experienced at length, is perhaps unlikely to appeal to the modern reader (cf. Reid: *ODNB*). The sheer quantity of his literary production is impressive, and his reputation stood high among his contemporaries. Alexander was born at Menstrie (Clackmannanshire), was knighted in 1608/9, in 1630 was ennobled as Viscount Stirling and Lord Alexander of Tullibody, and in 1633 was raised to Earl of Stirling and Viscount Canada. He was successful at Court, first under Prince Henry and after 1612 under Prince Charles, and he enjoyed good relations with both King James and his successor. Alexander prospered in the sphere of public administration, though rather less so in his financial schemes.

In 1604 he published *Aurora*, a sequence of sonnets written in his early years, interspersed with songs, madrigals and elegies, following the examples set by Petrarch and Sidney. The specimen selected here (WA1) is the final item thereof, in which the poet-persona moves the focus from the unreachable *inamorata* of convention to the lady whom he is about to marry. On this count, the poem may therefore mark a new departure, and may well allude to Alexander's relations with Janet Erskine, who became his wife in 1601 (cf. WQ2).

Alexander's connections with Prince Henry elicited his *Parænesis* [Poem of advice] in 1604, and in 1612 his *Elegie on the Death of Prince Henrie.* Nonetheless, his fame as poet rested largely on his four Seneca-inspired verse-dramas, *The Monarchicke Tragedies* (*Darius* in 1603; *Darius* with *Crœsus* in 1604; both in 1607 with *The Alexandræan Tragedie* and *Julius Cæsar*) and on his vast portrayal of the Apocalypse, *Doomes-Day* (four 'Houres' in 1614; expanded to twelve in 1637). Alexander was a close friend of William Drummond and of Walter Quin, and he also contributed liminary verses to publications by William Lithgow. He co-operated with James in the writing of vernacular psalm-versions, and in fact was responsible for the major part of *The Psalms of King David translated by King James* (Oxford, 1631).

Song. [WA1]

Farewell sweet fancies, and once deare delights,
The treasures of my life, which made me prove   *experience*
That unaccomplish'd joy that charm'd the sprights,   *spirits*
And, whilst by it I onely seem'd to move,
5   Did hold my ravish'd soule, big with desire,   *pregnant*
    That, tasting those, to greater did aspire.

Farewell, free thraldome, freedome that was thrall,
While as I led a solitary life,
Yet never lesse alone, whilst arm'd for all,
10 My thoughts were busied with an endlesse strife:
    For, then not having bound my selfe to any,
    I being bound to none, was bound to many.

Great god, that tam'st the gods, old-witted child,
Whose temples brests, whose altars are men's hearts,
15 From my heart's fort thy legions are exil'd,   *castle*
And Hymen's torch hath burn'd out all thy darts:
    Since I in end have bound my selfe to one,   *finally*
    That by this meanes I may be bound to none.

Thou daintie goddesse with the soft white skinne,
20 To whom so many offrings dayly smoke,
Were beautie's processe yet for to begin,   *trial*
That sentence I would labour to revoke,   *verdict*
    Which on Mount Ida as thy smiles did charme,
    The Phrigian shepheard gave to his owne harme.

25 And, if the question were referd to mee,
On whom I would bestow the ball of gold,
I feare me Venus should be last of three,
For with the Thunderer's sister I would hold,
    Whose honest flames, pent in a lawfull bounds,   *confined; limit*
30   No feare disturbs, nor yet no shame confounds.

I mind to speake no more of beautie's dove, *have decided*
The peacocke is the bird whose fame I'le raise;
Not that I Argos need to watch my love, *guard*
But so his mistris Juno for to praise:
35 And if I wish his eyes, then it shall be,
That I with many eyes my love may see.

Then farewell, crossing joys, and joyfull crosses, *frustrations*
Most bitter sweets, and yet most sugred sowers, *sournesses*
Most hurtfull gaines, yet most commodious losses,
40 That made my yeares to flee away like howers,
And spent the spring time of mine age in vaine,
Which now my summer must redeeme againe.

O welcome, easie yoke, sweet bondage, come:
I seeke not from thy toiles for to be shielded,
45 But I am well content to be orecome,
Since that I must commaund when I have yielded;
Then here I quit both Cupid and his mother,
And do resigne my selfe t'obtaine another. *surrender*

**Some verses written to his Majestie by the Authour at the time of
his Majestie's first entrie into England.   [WA2]**

Stay, tragick muse, with those untimely verses, *cease*
With raging accents and with dreadfull sounds,
To draw dead monarkes out of ruin'd herses,
T'affright th'applauding world with bloudie wounds:
5 Raze all the monuments of horrours past,
T'advance the publike mirth our treasures wast. *plunder*

And pardon, olde heroes, for O, I finde
I had no reason to admire your fates:
And with rare guiftes of body and of minde,
10　Th'unbounded greatnesse of evill-conquerd states:
　　More glorious actes then were atchiev'd by you,
　　Do make your wonders thought no wonders now.　　　　　　*esteemed*

For yee, the potentates of former times,
Making your will a right, your force a law,
15　Staining your conquest with a thousand crimes,
Still raign'd like tyrants but obey'd for awe:
　　And whilst your yoake none willingly would beare,
　　Dyed oft the sacrifice of wrath and feare.

But this age great with glorie hath brought forth
20　A matchlesse monarke, whom peace highlie raises,
Who, as th'untainted ocean of all worth,
As due to him hath swallow'd all your praises;
　　Whose cleere excellencies, long knowne for such,
　　All men must praise and none can praise too much.

25　For that which others hardly could acquire
With losse of thousands lives and endlesse paine,
Is heapt on him, even by their owne desire,
That thrist t'enjoy the fruites of his blest raigne;
　　And never conquerour gain'd so great a thing,
30　　As those wise subjects, gaining such a king.

But what a mightie state is this I see?
A little world, that all true worth inherites,
Strong without art, entrench'd within the sea,
Abounding in brave men full of great spirits:
35　　It seemes this ile would boast, and so she may,
　　To be the soveraigne of the world some day.

O generous James, the glorie of thir parts,   *territories*
In large dominions equall with the best,
But the most mightie monarke of men's harts,
40 That ever yet a diadem possest!
    Long maist thou live, well lov'd and free from dangers,
    The comfort of thine owne, the terrour of strangers.

Alexis to Damon. [WA3]

The love Alexis did to Damon beare
Shall witness'd bee to all the woodes, and plaines   *attested*
As singular, renown'd by neighbouring swains,   *unique*
That to our relicts Time may trophies reare.   *descendants*
5 Those madrigals wee song amidst our flockes,
With garlands guarded from Apollo's beames,
On Ochells whiles, whiles neare Bodotria's streames,   *sometimes*
Are registrate by echoes in the rockes.   *recorded*
Of forraine shepheardes bent to trie the states,   *conditions*
10 Though I, world's guest, a vagabond do straye,
Thou mayst that store, which I esteeme, survaye,   *quantity*
As best acquainted with my soule's conceits.   *thinking*
    What ever fate heavens have for mee design'd,
    I trust thee with the treasure of my mind.

Alexander Gardyne (c. 1590–c. 1642)

In some respects, the literary career of Gardyne is less one of a poet scaling Parnassus than of one climbing half-way up the mountain before sliding back down. His first published poetry was in *A Garden of Grave and Godlie Flowers* (Edinburgh, 1609), in which he planted sonnets and other literary species similar to those cultivated by his contemporaries. His subsequent crops were those of (a) local patriotism, in *The Lyf, Doings and Deathe of William Elphinston Bishop of Aberdeen*, (1619; unprinted before 1878), which was a poulter's measure versification made from a Latin prose *vita* of the famous late-medieval bishop, (b) quasi-Theophrastan moralising, in *Characters and Essayes* (Aberdeen, 1625), and (c) antiquarianism, in *The Theatre of Scottish Kings*, (1612x28; unprinted before 1709) and *The Theatre of Scottish Worthies* (c. 1628; unprinted before 1878). The rare critical notices of the *Theatres* are devastating: 'he has no originality or invention, no fancy, no ease or grace of versification, which are but poorly compensated for by pedantic words and extreme carelessness or poverty of rhymes' (Laing 1878: xv); another verdict, 'very dull', is only slightly less harsh (Spiller 1988: 152).

Yet though it may be conceded that Gardyne's later works are not undeserving of this negative criticism, the case is different with the 1609 *Garden*, which contains much passable verse. This collection is certainly of interest if viewed as a manifestation of the regional dimension within Jacobean culture, since many of the individuals addressed by Gardyne were prominent in Aberdeen and the North-East. Moreover, while much of the writing in his 1625 *Characters and Essayes* is uneven and lifeless, there are also some scintillations, such as the sketch of the bad man and atheist (AG10). Yet despite the rhetorical power of the latter and the calmer merit of some of the other poems, it is nevertheless true that the Aberdeen lawyer's garden of verses was liable to become choked with the wilder growths of rhetoric.

To the discret Reader. [AG1]   *discriminating*

I publish nought, nor put I to the Presse,   *not*
Thir poesies, to purchase me an praise,
Nor is my drift, nor my devise, to dresse   *plan; set up*
Elabrat lines, upon respects to raise,
5   And mount my Muse upon the front of Fame,   *vanguard*
  To get me gaine, or t'eternize my name.

Nor doe I on self-confidence or skill,
For price, or place, presumptuously aspyre.
My meaning much you doe mistake; my will
10 Is to get done my distich's last* desire.   *couplet*
  Slip all the smooth, sleik what you see unsound,   *accept; correct*
  Help whair they halt, abreadge when they abound.   *limp*

Thine if you merit,   *allow*
Alex. Gardyne.

Upon His Majestie's Armes quartered. [AG2]

Lord, be thy boundles bountie from above,   *by*
The British long tripartited throne   *in three*
United now, in pleasure, peace and love,
To thee and thine, great James, shal al-be-on.
5 Distractions, greefs, and grudges all ar gone,
  Competitors, that preast thy crowns to clame,   *contended*
Hes ceas'd their sutes, and leav's to thee alone,   *claims*
The Irish, French, and th'English Diademe,
Out of all doubt impertinent to them,   *not belonging*
10 And be all laws belonging unto thee,
As lo, my sacred Soveraigne supreme,
Behold here with thy royall eies and see:
The leopards, and the flowres of France they bring,
The harpe, to sport their lord, thee Lyon King.   *entertain*

To His Sacred Majestie, proclamed King of Great Britaine. [AG3]

Most magnanime, and high imperiall prince,
Whom Jova just undoubtedlie ordains   *Jehovah*
In peace, be a fore-pointed providence   *predetermined*
Of Al-be-on all, to rule the royall rains.   *power*
5 The bloudie broyls, where but th'ungodlie gains,   *troubles; only*
Great Jove, sweete time, and sacred soverain you
Have broght to end, and everie strength constrains   *resistance tames*
Before youre feete, debased, like to bow.   *humbled; alike*
The threatning storms of bold Bellona's brow,
10 To pleasant peace long intertain'd shall turne,   *cherished*
As may be noted evidentlie now,   *indeed*
Whill all your bounds with blasing bon-fires burne.   *lands*
  Amidst this mirth, and those triumphing things,
  Give God the glore, the creator of kings.

Congratulation for His Maiestie's deliverie from the Sulphurious Treason in the Parliament House. [AG4]

Lift up your hearts and hands unto the Lord,
Applaud, give praise, and with the Psalmist sing,
Unto His Majestie misericord,   *merciful*
For saif conserving of thee, soveraigne king.   *protection*
5 Give glore to God and thank him for this thing,
Laud we the Lord, with heavenlie hyms on hie,
That by that bloodie boutchrie did him bring,   *past; butchery*
Devisd for him with secret subtiltie.   *cunning*
Extend the truth, tell this eternallie,   *broadcast*
10 With mirrie minds conjunctlie all rejoes;   *together*
Jehova just, almightie, magnifie,
That fred him from the furie of his foes.   *rescued*
  Triumph, and sing for this deliverance sweet   *celebrate*
  Praise to the Father, Sonne, and Holy Sprit.

To the Cittie of Aberden, at the death of that excellent D[octor]
David, Bishop of Aberd[en].   [AG5]

The prince of preaching pastors in thir parts,
Thy archidoctor, dearest and divine,   *foremost teacher*
The light of learning in the liberall arts,
Thy senior sage, in every science sine,   *other knowledge*
5   Thy faithful father, and informer fine,   *priest; catechist*
Thy dearest David in the Lord is lost,
Thy Cipr'an, Ambrose, and thy Augustine,
The earth for heaven thy Cunninghame has cost: *yielded*
    Whill as religion with her loud laments
10   For his departure powreth out her plaints.

    To Church and King, what detriment and skaith   *harm*
The breaths-abridging burrio does bring,   *executioner*
Here in this death, is eminent to baith: *outstanding*
For lo, the church a columne, and the king   *pillar*
15 A consull grave, inlaiks in everie thing: *is deprived*
The people a platter of their publict pace,   *advocate; peace*
Ane symboll sure, and an assured signe   *trustworthy creed*
Of some approching perrell to the place,   *peril*
    Where he was wont divinely to indite   *expound*
20   The misteries of holy sacred write.   *scripture*

Invocation for seasonable weather.　[AG6]

prayer

O puissant prince, and king cunctipotent,　　　　*all-powerful*
Whose bodie rent was on the rack or Rude,　　　　*torn; Cross*
For man's great good, O Lord, thy selfe was shent,　　*destroyed*
Of that intent the devill to denude:　　　　*in order to; deprive*
5　Us to seclude, from that feirce fierie flood,　　　*protect*
Whilk reddie stood, to drink up, and demain　　　*drown; oppress*
That thou had then boght with thy blissed blood.　　*what; redeemed*
The heavenly foode that fed thy Isra'l faine,　　　*beloved*
Lord, send againe to nurish us, thy awne,　　　　*own*
10　Since floods of raine down falls out from the aer,
That we despaire to reape the fruites and graine,
Whairwith the plaine is now ore'spread alwhair.　　*ground; everywhere*
　My sute then, Lord, with spreit deprest, receave,　*prayer; contrite*
　Grant I may have, that heir I humbly crave.　　　*that which*

An description of the world.　[AG7]

What is this world, a theater of woe!　　　　　*how; spectacle*
A golfe of greif that still the greater growes,　　*abyss*
A faire where fooles are flitting to and fro,
A sea of sorrow that still ebs and flowes,　　　*continually*
5　A forge where Belial the bellowes blowes,
A shippe of sensuall soules, near sunke for sinn,　*almost*
Whair ramping rage is ruther-man and rowes,　　*wild; steersman*
A wratched vail, full of all vice within,　　　*vale*
A booth of busines where restles rin　　　　*stall; commerce*
10　To wrack himselfe, the wicked worldly worme,　　*ruin*
A deadly den of dolor and of din,　　　　　　*melancholy*
An onstai'd stage of state, a strife, a storme,　　*insecure*
　Th'unquiet Court of discontent and cair,
　The place of pride and well-spring of dispaire.　*residence*

Sighs of an sorrowfull soule. [AG8]

Sigh, sadly sigh, sob for thy sinnes and sound; *groan*
Weepe, waile, and woe, mourn, mirthless man, and mone;
Redouble thy dolor, till each den redound *sorrow; cave*
With noysome notes thy accents everie one. *painful*
5 Crie, carefull, crie, while every sensles stone,
Peirst with thy plaints, for pitie plead and pleane; *riven; lament*
With tragicke teares toone out thy griefs and grone, *declare*
While marble mazed at thy mones remaine. *till; bewildered*
Thou writes thy woes, thou weeps, thou vowes in vain,
10 Give not anon from straying thus, thou stay; *if; sinning*
Thou's drive thy daies in dateles deepe disdaine, *spend; misery*
Then sadly sigh, poore soule, and sighing say:
　　Sad be each sigh, moir noysome everie note,
　　That treads the tracture of my troubled throte. *exits; constriction*

🙰

The author his repentance fro wryting poesies prophane. [AG9] *worldly*

Could I, or this, my scattered skrols recall, *before now; papers*
Or my dispersed poesies repeit, *published; rewrite*
Most willinglie I wold revock them all,
And sound from singing of such toys retreit. *safe; vanities*
5 I wold envy 'gainst wanton verse, and writ *inveigh; write*
Invectivelie of all inventions vaine, *in denunciation*
For it infects the well desposed sprit *corrupts; ordered*
For to peruse such poesies prophane.
They breed abuse, and brings into the braine
10 Phantastick folies, and phanatick freats, *notions*
Which are in deed not bot presumptions plaine, *naught; utter*
Or at the most, but profite, poore conceats. *without; fancies*
　　Wherefore were those, else published, to pen, *already; write*
　　I should assume some sadder subject then. *more serious*

A bad man, or atheist. [AG10]

With God, with man, the world, himselfe, at warre,

And what not, all hee to damnation dare.   *may dare*

In nature like a dog, in wit an asse,   *intelligence*

And beast-like hee doth in his passion passe.   *excel*

5   Into his actions, which are always evill,

Hee is a corporall, incarnate devill.   *physical*

Hee maketh sinne a mocke, the Byble a bable,   *joke; trifle*

God's grace an humour; and his trueth a fable;   *whim*

And calles it cowardice for to keepe peace,

10   For troubled tymes hee holds his happinesse.   *keeps*

His castle hee doth call his sword, and Pride

The horse where-on this hell-hound haunts to ryde.   *is accustomed*

His purchase pyckrie is, his language lyes,   *pilfery*

His longing lust, his puncke his paradise.   *trull*

15   And, with a whore and a polluted punke,   *catamite*

His glorie is to bee debosht and drunke.   *debauched*

Hee is the patron of impietie,   *godfather*

And deadly danger of societie.

Hee vertue loathes, and loveth vanitie,

20   And is the horrour of humanitie.   *abomination*

In bawdrie and in barratrie h'abounds;   *vice; corruption*

Till bodie, soule, and fame hee all confounds.   *reputation; ruins*

Hee boasts the good, and hee upbraids them broadly,   *threatens*

And spights at all the gracious and godly.   *resents; religious*

25   His paunch is his prince, the taverne his towre,   *belly; refuge*

Mahound his master, his mistres, a whore.   *Satan*

Oathes are his graces and woundes are his badges;   *trade-mark*

Rebell, and Rogue, and Picke-purse his pages.   *attendants*

Hee knowes not God, nor goes where Grace doth dwell;

30   Bot walks through the world like a devill to hell.

Hee treacherous is and a truethlesse detractor,

The fellon, the foole, the Fiend's benefactor.   *criminal*

Untymely begotten and backwardly borne,

Unworthilie waxes and liveth forlorne.   *improperly grows*

35   A monster to men, a foole to the wise,

In doubting, Despare, and damned hee dyes.

William Drummond of Hawthornden
(1585-1649)

Drummond is the leading Scottish poet of the Jacobean (and Caroline) age, though the degree of attention paid to him in the last hundred years shows perhaps more of lukewarm duty than serious engagement and critical analysis. A Scottish patriot, he wrote a prose history of the first five kings James, but, though he was always deeply royalist in his views, he himself had little direct contact with the monarch. He favoured Episcopalian government of the Church, and in the struggles of the mid-century found himself increasingly at odds with the party of the Presbyterians and Covenanters. Like many Scottish poets of the day, he opted to write in English, despite being familiar with Older Scots and in his youth penning some verses in that language (MacDonald 1976: xix). He owned (and presumably commissioned) a personal manuscript copy of the poetry of Sir Richard Maitland of Lethington (d. 1586). Though he preferred residence at his Lothian country house of Hawthornden to the quest for advancement in London, he maintained good connections with his Scottish friends (e.g. David Murray and William Alexander) who did make the move south.

Drummond also enjoyed the respect and friendship of several eminent English poets, such as Ben Jonson and Michael Drayton: remarkably, Jonson walked all the way from London to converse with him, and a fascinating record of their conversation has been preserved. Drummond inspired many kindred spirits, both of his own generation (e.g. Alexander) and of a younger (e.g. George Lauder), and the esteem in which he was held can be measured from the verse tributes – not least Lauder's excellent pastoral elegy *Damon* – which introduce the posthumous edition of Drummond's poems (London, 1656). The latter volume was edited by Milton's nephew Edward Phillips, who in his prefatory address to the reader described Drummond as 'a Genius, the most polite and verdant that ever the Scottish Nation produced'. Until the middle of the nineteenth century, Drummond was considered as belonging essentially to the canon of English literature. This status is reflected in his relatively prominent presence in F. T. Palgrave's anthology, *The Golden Treasury* (1861), that witness to high Victorian taste, which ignores Donne and reproduces more of Drummond than of either Jonson or Herbert.

The present anthology sets the poetry of Drummond within the Scottish and Jacobean context. Like William Alexander, Walter Quin, Robert Ayton and Robert Allen, Drummond wrote on the death of Prince Henry (*Teares on the Death of Meliades*, 1613), and like Alexander Craig and William Mure he addressed a poem of welcome (*Forth Feasting*) to the king in 1617. These two compositions, together with many of the items in Drummond's *Poems* (1616), are among the indubitable masterpieces of Jacobean verse. The bibliography of Drummond's works is complicated: some were published without the name of poet, printer or place, and some were issued several times (even in the same year) with changes of title-page and ornamentation, and with ongoing minor revisions to the text of the poems (cf. Kastner 1913: xlv–xcvi). While Drummond normally had his sonnets set in roman type, his songs, madrigals and sextains (*sestine*) were in italic, and he was characteristically careful to ensure that his poetry appear in optimal form, both visually and verbally. His habitual tinkering is, for example, visible in the differences between the two versions of WD2; alas, he would seem to have been entirely satisfied with neither attempt, and this poem was not included in the *Poems* of 1616.

Drummond was one of many early modern English and Scottish poets to be fascinated by the genre of the sonnet, and he brought to it an exceptional degree of thoughtful sentiment and refined elegance of expression. This is true not only of his amatory sonnets, but also of those on religious themes, as in the *Flowres of Sion* (Edinburgh, 1623). He was deeply influenced by the contemporary Europe-wide enthusiasm for neo-Latin poetry, and was a close friend (and brother-in-law) of Sir John Scot of Scotstarvet (1585–1670), the editor of the *Delitiae poetarum Scotorum* [Delights of the Scottish poets] (Amsterdam, 1637); Scotstarvet would ultimately be responsible for collecting the scattered manuscripts of Drummond's works. Many Scottish Jacobean poets were aware of the literary fashions cultivated in Italy and France, but such vernacular productions impacted more thoroughly upon Drummond than upon any of his contemporaries. His accumulated books, now in Edinburgh University Library, demonstrate his enthusiastic reception of foreign literary influences (cf. MacDonald 1971).

Drummond's employment of the English language and his saturation in the Classics, in neo-Latin and in several European vernacular literatures in no way vitiates his status as one of the most significant poets of his homeland. Rather, such things testify to his significance as the outstanding representative of an age in which the traditional Scottish openness to European culture was broadened and intensified. Unfortunately, tastes changed with circumstances in the great crisis of the mid-seventeenth century, with its factionalism, armed conflict and cultural, political and religious upheaval. Nonetheless, the Jacobean age remains as something of a brave new literary world, with Drummond enthroned on the summit of Parnassus.

Teares on the Death of Mœliades. [WD1]

O heavens! Then is it true that thou art gone,
And left this woefull ile her losse to mone,
Mœliades,[†] bright day-starre of the west,
A comet, blazing terrour to the east;   *proclaiming*
5 And neither that thy spright so heavenly wise,   *spirit*
Nor bodie – though of earth – more pure than skies,
Nor royall stemme, nor thy sweet tender age,   *descent*
Of adamantine fates could quench the rage?
O fading hopes! O short-while-lasting joy
10 Of earth-borne man, which one houre can destroy!
Then even of vertue's spoyles Death trophees reares,   *sets up*
As if he gloried most in many teares;
Forc'd by grimme destines, heavens neglect our cryes,   *destinies*
Starres seeme set only to acte tragœdies.
15 And let them doe their worst, since thou art gone,
Raise whom they list to thrones, enthron'd dethrone,
Staine princely bowres with blood, and, even to Gange,   *chambers; Ganges*
In cypresse sad glad Hymen's torches change.
Ah! thou hast left to live, and in the time   *ceased; season*
20 When scarce thou blossom'd in thy pleasant prime.   *spring*
So falles by northerne blast a virgine rose,
At halfe that doth her bashfull bosome close;   *half-way*
So a sweet flourish languishing decayes,
That late did blush when kist by Phœbus' rayes;

25	So Phœbus, mounting the meridian's hight,	*mid-day*
	Choack'd by pale Phœbe, faints unto our sight;	*obscured; fades*
	Astonish'd Nature sullen stands to see	*gloomily*
	The life of all this all, so chang'd to bee;	*entire world*
	In gloomie gownes the starres about deplore,	*surrounding; lament*
30	The sea with murmuring mountains beats the shore;	
	Blacke darknesse reeles o're all; in thowsand showres,	*wheels*
	The weeping aire on earth her sorrow powres,	*pours*
	That, in a palsey, quakes to find so soone	
	Her lover set, and night burst foorth ere noone.	*sunk from sight*
35	If heaven, alas, ordain'd thee young to die,	
	Why was it not where thou thy might didst trie,	*power*
	And to the hopefull world at least set forth	
	Some little sparke of thy expected worth?	
	Mœliades, O that by Ister's streames,	
40	Amongst shrill-sounding trumpets, flaming gleames	
	Of warm encrimson'd swords, and cannons' roare,	*blood-stained*
	Balls thicke as raine pour'd by the Caspian shore,	
	Amongst crush'd lances, ringing helmes and shields,	
	Dismembred bodies ravishing the fields,	*desecrating*
45	In Turkish blood, made red like Mars'es starre,	
	Thóu ended hadst thy life, and Christian warre!	
	Or, as brave Burbon, thou hadst made old Rome,	
	Queene of the world, thy triumphe's place, and tombe!	
	So heaven's faire face, to the unborne which reads,	
50	A booke had beene of thy illustrious deedes;	
	So to their nephews aged syres had told	*ancestors*
	The high exploits perform'd by thee of old,	
	Townes raz'd, and rais'd, victorious, vanquish'd bands,	*relieved*
	Fierce tyrants flying, foyl'd, kill'd by thy hands,	*stopped*
55	And in deare arras virgins faire had wrought	*tapestry*
	The bayes and trophees to thy country brought,	*laurels*
	While some new Homer, imping pennes to fame,	*adding feathers*
	Deafe Nilus dwellers had made heare thy name.	
	That thou didst not attaine those honour's spheares,	
60	It was not want of worth, O no, but yeares.	

A youth more brave, pale Troy with trembling walles
Did never see, nor shee whose name apalles   *makes pale*
Both Titan's golden bowres, for bloody fights
Mustring on Mars'es field such Marse-like knights.
65 The heavens had brought thee to the highest hight
Of wit and courage, shewing all their might
When they thee fram'd – Ay mee! – that what is brave   *made*
On earth, they as their owne so soone should crave.
Mœliades, sweet courtly nymphes, deplore   *weep for*
70 From Thuly to Hydaspes' pearlie shore.
        When Forth, thy nurse – Forth, where thou first didst passe
Thy tender dayes, who smyl'd oft on her glasse   *smooth surface*
To see thee gaze, meandering with her streames –
Heard thou hadst left this round, from Phœbus' beames   *world*
75 Shee sought to flie, but forced to returne
By neighbour brookes, shee gave herself to mourne;
And, as shee rush'd her Cyclades among,
Shee seem'd to plaine that heaven had done her wrong.   *mourn*
With a hoarse plaint, Cleyd downe her steepie rockes,   *lament*
80 And Tweed through her greene mountaines cled with flockes,
Did wound the ocean, murmuring thy death,   *bewailing*
The ocean that roar'd about the earth,
And it to Mauretanian Atlas told,
Who shrunke through griefe, and downe his white haires roll'd
85 Hudge streames of teares, that changed were in floods,
With which hee drown'd the neighbour plaines and woods.
The lesser brookes, as they did bubbling goe,
Did keepe a consort unto publike woe.   *accompaniment*
The shepheardes left their flockes with downe-cast eyes,
90 Disdaining to looke up to angrie skies;
Some broke their pipes, and some in sweet-sad layes,
Made senslesse things amazed at thy praise;
His reed Alexis hung upon a tree,   *shepherd's pipe*
And with his teares made Doven great to bee.   *high-flowing*
95 Mœliades, sweet courtly nymphes, deplore
From Thuly to Hydaspes' pearlie shore.

Chaste maides which haunt faire Aganippe well,
And you in Tempe's sacred shade who dwell,
Let fall your harpes, cease tunes of joy to sing,
100 Discheveled, make all Parnassus ring   *with hair untidy*
With antheames sad; thy musicke, Phœbus, turne
In dolefull plaints, whilst joy it self doth mourne.
Dead is thy darling, who decor'd thy bayes,   *embellished; garlands*
Who oft was wont to cherish thy sweet layes,
105 And to a trumpet raise thine amorous stile,
That floting Delos envie might this ile.
You Acidalian archers breake your bowes,
Your brandons quench, with teares blot beautie's snowes,   *torches*
And bid your weeping mother yet againe
110 A second Adon's death, nay, Mars'es, plaine.   *lament*
His eyes were once your darts, nay, even his name   *arrows*
Where ever heard, did every heart inflame:
Tagus did court his love, with golden streames,
Rhein with his townes, faire Seine, with all shee claimes,
115 But ah, poore lovers, death did them betrey,
And, not suspected, made their hopes his prey!
Tagus bewailes his losse, with golden streames,
Rhein with his townes, faire Seine with all shee claimes.
Mœliades, sweet courtly nymphes, deplore
120 From Thuly to Hydaspes' pearlie shore.
   Delicious meads, whose checkred plaine foorth brings   *fair; variegated*
White, golden, azure flowres, which once were kings,
In mourning blacke their shining colours dye,
Bow downe their heads, whilst sighing zephyres flye.
125 Queene of the fields, whose blush makes blushe the morne,
Sweet rose, a prince's death in purple mourne;
O hyacinthes, for ay your AI keepe still,   *Alas!; always*
Nay, with moe markes of woe your leaves now fill;
And you, O flower of Helen's teares first borne,
130 Into those liquide pearles againe you turne.
Your greene lockes, forests, cut, in weeping myrrhes,
The deadly cypresse, and inke-dropping firres

Your palmes and mirtles change; from shadowes darke,
Wing'd syrens, waile, and you, sad echoes, marke
135 The lamentable accents of their mone,
And plaine that brave Mœliades is gone.
Stay, skie, thy turning course, and now become   *stop*
A stately arche, unto the earth his tombe;
Over which ay the watrie Iris keepe,   *always; guard*
140 And sad Electra's sisters which still weepe.
Mœliades, sweet courtly nymphes, deplore
From Thuly to Hydaspes' pearlie shore.
      Deare ghost, forgive these our untimely teares,
By which our loving minde, though weake, appeares.
145 Our losse not thine, when wee complaine, wee weepe,
For thee the glistering walles of heaven doe keepe,   *shining*
Beyond the planets' wheeles, above that source   *orbits*
Of spheares, that turns the lower in its course,
Where sunne doth never set, nor ugly night
150 Ever appeares in mourning garments dight;   *apparelled*
Where Boreas' stormie trumpet doth not sound,
Nor cloudes, in lightnings bursting, minds astound.
From care's cold climates farre, and hote desire,
Where time is banish'd, ages ne're expire,
155 Amongst pure sprights environed with beames,   *spirits; light*
Thou think'st all things below to bee but dreames,
And joy'st to looke downe to the azur'd barres   *layers*
Of heaven, indented all with streaming starres,   *set; effulgent*
And in their turning temples to behold,
160 In silver robe the moone, the sunne in gold,
Like young eye-speaking lovers in a dance,
With majestie by turns retire, advance.
Thou wondrest earth to see hang like a ball,
Clos'd in the gastly cloyster of this all,   *wretched; world*
165 And that poore men should prove so madly fond,   *deluded*
To tosse themselves for a small foot of ground;   *vex*
Nay, that they even dare brave the powers above,
From this base stage of change, that cannot move.   *low place*

All worldly pompe and pride thou seest arise
170 Like smoake, that scattreth in the emptie skies.   *dissipates*
Other hilles and forests, other sumptuous towres,   *different*
Amaz'd thou find'st, excelling our poore bowres,
Courts voyde of flattrie, of malice mindes,
Pleasure which lasts, not such as reason blindes:
175 Farre sweeter songs thou hear'st and carrolings,
Whilst heavens doe dance, and quire of angels sings,
Than moldie mindes could faine; even our annoy   *earthy; pain*
If it approach that place, is chang'd in joy.
Rest blessed spright, rest saciate with the sight   *fulfilled*
180 Of him, whose beames both dazell and delight,
Life of all lives, cause of each other cause,
The spheare, and center, where the minde doth pause:
Narcissus of himselfe, himselfe the well,
Lover, and beautie, that doth all excell.
185 Rest happie ghost, and wonder in that glasse,   *marvel; mirror*
Where seene is all that shall be, is, or was,
While shall be, is, or was doe passe away,   *until*
And nought remaine but an eternall day.
For ever rest, thy praise Fame may enroule   *record*
190 In golden annalles, whilst about the Pole
The slow Boötes turns, or sunne doth rise
With skarlet scarfe, to cheare the mourning skies.   *mantle*
The virgines to thy tombe may garlands beare
Of flowres, and on each flowre let fall a teare.
195 Mœliades, sweet courtly nymphes, deplore
From Thuly to Hydaspes' pearlie shore.

[WD2] (a)

Stay passenger, see where enclosed lyes,   *stand still*
Wit's paragone and nature's daintiest frame,   *form*
Vertue's faire temple, wonder unto fame,
In whome was found the best heaven could devise –   *create*
5 At least that part the earth of him could claime,
Of elements combind that did arise,
For as to his brave spirit and glorious name,
The one the world, the other fills the skyes.
Arabian odours, mirtles, youthfull bayes,
10 Roses and that sweet flowre that mourning beares,
Spred on this stone, while I these dolefull layes
Sigh forth, and wash it over with my teares.
    Then goe and tell from Gades unto Inde,   *Cadiz; India*
    Thow saw where earth's perfections were confinde.

(b)

Stay passenger, see where enclosed lyes,
The paragon of princes, fairest frame
Time, nature, place could show to mortal eyes,
In worth, wit, vertue, miracle to fame –
5 At lest that part the earth of him could clame,
This marble holds, hard like the Destinies,   *Fates*
For as to his brave spirit, and glorious name,
The one the world, the other fills the skies.
Th'immortall amaranthus, princely rose,
10 Sad violet, and that sweet flowre that beares
In sanguine spots the tenor of our woes,   *blood-red*
Spred on this stone, and wash it with thy teares.
    Then go and tell from Gades unto Inde,
    Thou saw where earth's perfections were confinde.

[WD3]

I know that all beneath the moone decayes,
And what by mortalles in this world is brought, *imported*
In time's great periods shall returne to nought;
That fairest states have fatall nights and dayes. *terminal*
5 I know how all the Muses' heavenly layes,
With toyle of spright which are so dearely bought, *spirit; acquired*
As idle sounds, of few or none are sought, *appreciated*
And that nought lighter is than airie praise.
I know fraile beautie like the purple flowre,
10 To which one morne of birth and death affords, *supplies*
That love a jarring is of mindes' accords, *clashing; harmonies*
Where sense and will invassall reason's power. *enslave*
  Know what I list, this all can not mee move, *whatever; choose*
  But that – O mee! – I both must write, and love.

[WD4]

That learned Græcian – who did so excel
In knowledge passing sense, that hee is nam'd *transcending*
Of all the after-worlds 'divine' – doth tell,
That at the time when first our soules are fram'd, *formed*
5 Ere in these mansions blinde they come to dwell, *dark dwellings*
They live bright rayes of that eternall light,
And others see, know, love, in heaven's great hight,
Not toylde with ought to reason doth rebell. *encumbered*
Most true it is, for straight at the first sight
10 My minde mee told, that in some other place
It elsewhere saw the idea of that face,
And lov'd a love of heavenly pure delight.
  No wonder, now I feele so faire a flame,
  Sith I her lov'd, ere on this earth shee came. *since*

[WD5]

Now while the night her sable vaile hath spred,
And silently her restie coach doth rolle,   *unstoppable*
Rowsing with her from Tethis' azure bed
Those starrie nymphes which dance about the Pole;
5 While Cynthia, in purest Cipres cled,   *finest linen*
The Latmian shepheard in a trance descries,
And whiles lookes pale from hight of all the skies,   *sometimes*
Whiles dyes her beauties in a bashfull red;
While sleepe, in triumph, closed hath all eyes,
10 And birds and beastes a silence sweet doe keepe,
And Proteus' monstrous people in the deepe,
The winds and waves, husht up, to rest entise;   *entice*
    I wake, muse, weepe, and who my heart hath slaine
    See still before me, to augment my paine.

Madrigall. [WD6]

A dedale of my death,   *emblem*
Now I resemble that subtile worme on earth   *skilled creature*
Which, prone to its owne evill, can take no rest.   *bound to; harm*
For with strange thoughts possest,
5 I feede on fading leaves
Of hope, which me deceaves,
And thousand webs doth warpe within my brest.   *spin*
And thus in end unto my selfe I weave   *ultimately*
A fast-shut prison, no, but even a grave.

[WD7]

O sacred blush, impurpling cheekes' pure skies,
With crimson wings which spred thee like the morne,
O bashfull looke, sent from those shining eyes,
Which, though cast down on earth, couldst heaven adorne;
5 O tongue, in which most lushious nectar lies,
That can at once both blesse and make forlorne,
Deare corall lip, which beautie beautifies,
That trembling stood, ere that her words were borne;
And you her words, words no, but golden chaines,
10 Which did captive mine eares, ensnare my soule,
Wise image of her minde, minde that containes
A power, all power of senses to controule:
    Yee all, from love, disswade so sweetly mee
    That I love more, if more my love could bee.

[WD8]

With flaming hornes the Bull now brings the yeare,
Melt doe the horride mountaines' helmes of snow,
The silver flouds in pearlie channells flow,
The late-bare woods greene anadeams doe weare.   *crowns*
5 The nightingall, forgetting winter's woe,
Calls up the lazie morne her notes to heare,
Those flowrs are spred which names of princes beare,
Some red, some azure, white, and golden grow.
Here lowes a heifer, there bea-wailing strayes   *bleating*
10 A harmelesse lambe, not farre a stag rebounds,   *gives answer*
The sheepe-heards sing to grazing flockes sweet layes,
And all about the echoing aire resounds.
    Hills, dales, woods, flouds, and every thing doth change,
    But shee in rigour, I in love am strange.   *unyielding*

[WD9]

Like the Idalian queene,
Her haire about her eyne,
With necke and brests ripe apples to be seene,
At first glance of the morne
5 In Cyprus gardens gathering those faire flowrs
Which of her bloud were borne,
I saw, but fainting saw, my paramours.   *beloved*
The Graces naked danc'd about the place,
The winds and trees, amaz'd,   *marvelling*
10 With silence on her gaz'd,
The flowrs did smile, like those upon her face;
And as their aspine stalkes those fingers band,   *delicate; clasped*
    That shee might read my case   *understand*
    A hyacinth I wisht mee in her hand.

[WD10]

Trust not, sweet soule, those curled waves of gold,
With gentle tides which on your temples flow,
Nor temples spread with flackes of virgine snow, *flakes*
Nor snow of cheeks with Tyrian graine enroll'd;   *dye; suffused*
5 Trust not those shining lights which wrought my woe,
When first I did their burning rayes beholde,
Nor voyce, whose sounds more strange effects doe show   *unusual*
Than of the Thracian harper have beene tolde;
Looke to this dying lillie, fading rose,   *consider*
10 Darke hyacinthe, of late whose blushing beames   *faded*
Made all the neighbouring herbes and grasse rejoice,
And think how litle is twixt life's extreames.
    The cruell tyrant that did kill those flowrs,
    Shall once – aye mee! – not spare that spring of yours.

[WD11]

Slide soft, faire Forth, and make a chrystall plaine,   *surface*
Cut your white lockes, and on your foamie face   *spray*
Let not a wrinckle bee, when you embrace   *ripple*
The boat that earth's perfections doth containe.
5 Windes, wonder, and through wondering holde your peace,   *marvel*
Or, if that yee your hearts cannot restraine
From sending sighes, mov'd by a lover's case,   *condition*
Sigh, and in her faire haire your selves enchaine;
Or take those sighes, which absence makes arise,
10 From mine oppressed brest and wave the sailes,   *swell*
Or some sweet breath new brought from Paradise:
Flouds seeme to smile, love o're the winds prevails,
    And yet hudge waves arise: the cause is this,
    The ocean strives with Forth the boate to kisse.

[WD12]

Are these the flowrie bankes? Is this the mead
Where shee was wont to passe the pleasant hours?
Did here her eyes exhale mine eyes' salt showrs,   *draw out*
When on her lap I laide my wearie head?
5 Is this the goodly elme did us o'respread,
Whose tender rine, cut out in curious flowrs   *bark; fancy*
By that white hand, containes those flames of ours?
Is this the rusling spring us musicke made?   *purling brook*
Deflourish'd mead, where is your heavenly hue?   *bare meadow*
10 Banke, where that arras did you late adorne,   *tapestry; formerly*
How looke yee, elme, all withered and forlorne?
Onely, sweet spring, nought altered seemes in you.   *fount*
    But while, here chang'd, each other thing appears,   *something else*
    To sowre your streames, take of mine eyes these teares.

[WD13]

Mine eyes, dissolve your globes in brinie streames,
And with a cloud of sorrow dimme your sight,
The sunne's bright sunne is set, of late whose beames
Gaue luster to your day, day to your night.
5 My voyce, now deafen earth with anatheames,   *imprecations*
Roare foorth a challenge in the world's despight: *defiance*
Tell that disguised griefe is her delight,
That life a slumber is of fearfull dreames;
And, woefull minde, abhorre to thinke of joy,   *refuse*
10 My senses all, now comfortlesse you hide,
Accept no object but of blacke annoy,   *gloomy pain*
Teares, plaints, sighs, mourning weeds, graves gaping wide.
    I haue nought left to wish, my hopes are dead,   *nothing*
    And all with her beneath a marble laide.

[WD14]

Sweet soule, which in the Aprill of thy yeares,
So to enrich the heaven mad'st poore this round,   *world*
And now, with golden rayes of glorie crown'd,
Most blest abid'st above the spheare of spheares;
5 If heavenly lawes – alas – have not thee bound   *restricted*
From looking to this globe that all upbeares,   *supports*
If rueth and pittie there above bee found,
O daigne to lend a looke unto those teares.
Doe not disdaine, deare ghost, this sacrifice,
10 And, though I raise not pillars to thy praise,
Mine offerings take. Let this for mee suffice:
My heart a living piramide I raise.
    And whilst kings' tombes with lawrels flourish greene,
    Thine shall with mirtles, and these flowrs bee seene.

Song. [WD15]

Sad Damon – beeing come
To that for-ever lamentable tombe,
Which those eternall powers that all controule
Unto his living soule
5 A melancholie prison had prescriv'd –
Of hue, of heate, of motion quite depriv'd
In armes wake, trembling, cold,   *weak*
A marble hee, the marble did infold;   *embrace*
And having made it warme with many a showre,
10 Which dimmed eyes did powre,   *pour*
When griefe had given him leave, and sighes them stay'd,   *detained*
Thus, with a sad alas, at last he said:
   "Who would have thought, to mee
The place where thou didst lie could grievous bee,
15 And that, deare body, long thee having sought –
O mee! Who would haue thought? –
Thee once to finde, it should my soule confound,
And give my heart than death a deeper wound?
Thou didst disdaine my teares,
20 But grieve not that this ruethfull stone them beares,
Mine eyes serve only now for thee to weepe;
And let their course them keepe,
Although thou never wouldst them comfort show;
Doe not repine, they have part of thy woe.   *regret*
25   Ah wretch! Too late I finde,   *unfortunate*
How Vertue's glorious titles prove but winde;
For if shee any could release from death,
Thou yet enjoy'd hadst breath;
For if shee ere appear'd to mortall eine,   *ever*
30 It was in thy faire shape that shee was seene.
But O! If I was made
For thee, with thee why too am I not dead?
Why doe outragious fates, which dimm'd thy sight,
Let mee see hatefull light?

35 They without mee made death thee to surprise –
Tyrants, perhaps, that they might kill mee twise.
     O griefe! And could one day
Have force such excellence to take away?
Could a swift flying moment, ah, deface   *despoil*
40 Those matchlesse gifts, that grace,
Which Art and Nature had in thee combinde,
To make thy body paragone thy minde?   *equal*
Have all past like a cloud,
And doth eternall silence now them shroud?
45· Is what so much admir'd was, nought but dust
Of which a stone hath trust?   *keeping*
O change! O cruell change! Thou to our sight
Shewes destines' rigour equall doth their might.   *Fates*
     When thou from earth didst passe,
50 Sweet nymph, perfection's mirrour broken was,
And this of late so glorious world of ours,
Like meadow without flowrs,
Or ring of a riche gemme made blind, appear'd,   *deprived*
Or night by starre nor Cynthia neither clear'd.   *lit up*
55 Love, when he saw thee die,
Entomb'd him in the lidde of either eye,
And left his torch within thy sacred urne,
There for a lampe to burne:
Worth, honour, pleasure, with thy life expir'd,   *virtue*
60 Death since, growne sweet, beginnes to bee desir'd.
     Whilst thou to us wast given,
The earth her Venus had, as well as heaven,
Nay, and her sunne, which burnt as many hearts,
As hee doth easterne parts;
65 Bright sunne which, forc'd to leave these hemispheares,
Benighted set into a sea of teares.
Ah Death! Who shall thee flie,   *flee from*
Sith the most worthie bee o'rethrowne by thee?   *since*
Thou spar'st the ravens, and nightingalles dost kill,
70 And triumphes at thy will:

But give thou canst not such an other blow,   *strike*
Because like her earth can none other show.
    O bitter-sweets of love!
How better is't at all you not to prove,   *taste*
75 Than, when wee doe your pleasure most possesse,
To find them then made lesse?
O that the cause which doth consume our joy,
Remembrance of it too, would too destroy!
What doth this life bestow   *grant*
80 But flowrs on thornes which grow?
Which, though they sometime blandishing delighte,   *seductively*
Yet afterwards us smite?
And if the rising sunne them faire doth see,
That planet setting, too beholdes them die.   *also*
85   This world is made a hell,
Depriv'd of all that in it did excel.
O Pan, Pan, winter is fallen in our May,
Turn'd is in night our day.
Forsake thy pipe, a scepter take to thee,
90 Thy lockes disgarland, thou blacke Jove shalt bee.   *ungarland*
The flockes doe leave the meads,
And, loathing three-leaf'd grasse, hold up their heads.   *clover*
The streames not glide now with a gentle rore,   *murmur*
Nor birds sing as before,
95 Hilles stand with clouds like mourners, vail'd in blacke,
And owles on caban roofes fore-tell our wracke.   *hovels; ruin*
    That Zephyre everie yeere
So soone was heard to sigh in forrests here,
It was for her; that, wrapt in gownes of greene,
100 Meads were so earelie seene,
That in the saddest months oft sung the mearles,   *blackbirds*
It was for her; for her trees dropt foorth pearles;
That prowde, and statelie courts
Did envie those our shades, and calme resorts,
105 It was for her; and she is gone, O woe!
Woods cut, againe doe grow,

Budde doth the rose, and dazie, winter done;   *daisy; past*
But wee once dead no more doe see the sunne.
    Whose name shall now make ring
110 The ecchoes? Of whom shall the nymphettes sing?   *maidens*
Whose heavenlie voyce, whose soule-invading straines,   *piercing*
Shall fill with joy the plaines?
What haire, what eyes, can make the morne in east
Weepe, that a fairer riseth in the west?
115 Faire sunne, poste still away,   *hasten*
No musicke here is found thy course to stay.   *detain*
Sweet Hybla swarmes with wormewood fill your bowrs,
Gone is the flowre of flowrs:
Blush no more, rose, nor Lillie pale remaine;
120 Dead is that beautie which yours late did staine.   *outshine*
    Aye mee! To waile my plight,
Why have not I as many eyes as night?
Or as that shepheard which Jove's love did keepe,   *guard*
That I still still may weepe?   *ever; quietly*
125 But though I had, my teares unto my crosse   *misfortune*
Were not yet equall, nor griefe to my losse.
Yet, of you brinie showrs,
Which I heere powre, may spring as many flowrs,
As came from those which fell from Helen's eyes,
130 And when yee doe arise,
May everie leafe in sable letters beare
The dolefull cause for which yee spring up here."

[WD16]

Thrise happie hee, who by some shadie grove
Farre from the clamarous world doth live his owne,   *by himself*
Though solitare, yet who is not alone,
But doth converse with that eternall love.
5   O how more sweet is birds' harmonious mone,
Or the soft sobbings of the widow'd dove,
Than those smoothe whisp'rings neare a prince's throne,
Which good make doubtfull, doe the evill approve.
O how more sweet is Zephyre's wholesome breath,
10 And sighs perfum'd, which doe the flowres unfold,   *make*
Than that applause vaine honour doth bequeath;
How sweet are streames to poyson drunke in gold!   *contrasted*
      The world is full of horrours, falshoods, slights,
      Woods' silent shades have only true delights.

Forth Feasting: a Panegyricke to the King's most   *address*
excellent Majesty.   [WD17]

Flumina senserunt ipsa

What blustring noise now interrupts my sleepe?
What echoing shouts thus cleave my chrystal deep,   *pierce*
And call me hence from out my watrie court?
What melodie, what sounds of joye and sport,
5   Bee these, heere hurl'd from ev'rie neighbour spring?
With what lowd rumours doe the mountaines ring,
Which in unusuall pompe on tip-toes stand,   *ceremony*
And, full of wonder, over-looke the land?
Whence come these glittring throngs, these meteors bright,
10 This golden people set unto my sight?
Whence doth this praise, applause, and love, arise?

What load-starre east-ward draweth thus all eyes?
And doe I wake? Or have some dreames conspir'd
To mocke my sense with shadowes much desir'd?
15 Stare I that living face, see I those lookes,   *behold*
Which with delight wont to amaze my brookes?   *used*
Doe I behold that worth, that man divine,   *greatness*
This age's glorie, by these bankes of mine?
Then is it true, what long I wish'd in vaine,
20 That my much-loving prince is come againe?
So unto them whose zenith is the Pole,   *heaven*
When six blacke months are past, the sunne doth rolle: *emerge*
So after tempest, to sea-tossed wights,
Faire Helen's brothers show their chearing lights:
25 So comes Arabia's mervaile from her woods,   *marvel*
And farre farre off is seene by Memphis floods,
The feather'd sylvans clowd-like by her flie,   *wood-fowl*
And with applauding clangors beate the skie,
Nyle wonders, Serap's priests entranced rave,
30 And in Mygdonian stone her shape ingrave,
In golden leaves write down the joyfull time
In which Apollo's bird came to their clime.
    Let mother earth now deckt with flowrs bee seene,
And sweet-breath'd zephyres curle the medowes greene;
35 Let heavens weepe rubies in a crimsin showre,
Such as on Indie's shores they use to powre;   *habitually pour*
Or with that golden storme the fields adorne,
Which Jove rain'd, when his blew-eyed maide was borne.
May never Houres the webbe of day out-weave,   *complete*
40 May never night rise from her sable cave.
Swell prowd, my billowes, faint not to declare
Your joyes, as ample as their causes are,   *great*
For murmure's hoarse sound, like Arion's harpe,
Now delicatlie flat, now sweetlie sharpe.
45 And you, my nymphes, rise from your moyst repaire,   *abode*
Strow all your springs and grotts with lillies faire,   *caverns*
Some, swiftest-footed, get her hence, and pray   *set off*

Our floods and lakes come keepe this holie-day.
What e're beneath Albania's hills doe runne,
50   Which see the rising or the setting sunne,
Which drinke sterne Grampius mists, or Ochelles snows:
Stone-rowling Taye, Tine, tortoyse-like that flows,
The pearlie Done, the Deas, the fertile Spay,
Wild Neverne which doth see out longest day,
55   Nesse smoaking-sulphure, Leave with mountains crown'd,
Strange Loumond, for his floting isles renown'd: *mysterious*
The Irish Rian, Ken, the silver Aire,
The snakie Dun, the Ore with rushie haire,   *sinuous*
The chrystall-streaming Nid, lowd-bellowing Clyd,
60   Tweed which no more our kingdomes shall divide:
Rancke-swelling Annan, Lid with curled streames,   *swift*
The Eskes, the Solway where they loose their names,
To ev'rie one proclaime our joyes, and feasts,
Our triumphes; bid all come, and bee our guests;
65   And, as they meet in Neptune's azure hall,
Bid them bid sea-gods keepe this festivall.
This day shall by our currents bee renown'd;
Our hills about shall still the day resound.   *around; echo*
Nay, that our love more to this day appeare,
70   Let us with it hencefoorth begin our yeare.
       To virgins flowrs, to sunne-burnt earth the raine,
To mariners faire winds amidst the maine,
Coole shades to pilgrimes, which hote glances burne,   *rays*
Please not so much, to us as thy returne.
75   That day, deare Prince, which reft us of thy sight,
– Day, no, but darknesse, and a duskie night –
Did fraight our brests with sighs,* our eyes with teares,   *load*
Turn'd minutes in sad months, sad months in yeares.
Trees left to flowrish, meadows to beare flowrs,   *ceased*
80   Brookes hid their heads within their sedgie bowrs,   *reedy*
Faire Ceres curst our fields with barren frost,
As if againe shee had her daughter lost:
The Muses left our groves, and, for sweete songs,   *in place of*

Sate sadlie silent, or did weepe their wrongs;
85 Yee know it, meads, yee murmuring woods it know,
Hilles, dales, and caves, copartners of their woe;
And yee it know, my streames, which from their eine
Oft on your glasse reciev'd their pearled brine;   *surface; tears*
'O Naïds deare', said they, 'Napæas faire,
90 O nymphes of trees, nymphes which on hills repaire,   *dwell*
Gone are those maiden glories, gone that state,   *splendour*
Which made all eyes admire our hap of late.   *fortune; former*
As lookes the heaven when never starre appears,
But slow and wearie shroude them in their spheares,
95 While Tithons' wife embosom'd by him lies,
And world does languish in a drearie guise:
As lookes a garden of its beautie spoil'd,
As wood in winter by rough Boreas foil'd;   *devastated*
As pourtraicts raz'd of colours use to bee: *drained; tend*
100 So lookt those abject bounds depriv'd of thee.'   *desolate lands*
    While as my rills enjoy'd thy royall gleames,   *as long; aura*
They did not envie Tyber's haughtie streames,
Nor wealthie Tagus with his golden ore,
Nor cleare Hydaspes which on pearles doth rore,   *roar*
105 Empampred Gange, that sees the sunne new borne,   *worshipped*
Nor Acheloüs with his flowrie horne,
Nor floods which neare Elysian fields doe fall: *rivers*
For why? Thy sight did serve to them for all.
No place there is so desert, so alone,
110 Even from the frozen to the torrid zone,
From flaming Hecla to great Quincys lake,
Which thine abode could not most happie make.
All those perfections which by bounteous heaven
To diverse worlds in diverse times were given,
115 The starrie senate powr'd at once on thee,   *gods; poured*
That thou examplare mightst to others bee.
    Thy life was kept till the thre Sisters spunne   *protected*
Their threedes of gold, and then it was begunne:
With curled clowds when skies doe looke most faire,

And no disordred blasts disturbe the aire;
When lillies doe them decke in azure gownes,
And new-borne roses blush with golden crownes,
To bode how calme wee under thee should live,   *indicate*
What Halcyonean dayes thy reigne should give,
125 And to two flowrie diadems, thy right,   *crowns*
The heavens thee made a partner of the light.
Scarce wast thou borne, when, joyn'd in friendly bands,   *league*
Two mortall foes with other clasped hands;
With Vertue Fortune strove, which most should grace
130 Thy place for thee, thee for so high a place;
One vow'd thy sacred brest not to forsake,
The other on thee not to turne her backe,
And, that thou more her love's effects mightst feele,
For thee shee rent her sayle, and broke her wheele.   *tore*
135   When yeares thee vigour gave, O then, how cleare   *strength*
Did smother'd sparkles in bright flames appeare?   *hidden sparks*
Amongst the woods to force a flying hart,   *drive*
To pearce the mountaine wolfe with feathred dart,
See faulcons climbe the clowds, the foxe ensnare,
140 Out-runne the winde-out-running dædale hare,   *nimble*
To loose a trampling steede alongst a plaine,   *prancing*
And in meandering gyres him bring againe.   *winding circles*
The preasse, thee making place, were vulgar things,   *ordinary horde*
In admiration's aire, on glorie's wings;
145 O thou farre from the common pitch didst rise,
With thy designes to dazell Envie's eyes.
Thou soughtst to know this all's eternall source,   *universe*
Of ever-turning heavens the restlesse course,
Their fixed eyes, their lights which wandring runne,
150 Whence moone her silver hath, his gold the sunne,
If destine bee or no, if planets can   *destiny*
By fierce aspects force the free-will of man: *dominating*
The light and spyring fire, the liquid aire,   *ascending*
The flaming dragons, comets with red haire,   *trains*
155 Heaven's tilting launces, artillerie, and bow,

Lowd-sounding trumpets, darts of haile and snow,
The roaring element with people dombe,
The earth with what conceiv'd is in her wombe,
What on her moves, were set unto thy sight,
160 Till thou didst find their causes, essence, might. *function*
But unto nought thou so thy mind didst straine
As to bee read in man, and learne to raigne; *well-learned*
To know the weight, and Atlas of a crowne, *responsibility*
To spare the humble, prowdlings pester downe. *control grandees*
165 When, from those pearcing cares which thrones invest *painful; beset*
As thornes the rose, thou weari'd wouldst thee rest,
With lute in hand, full of cœlestiall fire,
To the Pierian groves thou didst retire:
There, garlanded with all Urania's flowrs,
170 In sweeter layes than builded Thæbes' towrs,
Or them which charm'd the dolphines in the maine,
Or which did call Euridice againe,
Thou sungst away the houres, till from their spheare
Starres seem'd to shoote, thy melodie to heare.
175 The god with golden haire, the sister maides,
Left nymphall Helicon, their Tempe's shades, *having left*
To see thine isle, here lost their native tongue,
And in thy world-divided language sung.
    Who of thine after-age can count the deedes, *maturity*
180 With all that Fame in time's hudge annals reedes?
How by example, more than anie law,
This people fierce thou didst to goodnesse draw;
How while the neighbour worlds, tows'd by the Fates, *stirred up*
So many Phaëtons had in their states,
185 Which turn'd in heedlesse flames their burnish'd thrones,
Thou, as ensphear'd, keep'dst temperate thy zones. *in orbit; cool*
In Africke shores the sands that ebbe and flow,
The speckled flowrs in unshorne meads that grow,
Hee sure may count, with all the waves that meet *come together*
190 To wash the Mauretanian Atlas' feet,
Though thou were not a crowned king by birth, *had you not been*

Thy worth deserves the richest crowne on earth:
Search this halfe-spheare and the opposite ground,
Where is such wit and bountie to bee found?
As into silent night, when neare the Beare
The Virgine Huntresse shines at full most cleare, *full size*
And strives to match her brother's golden light,
The hoast of starrs doth vanish in her sight,
Arcturus dies, cool'd is the Lyon's ire,
Po burnes no more with Phaëtontall fire,
Orion faints to see his armes grow blacke, *dull*
And that his flamming sword hee now doth lacke:
So Europe's lights, all bright in their degree, *luminaries*
Loose all their lustre paragond with thee. *compared*
By just discent thou from moe kings dost shine, *more*
Then manie can name men in all their line.
What most they toyle to find, and finding hold *retain*
Thou scornest, orient gemmes and flattring gold,
Esteeming treasure surer in men's brests, *safer*
Than when immur'd with marble, closd in chests.
No stormie passions doe disturbe thy mind,
No mists of greatnesse ever could thee blind.
Who yet hath beene so meeke? Thou life didst give
To them who did repine to see thee live; *regret*
What prince by goodnesse hath such kingdoms gain'd?
Who hath so long his people's peace maintain'd?
Their swords are turn'd in sythes, in culters speares, *ploughshares*
Some giant post their anticke armour beares. *column; venerable*
Now, where the wounded knight his life did bleed,
The wanton swaine sits piping on a reed, *carefree*
And where the canon did Jove's thunder scorne, *challenge*
The gawdie hunts-man windes his shrill-tun'd horne. *green-clad*
Her greene lockes Ceres, void of feare, doth die, *re-colour*
The pilgrime safelie in the shade doth lie,
Both Pan and Pales, carelesse, keepe their flockes, *free of cares*
Seas have no dangers save the winds and rockes.

Thou art this isle's Palladium, neither can,
While thou are kept, it bee o're-throwne by man.   *preserved*
   Let others boast of blood and spoyles of foes,
230 Fierce rapines, murders, Iliads of woes,   *raids; epic tales*
Of hated pompe, and trophæes reared faire,   *set up*
Gore-spangled ensignes streaming in the aire,   *stained banners*
Count how they make the Scythian them adore,   *retell*
The Gaditan, the souldiour of Aurore.
235 Unhappie vauntrie! – to enlarge their bounds,   *boasting*
Which charge themselves with cares, their frends with wounds,   *load*
Which have no law to their ambitious will,
But – man-plagues – borne are humane blood to spill.
Thou a true victor art, sent from above,
240 What others straine by force to gaine by love:
World-wandring Fame this prayse to thee imparts,
To bee the onelie monarch of all hearts.
They many feare who are of many fear'd,
And kingdoms got by wrongs by wrongs are tear'd,   *ruined*
245 Such thrones as blood doth raise blood throweth downe,
No guard so sure as love unto a crowne.
   Eye of our westerne world, Mars-daunting king,
With whose renowne the earth's sevene climats ring,
Thy deeds not only claime these diademes,
250 To which Thame, Liffy, Taye, subject their streames,
But to thy vertues rare, and gifts, is due
All that the planet of the yeere doth view;
Sure if the world above did want a prince,   *lack*
The world above to it would take thee hence.
255   That murder, rapine, lust, are fled to hell,   *plunder*
And in their roomes with us the Graces dwell,   *place*
That honour more than riches men respect,
That worthinesse than gold doth more effect,   *achieve*
That pietie unmasked showes her face,   *uncovered*
260 That innocencie keepes with power her place,   *maintains*
That long-exil'd Astrea leaves the heaven,

And turneth right her sword, her weights holds even,   *are true*
That the Saturnian world is come againe,
Are wish'd effects of thy most happie raigne.

265   That daylie peace, love, truth, delights encrease,
And discord, hate, fraude, with incombers cease,   *troubles*
That men use strength not to shed others' blood,
But use their strength now to doe other good,
That furie is enchain'd, disarmed wrath,
270 That, save by Nature's hand, there is no death,
That late grimme foes like brothers other love,   *former*
That vultures prey not on the harmlesse dove,
That wolves with lambs doe friendship entertaine,
Are wish'd effects of thy most happie raigne.

275   That townes encrease, that ruin'd temples rise,
And their wind-moving vanes plante in the skies,
That ignorance and sloth hence runné away,
That buri'd arts now rowse them to the day,
That Hyperion, farre beyond his bed,
280 Doth see our lyons rampe, our roses spred,
That Iber courtes us, Tyber not us charmes,
That Rhein with hence-brought beams his bosome warmes,
That evill us feare, and good us doe maintaine,
Are wish'd effects of thy most happie raigne.

285   O vertue's patterne, glorie of our times,
Sent of past dayes to expiate the crimes,
Great Kinge, but better farre than thou art greate,
Whom state not honours, but who honours state,
By wonder borne, by wonder first enstall'd,   *miracle*
290 By wonder after to new kingdomes call'd,
Young, kept by wonder neare home-bred alarmes,   *preserved*
Old, sav'd by wonder from pale traitours' harmes,
To bee for this thy raigne which wonders brings,
A king of wonder, wonder unto kings.
295 If Pict, Dane, Norman, thy smooth yoke had seene,   *gentle*
Pict, Dane, and Norman, had thy subjects beene:

If Brutus knew the blisse thy rule doth give,   *had known*
Even Brutus joye would under thee to live: *rejoice*
For thou thy people dost so dearlie love,
300 That they a father, more than prince, thee prove.   *experience*
    O dayes to bee desyr'd! Age happie thrice!
If yee your heaven-sent-good could duelie prize.   *appropriately*
But yee, halfe-palsie-sicke, thinke never right
Of what yee hold, till it bee from your sight,
305 Prize onlie summer's sweet and musked breath,   *perfumed*
When armed winters threaten you with death,   *hostile*
In pallid sicknesse doe esteeme of health,
And by sad povertie discerne of wealth.   *value*
I see ane age when, after manie yeares
310 And revolutions of the slow-pac'd spheares,
These dayes shall bee to other farre esteem'd,   *present; preferred*
And like Augustus' palmie raigne bee deem'd.   *victorious*
The names of Arthure, fabulous palladines,   *knights*
Grav'n in time's surlie brows in wrinckled lines,   *frowning*
315 Of Henries, Edwards, famous for their fights,
Their neighbour conquests, orders new of knights,
Shall by this prince's name be past as farre   *exceeded*
As meteors are by the Idalian starre.
If gray-hair'd Proteüs' songs the truth not misse,
320 And gray-hair'd Proteüs oft a prophet is,
There is a land hence-distant manie miles,
Out-reaching fiction and Atlanticke isles,   *going beyond*
Which – homelings – from this little world wee name,   *kinsmen; land*
That shall imblazon with strange rites his fame,
325 Shall reare him statues all of purest gold,
Such as men gave unto the gods of old,
Name by him fanes, prowd pallaces, and townes,   *shrines*
With some great flood, which most their fields renownes.   *makes famous*
This is that king who should make right each wrong,
330 Of whome the bards and mysticke Sybilles song,
The man long promis'd, by whose glorious raigne,

This isle should yet her ancient name regaine,
And more of Fortunate deserve the stile,
That those where heavens with double summers smile.

335 Runne on, great Prince, thy course in glorie's way, *path*
The end of life, the evening crownes the day;
Heape worth on worth, and stronglie soare above
Those heights which made the world the first to love; *thee*
Surmount thy selfe, and make thine actions past

340 Bee but as gleames or lightnings of thy last; *intimations; future*
Let them exceed them of thy younger time,
As farre as autumne doth the flowrie prime. *spring*
Through this thy empire range, like world's bright eye,
That once each yeare survayes all earth and skie,

345 Now glaunces on the slow and restie Beares, *turning*
Then turns to drie the weeping Auster's teares,
Just unto both the Poles, and moveth even *in regularity*
In the infigur'd circle of the heaven. *zodiac*
O long, long haunt these bounds, which by thy sight *territories*

350 Have now regain'd their former heate and light:
Heere grow greene woods, heere silver brookes doe glide,
Heere meadowes stretch them out with painted pride, *colourful*
Embrodring all the banks, heere hilles aspire *embroidering*
To crowne their heads with the ætheriall fire,

355 Hills, bullwarks of our freedome, giant walls,
Which never fremdlings' slight nor sword made thralls. *foreigners' scorn*
Each circling flood to Thetis tribute payes, *winding river*
Men here, in health, out-live old Nestor's dayes;
Grimme Saturne yet amongst our rockes remains,

360 Bound in our caves with many mettald chaines;
Bulls haunt our shades like Leda's lover white,
Which yet might breede Pasiphaë delight;
Our flocks faire fleeces beare, with which for sport,
Endemion of old the moone did court;

365 High-palmed harts amidst our forests runne, *big-antlered*
And, not impall'd, the deepe-mouth'd hounds doe shunne; *freely running*

The rough-foote hare him in our bushes shrowds,
And long-wing'd haulks doe pearch amidst our clowds.   *hawks; hover*
The wanton wood-nymphes of the verdant spring,   *lively*
370 Blew, golden, purple flowres shall to thee bring;
Pomona's fruits the Paniskes; Thetis' gyrles
Thy Thuly's amber, with the ocean pearles;
The Tritons, heards-men of the glassie field,   *oceans*
Shall give thee what farre-distant shores can yield,
375 The Serean fleeces, Erythrean gemmes,
Vaste Plata's silver, gold of Peru streames,
Antarticke parrots, Æthiopian plumes,
Sabæan odours, myrrhe, and sweet perfumes.
And I my selfe, wrapt in a watchet gowne,   *light-blue*
380 Of reedes and lillies on mine head a crowne,
Shall incense to thee burne, greene altars raise,   *fresh*
And yearly sing due pæans to thy praise.
    Ah, why should Isis onlie see thee shine?
Is not thy Forth, as well as Isis, thine?
385 Though Isis vaunt shee hath more wealth in store,
Let it suffice thy Forth doth love thee more:
Though shee for beautie may compare with Seine,
For swannes and sea-nymphes with imperiall Rhene,
Yet in the title may bee claim'd in thee,
390 Nor shee, nor all the world, can match with mee.
Now when, by honour drawne, thou shalt away
To her, already jelous of thy stay,
When in her amourous armes shee doth thee fold,   *clasp*
And dries thy dewie haires with hers of gold,
395 Much questioning of thy fare, much of thy sport,   *journey*
Much of thine absence, long, how e're so short,
And chides, perhaps, thy coming to the north,
Lothe not to thinke on thy much-loving Forth.
O love these bounds, wherof thy royall stemme   *lands; ancestors*
400 More than an hundredth wore* a diademe.
So ever gold and bayes thy browes adorne,   *laurel*

So never time may see thy race out-worne;   *dynasty*
So of thine owne still mayst thou bee desir'd,
Of strangers fear'd, redoubted, and admir'd;   *revered*
405 So Memorie the praise, so pretious Houres
May character thy name in starrie flowres;   *inscribe*
So may thy high exployts at last make even   *equal*
With earth thy empire, glorie with the heaven.

[The Blessednesse of Faithfull Soules by Death.]   [WD18]

Let us each day enure our selves to dye,   *train*
If this – and not our feares – be trulie death:
Above the circles both of hope and faith
With faire immortall pinniones to flie.   *wings*
5 If this be death, our best part to untie,   *is to disconnect*
By ruining the jaile, from lust and wrath,   *imprisonment*
And everie drowsie languor heere beneath,   *sluggish passion*
It turning deniz'd citizen of skie;   *making it*
To have more knowledge than all bookes containe,
10 All pleasures even surmounting wishing powre,   *to be wished*
The fellowship of God's immortall traine,   *company*
And these that time nor force shall e're devoure.
    If this be death, what joy, what golden care
    Of life, can with deathe's ouglinesse compare?   *ugliness*

To the obsequies of the blessed Prince, James, King of Great Britaine. [WD19]

Let holie David, Salomon the wise,
That king whose brest Ægeria did inflame,
Augustus, Helene's sonne, great in all eyes,
Doe homage low to thy mausolean frame, *entombed body*
5 And bow before thy laurell anadeame; *crown*
Let all those sacred swannes, which to the skies
By never-dying layes have rais'd their name,
From North to South, where sunne doth set and rise.
Religion, orphan'd, waileth o're thine urne,
10 Out justice weepes her eyes, now truly blind;
In Niobe'es the remnant vertues turne:
Fame, but to blaze thy glories, lives behind. *only; proclaim*
    The world, which late was golden by thy breath, *formerly*
    Is iron turn'd, and horrid by thy death. *fearsome*

Of a Bee. [WD20]

Ingenious was that bee
In lip that wound which made,
And kind to others, though unkind to thee;
    For by a just exchange,
5   On that most livlie red *living*
    It gives to those revenge,
Whom that delitious, plump, and rosie part,
All pittilesse, perhaps, now wounds the hart.

Sir William Mure of Rowallan (1594–1657)

Mure's reputation as a sternly Calvinist poet derives from the very sober and serious verse of his mature years, published during the reign of Charles I. However, as a young man he wrote on the theme of love, and some of his lyrics were designed to fit the tunes of existing secular songs. He gave the manuscript containing his early work the very un-Calvinistic title (borrowed from Ronsard) of 'Livre des amours' [Book of love-poems], with the motto 'Mon amour et ma douleur sont sans comparaisoun.' [My love and sorrow are without comparison]. Several other manuscripts belonging to him, containing musical notation and tablature for lute-accompaniment, give an indication of the culture prevalent in the family household at Rowallan (Shire 1969: 207–14). The only large-scale work from his youth is an excellent translation and recasting (1614) of the first and fourth books of Virgil's Æneid, which tell of the tragic love of Dido and Æneas. Mure embroidered upon the Classical story, and passages with his additions have been included here (WM2, 3). This early masterpiece, an epyllion in three books, betrays influence from the manner of Ariosto and Boiardo, from Marlowe, and from Shakespeare's *Venus and Adonis*, which uses the same stanza-form. However, despite the powerful appeal of love in Mure's poem, the ultimate rejection of passion in favour of duty seems an advance signal of the moral seriousness of his subsequent writing. There is no clear sign that Mure was familiar with the *Eneados* (1513) of Gavin Douglas, but he may well have known Sir David Murray's *Sophonisba* (1611) – this being another poem set in Carthage, with a famous love-lorn queen as eventual suicide, and having as its underlying theme the conflict between human passion and higher duty. Dido's reproachful speech to Æneas has a real sense of drama, almost in a high-operatic style, and is without parallel in the work of Mure's Scottish contemporaries.

Mure's 1617 poem in honour of King James (WM4), delivered at Hamilton towards the end of the royal progress and printed in the *Muses' Welcome* of the following year, is the work of one who is fully comfortable with the role and person of the monarch. Unlike many of his Scottish contemporary poets, Mure did not move to London, but stayed at home at Rowallan (Ayrshire). In later years his moral, political and religious views hardened, and he increasingly occupied himself with national and religious politics. This led to the literary, religious and moral identity for which he is now remembered, as in the sonnets of his 'Fancies Farewell' of *A Spirituall Hymne* (Edinburgh, 1628), in *The True Crucifixe for true Catholickes* (1629), in his vernacular versions of the Psalms, in *The Joy of Tears* (1635), and in the several publications in which he attacked the innovations which Charles I was tactlessly imposing on the church in Scotland. Such convictions induced the poet to participate in military resistance in support of the National Covenant. Nonetheless, his swan-song, *The Cry of Blood and of a Broken Covenant* (1650), dedicated to Charles II, was a declaration of Mure's instinctive and abiding loyalty to the royal family, and in particular to the new King's martyred father.

[The poet's muse.]   [WM1]

Some gallant spreits, desyrouse of renowne,
To climb with pain Parnassus do aspyre,
By natour some do weir the lawrell croun,   *nature*
And some the poet proves for hoip of hyre.   *try out; hope of gain*
5 Bot none of those my spirits doth inspire,
My muse is more admir'd then all the nyne,
Quho doth infuse my breast with sacred fyre   *fill*
To paint hir foorth most heavinly and dewyne.
Hir worth I raise in elegiak lyne;
10 In lyricks sweit hir beuties I extoll;
The brave heroik doth hir rair ingyne   *rare mind*
In Tyme's immortal register enroll:
     Since thou of me hath maid thy poet, then
     Be bold, sweit lady, to imploy my pen.

[Dido and Æneas in the cave.]   **[WM2]**   *[Book II]*

One cave, whil al the tempest dark do shield,
The Trojane duke and Dido both contained.
Prodigious presages sad earth did yield,   *omens*
With them when Juno in the cave convein'd.   *came together*
   The guilty air gave light; the fire did glance;   *shone; flashed*
300   And montaine faryes did bewaile the chance.   *occasion*

Looke, how a comet, whose bright flaming haire   *trail*
Bringes tidinges sad of dearth, or death of kinges,
Drawes all men's eyes to gaze amidst the aire,
Conjecturing thereby of future thinges;
305   So, whil at first, the princes' beauty shin'd,
   Æneas, wond'ring, ravish't was in minde.   *marvelling*

Her pure unborrowed blush, her native white,   *natural*
The piercing rayes of her victorious eyes
Bred in his soule such singular delight,
310 And did his senses suddainely supprise,
   In such a sort, that of all sense denude,
   He long a lifles, senseless statue stoode.

But soone her looks, of pow'r t'awaken death,
And ravish with amazement hardest hearts,
315 Reviv'd him frome his traunse, recal'd his breath,   *trance*
And to his sleeping senses life empartes;
   Who instantly confines within his armes,   *embraces*
   His sweetest siren, who his fancie charmes.

Sie now, how honour, love, and modesty
320 With diverse colours dye her blushing cheeks!
When, lay'd aside respect of majesty,
The fort to render proud Æneas seeks.   *overcome*
   And whil, desire rul'd by the blinded boy,   *being controlled*
   Love's sweet-stolne sport he labours to enjoy.

325 With faint repulses and denialls sweet,
Lo, how she, shrinking, strives his sutes to shune;
But he now offers force, now doth entreate,
And still persewes, till last the prise is wonne, *goes on*
  The jemme enjoy'd, which women hold so deare, *jewel*
330 And honour, prostrate, blushing did reteare. *retire*

Can words, can vowes, can feeble hands resist,
With hote desire whil yowthfull blood doth boyle?
Though she repine, do his assaults desist? *regret*
Small glory is a yielded foe to foyle. *vanquish*
335 Women must still deny and use defences,
  Till charming Cupid lull a-sleep the senses.

This wrought to sin, anone she waxeth bold, *thus*
And mutually her mate doth entertaine;
Loe, how her strict embraces him enfold,
340 Whil as they issue frome the cave againe, *when*
  Nothing asham'd to come in open sight,
  Thus use of sinning soone maks sin seame light. *custom*

This disemall day did Dido'es death begin,
This day of all her sorrowes was the source:
345 Now neither fame she cares, nor shame, nor sin,
Nor more devises any secrete cowrse
  To cloake her love, but marriage; this she thinks, *thus*
  And at this foule offence, effronted, winks. *connives*

[Dido's reproach to Æneas.]   [wm3]

[Book II]

With boundles rage, thus overrul'd a space,   *for a while*
Anger and furie in her face did flame;
Mad passions did her patience displace,
580 Despight and rancour reason overcame;
  Wraith keipt in words, sighs only passage finde,   *anger impeded*
  Whose vapours, vented, ease her burden'd minde.   *released*

At last, more calme, she thus begowth to speak,   *began*
(Extremity to words a way affords):
585 "Dost thow intend, deir lord," quoth she, "to break
Thy solemne vowes, and violate thy words?
  Thy sad departure frome thy love to hyd,
  And frome thir shoares thus secretly to slyde?   *decamp*

"Whither, O cruell? Whither dost thow flie?
590 What discontent thus change in the doth move?   *thee; cause*
What wrong, alas, or what offence in me,
Thus maks the loath and vilipend my love?   *contemn*
  With too much kindnes art thow overcloyed?   *sated*
  Or, ar my favours hated, 'cawse enjoyed?   *because*

595 "Ah, 'twas not so, when thow didst pensive sit,
Sigh, faine to die, look pale, protest, and sweare,   *feign*
Vowing thy service at my feet, whil yit
For all thy oathes thy policies appear.   *schemes*
  By sad experience, O I find it true,
600 That seldome lust delights in what is due.   *fitting*

"But yit the world in me some fault may deeme,
For poore, weak women ever bear the blame,
Why thow my bed, as stayn'd, dost disesteeme,   *stained; spurn*
Regardles of my favour, thy defame.   *dishonour*
605 But I to the appeal, if ere my yowth   *ever*
  Gave proofe of ought butt undistained trewth.   *unsullied*

"Did my cold breast so long unwarm't remaine,
From men's deceites and charming flatterings free,
Nor once one thought of love did intertaine?
610 Cruell to all, but kinde alone to the,
　　Keipt I so long my marble minde unshaken,
　　To be by the disdain'd, and thus forsaken?

"Stay yit, O stay, my deir, possesse in peace
The jewell, which of laite so dear thow prised;
615 And be not author of her sad disgrace,
Who cannot breath and be by the despised.
　　Returne, deir lord, leave not thy halfe behind,
　　What I entreate with tears thy oathes do bind.

"Oh, hast thow ells forgot, when in the cave
620 Thy guilded words and vowes first wan the field,
When to thy sutes consent my silence gave　　　　*importunities*
And poore beleving I myself did yeild,
　　How thow did swear, resolve, protest, and vow,
　　Still to be hers, whom thow disdainest now?

625 "How can I think those sighs so feeling, fained?　　*pretended*
Those passionat regrates but arm'd with airt?　　*longings; only*
Those looks so sad but for the fashion fraimed,　　*serious; adopted*
To melt with pitty my relenting heart?
　　Whil thow beneath thy passione seam'd to faint,
630　　And thowsand colours thy pale cheiks did paint.

"Those sighs, regrates, lookes, passions, colours strange,
Though fayn'd, in me produc't no false effects;　　*feigned*
By those betray'd, I from myself did range,
Too prodigall of what thow now neglects,
635　　And headlesly to thy desires consenting;
　　Whilk breeds in the dislike, in me lamenting.

[151]

"If thow object thy love was then entire,
What owtward virtues now in me do want?   *lack*
Do not thir beautyes even the same appeare,
640   That did attract thine heart of adamant?
        No stolne vermilion blush, to charme delight,   *artificial*
        With false allurements, did bewitch thy sight.

"That bastard beauty and adult'rate dye,
That new-found falshood, counterfoot of nature,   *counterfeit*
645   Shame of owr sexe, the stayne of modesty,   *pollution*
Fewell to lust, to chastity a traitoure,   *fuel*
        That mystery to me was still unknowne,
        This red and white was then, as now, mine owne.

"Though loathed beauty lack perswading force,
650   Now overclouded with affliction's vaile;
Though sutes, nor sighes find pitty nor remorce;
Though passions, plaints, and prayers nought prevaile;   *nothing*
        And though thir eyes' bright sunne obscur'd with smarte,
        Lack piercing rayes to penetrate thy heart;

655   "Yit cannot my affection nor thy faith,
My constant love, thy promise and right hand,
Nor thine owne Dido'es miserable death,
Can none of those deteine the in this land?   *detain*
        But ah, whil winter's stormes thus raigeing be,
600   Wilt thow endanger both thy self and me?

"Wilt thow, O cruell thow, to saile mak haste,
Whil boystrows Boreas threats the swelling seas?
Suppone, though Troy yit undestroy'd did last,   *suppose*
And to no forraine countrey now thow flyes,
665   Whil furiows Neptune rageing doth remaine,
        Thy native Troy should thow by shipping gaine.

"Ah, fleest thow me? Yit by those streaming teares,
Which leave affliction's furrowes on my face,
By thy right hand, by all the hopes and feares
670 Possesse poore lovers, by those oaths, alace,
    Which me betrayed, by owr espousall day:
    And by that love thow bar'st me once, I pray,   *bore*

"If ever I of the did well deserve,
To the ought dear if ever Dido gave,   *anything*
675 Showe now compassion, firme thy faith observe,
My life and croune from death and ruine save.
    O let my prayers yit relent thy minde,   *mollify*
    If any place with the my sutes may finde.

"For thee, the Libian kinges conspire my wrack,   *ruin*
680 For thee, the hatred of mine owne I beare;   *my people*
For thee alone, my shamefast lyf I brack,   *virtuous; broke*
And fame I lost, to me nor life more deare.   *reputation*
    To whom thus leavest thow me to die with shame?
    O ghuest? I dar no more the 'husband' name.   *thee*

685 "Ah, loathed Dido, must thow live to sie
Thy foes triumph, thy self detained a slave?
Yit, if at least before thy flight from me,
My luck had been succession sweet to have: *descendants*
    If any small Æneas heir did play,
690   Within this hall, thy face who might bewray,   *reveal*

"Those sorrowes then I should not shrink to prove,   *experience*
Nor utterly forsaken should I seeme."
Thus clos'd she weeping, but no words culd move
His marble minde, he doth so much esteime   *unflinching*
695   The Thund'rer's will. With stedfast eyes he stair'd,   *gazed*
    And obstinate for answere thus prepar'd.

The King's Majestie came to Hamilton.　[wm4]

Burst furth, my Muse, too long thou holds thy peace;
Paint furth the passions of thy new-borne joy.
Forbear to sing thy lovelie layes a space,
Leave wanton Venus and her blinded boy.
5　　Raise up thy voice and now, deare Muse, proclaime
　　A greater subject and a graver theame.

Since our much lov'd Apollo doth appeare
In pompe and pow'r, busked with golden rayes,　　　　*nimbed*
More brigt heir shyning on our hemispheare,　　　　*here*
10　Nor that great planet, father of the dayes,
　　With boldness offer at his sacred shrine
　　These firstlings of thy weake and poore ingyne.　　*first-fruits; talent*

Great James, whose hand a thre-fold sceptre swayes,
By heavens exalted to so high a place,
15　Both crown'd with gold and never fading bayes,　　*laurels*
Who keps three kingdoms in so still a peace,　　　　*steady*
　　Whose love, cair, wisdom, grace and high deserts
　　Have maid thee monarch of thy subjects' harts.

Thogh thou by armes great empyrs may'st surprise,
20　Mak Europ thrall and over Asia reigne;
Yet at thy feete, despised, Bellona lyes,
No crownes thou craves which bloodie conqueis staine.
　　Whil others aime at greatnes boght with blood,
　　Not to bee great, thou strives, bot to bee good.

25　Whome snakie hatred, soule conceav'd disdaine,　　*venemous*
Hart-rooted rancor, envy borne in hell
Did long in long antipathie detaine
To either's ruine, as they both can tell,
　　Uniting them, thou hast enlarged thy throne,
30　　And maid devyded Albion all bee one.

O heavenlie union! O thryse happie change
From bloodie broyles, from battells and debait;   *feuds; contest*
From mischeifs, cruelties and sad revenge
To love and peace thou hes transformd our stait,
35   Which, now confirmed, by thee before begunne,
     Shall last till earth is circuit with the sunne.   *circled by*

Jov's great vice-gerent, Neptun's richest treasure,   *deputy*
Earth's glorie, Europ's wonder, Britann's pryde,
Thy wit, lyk heaven, is such a divyne measure   *wisdom*
40 This little world so happily doth guyd,
     That Cæsar, Trajan, Pompey, Alexander,
     If now they liv'd, the place to thee might rander.   *cede*

What wants in the, O King, heavens could impairt;   *lacks; grant*
Or what is in thee not of highest pryce?
45 A liberall hand, a most magnifick hart,
A readie judgment, and a prompt advyse,   *decision*
     A mynd onconquered fearcest foes to thrall,   *subjugate*
     Bright eye of knowledge, singular in all.   *unique*

Thy waitchfull caire, thy zeale, and fervent love,
50 The Church, the laye, each high or low estaite   *laity*
Long-since by many worthie deeds did prove;   *experience*
Bot most of all by these effects of laite,
     For thou affects amongst thy high design's   *intends*
     To build the sanctuarie of the King of Kings.

55 Heavens therefore did thy royall grandeur guaird,
Thy royall person from the cradle keap'd   *protected*
From thousand plots t'eclips thy sunne, prepair'd
By these who horror upon horror heap'd,
     Their barbarous hands into thy blood to bathe
60   And mak thee, guiltles, object of their wrathe.

Thogh Anak's cursed children did repyne,   *grumble*
Yet heavens made Josua over them prevaill;
Thogh hellish harts envy'd* thy glorie's shyne,   *envied*
Yet in the practise their attempts did faill.
65   But loe, thy mercie still to be admir'd!   *always*
      Thou spared them, against thee who conspyr'd.

For, as in all thou second art to none,
To thee all kings in clemencie give place.
Thryce happie people rul'd by such a one,
70 Whose lyfe both this and after-tymes shall grace.
      Long may thy subjects, ere thy glasse outrunne,
      Enjoy the light of thee, their glorious sunne.

What load-stone strange had such attractive force   *magnet*
To draw thee home-ward to these northerne parts?
75 Whill Mars the world affrights with trumpets hoarse,
Broyls inhumaine devyding humane harts;   *conflicts*
      Whill Belgium braine-sick is, France mother-sick,   *mad; hysterical*
      And with Iberian fyres the Alpes doe reik.   *smoke*

Most lyk that fishe, whose golden shape of late
80 Was to thee given, thy love to represent,
Which in the ocean, thogh she doe grow great
And many foraine floods and shelves frequent,   *rivers; shallows*
      Yet, not unmyndfull of her native burnes,   *streams*
      Thogh with great toyle, unto them back returnes.

85 Rejoyce then, Scotland, change thy mourning weed;
Now deck thyselfe into thy best attyre,
And lyk a bryd advance thy chearfull head;   *put forth*
Enjoy with surfet now thy soule's desire.   *surfeit*
      Uncessantlie with sighs importune heaven
90   That thou may long enjoy this gift new given.

Welcome, O welcome thryse, our glorious guyd,
A thousand tymes this soyle doth thee salute; *land*
Welcome, O welcome, Britann's greatest pryd,
By thee which happie doth it selfe repute. *consider*
95   Thogh all-where welcome, yet most welcome heir, *everywhere*
    Long haunt thir bounds, ere thou from hence retire. *inhabit; lands*

Heir plesant plain's alongst the crystall Clyd,
Which in a flowrie labyrinth her playes,
Heir blooming banks, heir silver brooks doe slyd,
100 Heir mearle and maves sing melodious layes, *blackbird; thrush*
    Heir heards of deer defy the fleetest hounds;
    Heir wods and vail's and echoes that resounds.

Stay then, O stay, and with thy presence grace
That noble race, which, famous by thy blood,
105 Long toyle and trouble glaidlie did embrace,
And wounded oft gusht furth a crimson flood.
    In hazards great defending with renowne
    The liberties and glorie of thy crowne.

But, leaving more to entertaine thyn ear's *desisting*
110 With airie accents, hoarse and homelie songs, *feeble*
My solitarie Muse her selfe reteirs, *draws back*
Un-usd abroad to haunt such pompous throngs.
    Swa renders place, that after emptie words *and so gives way*
    Thou may partack such as this soyle affords. *partake; yields*

Patrick Gordon (fl. 1613–15)

Uncertainty attaches to the family background of Gordon. Formerly labelled simply as 'unknown' (Shire 1969: 229), he has been discovered to be either of two persons of the same name (Stevenson, *ODNB*). One Patrick Gordon (d. before 1657) was descended from the Gordons of Braco (Inverurie parish), and became a diplomat, acting for King James in Poland and Prussia; the other (fl. 1606–1649), so-called of Ruthven, was a son of Thomas Gordon of Cluny and Lady Elizabeth Douglas, and was the historian who wrote on the Civil War campaigns of the Marquess of Montrose. Liminary verses (e.g. by Alexander Craig, Alexander Gardyne and Robert Gordon) addressed to Patrick Gordon in his *Penardo and Laissa,* a work said by the poet to be his 'firste borne' spiritual child, point to the connection with the North-East of Scotland, and this is also reflected by the poem's dedication to George, Earl of Enzie, Lord Gordon and Badenoch, and son of the Marquess of Huntly.

Gordon's first known printed poem was *Neptunus britannicus* [British Neptune] (London, 1614). In this Latin work, the poet assumes the typically pastoral (and proximately punning) identity of 'Corydon', in expressing his lament at the death of Henry (6 November 1612), in extending commiserations and good wishes to the prince's brother Charles, Duke of York, and at the same time addressing a marriage ode to Charles's sister Elizabeth, married on 14 February 1613 to Frederick, Elector of the Palatinate. In some introductory elegiac couplets, the entire poem is formally offered to David Murray, who was closely attached to Prince Henry. The poet's concluding declaration, that, should the King's Majesty ever call for him, Gordon will be found fighting to the death for his fatherland, seems to indicate on the poet's part an intention of military service. In its structure, the poem consists of an imagined exchange between the sea-god Neptune and his partner, Tethys. There is extravagant praise of the island of Albion and the surrounding seas, together with a catalogue of British rivers (Thames, Trent, Humber, Tweed, Forth, Tay, Dee and Don), European rivers and others even more remote, all of which join in the lament. Neptune (and through him King James) is finally consoled, and the poem contrives to end on a happy note.

The two other literary works by Gordon are on a much larger scale, and in the vernacular. *Penardo and Laissa* (1615) is a dizzying tale of adventures, set in an east-European fantasy-land. It does not lack its doughty hero, beautiful and virtuous heroine, cruel king, evil magician, castles, dungeons, dwarves, dragon, and cast of thousands, and is an enjoyable piece of escapism. The work owes something to Hellenistic romance and something to Spenser's *Faerie Queene*, but without the moral, religious and political seriousness of the latter work.

If, as the poet declares, *Penardo* was indeed Gordon's 'firste borne' it must – despite its date of printed publication – have been written before *Neptunus britannicus*. The same may be true of *The famous historie . . . of Bruce*, and both vernacular poems may initially have circulated in manuscript. Yet *The famous historie* may be presumed to have been complete when it was in 1613 granted a licence by the Archbishop of St Andrews, although, like *Penardo*, it was printed at Dort (Dordrecht) in the Netherlands and only in 1615. In their different ways, both these long works may have arisen from the poet's desire to please the taste of Prince Henry. Liminary poems by Alexander Gardyne and Alexander Craig suggest that Gordon's works were also known to, and had found favour among, his circle of Aberdeen friends.

Gordon's use of the story of the accession of Robert Bruce to the throne of Scotland may be understood as obliquely, tactfully and approvingly bearing on the accession of James Stewart to the throne of England. John Barbour's fourteenth-century foundational historical romance was not forgotten: it had been printed in 1571, and there would be several further reprints from 1616 onwards. *The famous historie* uses Barbour's work as the basis of its own narrative structure, though it omits the campaign of Edward Bruce in Ireland, and abandons the tetrameter couplets of the medieval poet for the Italianate fashion of stanzas in *ottava rima*. Gordon shows a notable interest in Stirling and the valley of the Forth (cf. PG3/97–136, 329–36), an area famous not only on account of the battle of Bannockburn, but also as the birthplace of Prince Henry in the castle there. The medieval poem is adapted to suggest a relevance to circumstances post-1603. Gordon supplies a new myth of royal mission, and in so doing takes as his model certain passages in Spenser's *Faerie Queene*, e.g. the chronicle of British kings (*FQ*, II, x) and Merlin's prophetic revelations (*FQ*, III, iii). The extract selected for the present anthology – the prophecy of Thomas the Rhymer – has no forerunner in Barbour. By inserting it into the already familiar overall historical narrative, Gordon instrumentalises the heroic literature of the Scottish past in order to promote a vision of yet greater prosperity in times to come, under the Stewart/Stuart dynasty.

[The Rhymer's Prophecy.]   [PG1]

[Chapter IV]

At last, arryving by a fontane syid,
Beneath a leavie aged oak he lyes;
115 A heartie draught of the colde streame he tryed,
Which for a daintie maill did him suffice.   *meal*
And now his cogitation deeplie weyghed   *mind; pondered*
Earthe's glorie vane and worldlie fantasies,
    Compairing all beneath heavn's sylver bowres
120   To cloudes of smook, to shaddowes, dreames or flowres.

Thus rap'd with admiration whill he lyes,   *amazement*
He vewes the starres and all the heavenlie lightes,
When as he heares a sound pas through the skyes
Lyik to the noyes of floodes' impetuous flightes,   *waterfalls*
125 Or, as when fearfull doves in numbers fleis,
Aer and their winges with noyes them selfes affrightes.   *noise*
    Suche was this noyes, yet nothing he perceaves,
    Nor was there wind to move the trembling leaves.

A dark gray clowde past furthe o're all the aire,
130 But nighte's pale queene cleird all the heavns at last,
When to him did an old grave man repair,
Whoes head and beard had youthe's freshe cullor past;
A cristall glob his trembling hand upbeare,   *orb; held*
Where heavne o're earth did move from east to west,
135   Their starres and planets shynd most bright and cleir,   *there*
    Which by a sprit was mov'd, as might appeare.

A spherik glob within hung lyk a ball,
That figurd rairlie furth the earth and sea,   *wonderfully*
Which round about was frie from heavn's cleir wall,   *shining*
140 Whose restles course round o're this glob did flie;
The glassie sea, now calme, then seemd to swell,   *gleaming*
Where wind-tost shipes with tydes and tempests be,
    Whill Neptune's azurd armes the earth embraceth,
    That cirquits yles, and shore from shore unlaceth.   *surrounds; divides*

145 Thus with a curious pinsell th'earth was drawne: *skilled pencil*
    Heir meidds, their floodes, heir wodes, their montanes were,   *meadows; there*
    Heir tounes, their towres, with flowrie gardenes showen,
    Heir vines, their figges, pomgranates, cydrons faire;   *lemons*
    Heir plowemen teill, their heards and flokes are knowne,   *recognised*
150 Heir bowres doth proyne their vines with wondrowes care,   *peasants; prune*
      Their sicles* cutts the corne, heir sythes the hay,
      Heir peace, their warrelyke armeis in array.

    Unto the Prince this aged syre drew neir,
    Whill chast Diana shynd more fair and bright;
155 Cled in a horye mantle white and cleir,   *ancient*
    He semd devote in prayers to spend the night.   *devoutly*
    Leane flesh, his wattrie blood, sweld vaines, appeir;   *swollen*
    His ghostlie lookes still offerd death his right,   *ghostlike*
      Whoe, pausing long with stedfast staering eyes,
160   This salutation did at last devyse.

    "Peace be to thee, my Lord and Prince," sayd he,
    "Whom great and mightie Jove has hither sent,
    That thow might kno his mercies great by me,
    And of thy bad and bypast lyfe repent.
165 The shame, the foyle, the losse that falles to thee   *harm*
    Is Jove's just doome, because thow gave consent   *verdict*
      Unto thy will, wrathe, vengeance, and defyld
      His sacred house with sinfull blood so wyld.

    Thy natione's foyle, their wrak, and their distres,   *suffering*
170 Thy countrie's shame, her woe, her desolation,
    Thy subjects' lose, in care all confortles,   *misfortune*
    Whom mightie Jove has had in detestation
    For their great sinnes, their faultes, their cairlesnes
    Of his soule feidding word; O wicked nation,   *nourishing*
175   That still, with folie, blindnes, pryde, abuse,
    Did sacred things apply to sinnefull use.

Their filthie life, their lewd lascivious lust,
Their walloweing in sensuall delight,
Threattens a dreadfull storme e're long, that must
180   Swellow them up in their owne sinnes' despight.   *engulf*
But leave we them and their affliction just,
And now behold this day, succeding night:
    These burning balles to thee and thyne shall prove   *spheres; show*
    Heavn's for-sight, wisdom, mercie, grace and love.   *providence*

185 This counterfite of those bright orbs behold;   *representation*
The earth and sea; but heavns of greatest wounder,
Whose restles course about the Poles is rold   *around; whirled*
With contrare motions, their first mobill under;   *first mover*
The firmament with fixed stares untold,   *innumerable*
190 Whoes various shapes and rare effects we pondre;
    Lynes, tropickes, circles, zones and zodiack,   *equinoctial points*
    Wherein Sol doeth the yeir's four seasones make.   *sun*

Almightie Jove, who made heavn's wondrous frame,
Has made man'es witt so rairlie excellent,   *wonderfully*
195 That he can vivelie counterfite the same   *copy to the life*
And his great maker's worke can represent,
With heavenlie furie, rap'd with sacred flamme   *inspiration*
Of artless arte's invention, noght content
    Of his all working wonders heir below,
200   But ev'n the heavenlie mansiones heir must show.   *zodiacal houses*

Lo, where the planets, each his sphere within,[†]
Keeps time and course with heavn'es trew planets all,   *faithful*
Forcd by their Primomobill for to rinn   *first mover*
In twice twelf houres about this earthlyk ball;
205 And their owne course they end and they beginne
With heavn's bright lampes, for thus they rise and fall.
    Chast Phebe's course just in a month goes right,   *exactly*
    Now poore, then wealthie of her brother's light.

Mercure and Venus follows Phebus' teame, *yoke*
210 His tender wings, her dows, on him depend, *doves*
Whose lead of light and life-reviving beame *progress*
Abowt a year his nat'rall course doth end;
And Mars in twice twelf months resums his game;
Saturn's mild sone in twelf twelf months rescend;[†] *son; returns*
215   Cold horie Saturn's leaden coach that rins,
In threttie years leav's aff wher he begins.

All these heavn's azure cannabie surrounds, *canopy*
Sprinkled with eies, spekled with tapers bright, *flashes; decked out*
Spangled with spangs thro all his boundles bounds, *sparkling; flashes*
220 Sowin all with glistring sparks of glansing light, *sown over; dazzling*
Sett with gilt stoods and golden skowchand grounds, *studs; heraldic gold*
Powdred with twinkling starrs, whoes kapring flight *scattered; skipping*
   Glanseth doune right, and with their myld aspects *shines; looks*
   Works in th'inferior bodeis strainge effects.

225 Those sparkling diamonds this ritche vaile contains, *veil*
Whoes numbers numberles ar past account,
Hath twalf that biasway's overthwart her lains, *crosses at an angle*
With powrfull virtue decks her glorious front; *influence*
And those ar signes, wherein the planets reignes
230 Whill they discend or rise, or fall or mount,
   For they pertake in their swift revolution
   From echo of those, strenth, virtue,[*] force and motion.

Beside all those, about the Polls yow sie *around*
Figurs of what almost on earth is found,
235 For the all-knawing-minde of majestie,
Before he fram'd this ritche embrowdred round, *embroidered orb*
The plot in his idea seemd to be *plan*
And forme of all his future works profound;
   Thus, wirking in his spreit divin'lie rare, *operating; exquisite*
240   Long ere the world was made, the world was their. *there*

Unfolding then that ritche and glorious tent,
He portrayd with a pinsell most divine   *pencil*
Upon the all-enlightning firmament
Those tabl's of his future works in fine;   *entirely*
245 Wheir lo, behold thy brave – most brave – descent,
That sollie in the letter aige sall shine,   *uniquely; latter*
      Bearing Christ's standerd and his churche defending,
      Bounding their empire with the world's ending.

Eathniks, not knowing God al provident,   *pagans; fore-seeing*
250 Have names of eathniks to these forms assign'd,
But lett it thee suffice and be content,
That I herein unfold what Jove design'd   *intended*
By these bright portraits, portreyd in the tent
Of azur gilded heavins' pavilion, sign'd
255   By his owne hand, and for himself their markit,   *marked*
      For ew'r immortaleisd, for heaven imbarkit.   *incorporated*

Greate architector of this wondrous frame,[†]   *construction*
Raise up my spreit to thy celestiall throne;
Let my poore soule contemplat in the flame
260 Of thy all dazling beautie, wheir alone
Thy glorious beams, reflecting, may o'erquhelme
My waikned sight, and more then sun-like shone   *weakened; than*
      On my poore soule's all darkned Cinthia's eyes,
      Mak her to earth ecclipst, cleir toward skyes."

265 Wheirwith the prophet's face began to shine,[†]
Hee suddanlie with sacred furie glows;
His soule cleiv's through the ten-fold orbs in fine,   *cuts; entirely*
And from sole Majestei's bright glorie drow's   *derives*
Her all celestiall sacred food divine;   *its*
270 A sun-like brightnes on his forehead grow's,
      A schining luster from his eyes furth sent   *luminescence*
      A firie glance of goldlyke blandishment.   *flash; attraction*

"First thow", said hee, "the rampand lyon tyis,†   *rampant; fasten*
Wha wandering from his den goes farre astray,
275   Intrap'd in snaires and foraigne subtilteis,
Whoe erst subdew'd all prays, becums a pray   *having first*
To craftie subtill foes, yet doth arise
With glorious triumph to their greate decay,
    And hee whoe scorned a strainger sould command,
280   Now yeelds his neck to thy victorious hand.

Heir saillis the schip wheirin thy young sone sitts,†
Slyceing the wavs of azur trembling plains,   *cutting; waves*
And wafts into a forren land, that fitts   *transports; suitable*
For greennish youth, wheir all delight remains,   *immature*
285   Whill heir sterne warrs remorsles furie fretts   *here; gnaws away*
And tears oure bowells asunder, strip's our vains;   *entrails; veins*
    Yet this blist bark our Jason brings from Greece,
    And of sweet peace brings home the Golden Fleece.

But lo, heir cums the loftie coach-man doune,†
290   That after him draw's furth suche lamps of light,
Such jems, such pearels and jewells for the crune,   *crown*
Such ornaments, such onlie rare delight,
That sun-lyke schyns with evir blest renowne
And all from Po to Ganges feiris their might;   *everyone; fear*
295   Yea, and him-self his chairge so weil discharges,
    Earth's sole impire Jove for his seed enlarges.†   *entire; extends*

Then cums that holie prince, grave, wise and old,
That for his children, murning still, laments,   *ever mourning*
Whoes spotles life heirby the swans foretold,
300   His thoghts and looks the eagill still presents;
For lo, his eies bent upwards still, behold,
Fixt on his Phebus, the one trine essence;   *threefold*
    Hee for his children plains to Jove above,   *laments*
    Whoe shall regaird his looks, his life, his love.†

305 Heir cums that prince, of wrongfull boundage frie,
    Who that myld virgin, Justice, did releace
    From that wild monster, raiging tyrannie,
    And seit her frie, to all his happie race.†
    Hee rewels the land with lawes and equitie,
310 In whoes blist regne flows knawlege, welth and grace;
      Of justice in his hand hee holds the heid,†   *head*
      Whois splender striks all malefactors deid.

    Heir monted, doth that valiant prince advance,†   *mounted*
    Whoes heavin-wrocht lance his enemies ov'rthrowis,   *made in heaven*
315 In whome shal schine pure virtue's radiance,
    Rais'd up on hie by Jove gainst all his foes;
    The ravening wolf hee foilles with temperance,   *frustrates*
    And the trew path to treew religion shois,
      Moveing his subjects' hearts, their minds and all,
320   Greate Jove to feare, and on his name to call.

    Now in thy time", quod he, "shall heir arrive†
    A worthie knight, that from his native land
    Shall flie, because he bravelie shall deprive   *flee; valiantly*
    In glorius fight a knight that shall withstand   *oppose*
325 Thy praises deu, whill he doth thee discrive.   *describe*
    Yea, evin this knight shall with victorious hand
      Come heir, whoes name his seid shill eternize,   *shall*
      And still they virteus line shall sympathize.   *thy virtuous; support*

    From this great man shall one far greater spring,†
330 Whom Fortune fair and Fate shall stil attend;   *always serve*
    Bellona fearce and Venus myld shall bring
    Laurells from Mars but, to greate love, shill send
    A garland ritche, sprung from this worthie king,
    Whose royall stem, unto the endles end†
335   Of his greate line, their tempels sall adorne,
      With never setting, ever rysing morne.

For lo, the daughter of this worthie prince[†]
Sall wed this knight, this lord of heigh renowne,
Whose hight, whose greatnes, and whose excellence,   *eminence*
340 Whose schulders seims ane Atlas to the crowne;
Of him shall come that mightie lord, whoe thence
Shall goe, and proud rebellious Danes beat downe;
      He, to obey his prince's great command,
      Shall tak this bold and wightie chairge in hand.   *important*

345 An armie and a navie he shall bring
Ou're Thetis' glassie montans' groundless deip;   *bottomless*
Under his wings that disinthroned king
Shall go, whose crowne rebellious Danes still keip;   *proceed*
Ou're all these northern worlds his name sall ring
350 Terror in evrie ear; whill he doth steip   *steep*
      His sword in their most valiant prince's blood,
      Whose might his all-commanding will ganestood.   *force; opposed*

And to his wounted height that king shall raise   *accustomed*
And inthroneize him, in dispight of foes;   *re-enthrone*
355 With fame, with glorie, and with endles praise,
He shall returne unto his land but lose.   *without loss*
When he hath spent in honor's height his dayes,   *apogee*
Favord by heav'ne, fred from untimlie woes;
      Of him discending, shall a greater rise,
360   And lift his glorie farr above the skyis.

He shall this land governe, protect, defend[†]
From forangne force, from home-bred civill broille,   *conflict*
And the emperiall swey shal swetlie bend,   *worthily exercise*
Whill the right heyre is yung in these great toille;   *heir; troubles*
365 Evne the Most Christian King sall seu in end   *sue at last*
For his greate freindschip and his favor, whills   *until*
      To dignitie aloft he shall him rear:
      Thus sall his greatnes schyn both heir and their.

Nor yet this prince allone shall be the last
370 That shall surmount his predicessors farr;
But this great famelie shall spred so fast,
As England shall in'vy that such a starr,   *envy*
Schot from their sphere, hath their cleir lichts surpast,   *bright*
And, like a comet, blazing blood and war,
375   Streams furth their beams, that each wheir purge from error,   *everywhere*
And warms their freinds, but burns their foes with terror.

This famous line shall floorish more and more,
Greate columns faire, rare pillars of the crowne,
Ritche ornaments that shall the land decore,
380 Sune-glistring-lights, with ever blisd renowne,   *luminaries; blessed*
Heavne-blazing lamps, whoes flame from virtue's store
Brings oill wheirin they hell-bred hydras drowne.
       But leave we them, and of thy royall race,
         Show heavin's-rare blessings, greatnes, hight, and grace.

385 Then comes that serpent berar furth in view,[†]   *bearer*
In base borne venamous blood to much delighted;
Our all the land their poysoned goir they spew,   *over; corruption*
And all his weill borne subjects much affrighted;
Wheirof great harme, great vengeance, doth ensew,
390 For those foull beasts, of eche so much dispighted,   *all; contemned*
       Shall be the cause of this greate prince's fall,
         Their poison so infects heart, minde and all.

And Archer-like the nixt doth martche on foot[†]
Amidst his armie, rashlie, to persew
395 His craftie fo'es, whill his brave minde, to stout,   *bold*
Shall scorne the counsal of his subjects trew.
Their shall unwars this war-like prince no dout   *unheedingly; wholly*
Be lost, whoes want thow, Scotland, long sall rew.   *lack; rue*
       For lo, too soone his sone of glorie bright   *sun*
400   Is chok'd with mists of Feat's untimelie night.   *Fate's*

And heir behold that magnanimious king,[†]
Most just in peace, most valorus in warr,
His royall scepter bravelie managing,   *wielding*
Whoes glorious fame shall pears all Europ's ear.
405 From him fair bewtei's faerest floure shill spring,[†]
Whom heir you sie, sett in a royall chear,   *throne*
    And their her dangling golden lockes intreyld;   *entwined*
    Much these have blist her, but much more her child."

The Argument. [PG2]

The south and north crownes joined by that great king,[†]
Who of all kinges hea'vns blissings most embrace:
His works, his witt, hea'ven's care him saif to bring
To happie end; his two rair impes of grace   *children*
5 In whom he is bles'd more then in anye thing;
By warr the youngest reules the earth in peace.
    The Prophet leaves the Prince amaizd at last;
    He foyles six knights, then to his armie past.   *overcomes*

[Prophecy of Stuart glory.]   [PG3]

Chapter V

"But heir, O Scotland, heir beginnes thy spring   *springtime*
Of honor, wealth, fame, glorie, praise, and blisse;
Evne now, and not til nou, high hea'vns doth bring
Thy happines, thy good, thy al, i-wish   *definitely*
5 Thy fame, thy name, for e're eternizing,
If sinfull pride beare not thy wayes amis;
    Hence shall thy glorie and thy greatnes grow
    Swelling o're seas and o're* all landes shall flow.   *expanding*

Their o're the glob of sea and earth he stands,†
10 Whiche to the north joynes sowthe's fair diadem,
And Boreas' spatious impire all commands,
And all wheir Titan coolls his firie team;   *everywhere*
If thow can number furth the occean sands,
Or all those spangled golden wonders name,   *sparkling; marvels*
15   In radiant coache that course heavns lifts a pace,   *procession*
    Then may'st thow compt his blisd and frutfull race.   *number*

This, this, is hee, ev'ne hee whome havin propoines   *heaven proposes*
Greate Jov's eternall motto for to beare,
Whoes soule refyning sighes, heart-scolding grones,   *soul-purifying*
20 Shall on this altar of devotion reare
Trew zeale, trew faith, and trew repenting moin'e,   *moan*
From whence ascends the sweit perfums of pra're   *prayer*
    To the One-trin, whoe from his mercie's throne   *Trinity*
    Shall rain doun plenteus showrs of greace anone.   *grace; forthwith*

25 From so great dangers shall the Lord him save,†
And to suche hight of happines him bring,
That, tho nogth els could eche one's ears bereave,   *nothing; capture*
Yet this shall be ane everlasting signe
For eche to sing his mild sweit virtues grave,
30 Without correction bent to eache designe,   *change*
    His bountie, clemencie and equitie,
    His constant minde and his stabilitie.

The least of nothing can my Muse record,
Whoes wings is lag'd with vapors gros and fatt,   *clogged; greasy*
35 But this I know, that his imperiall sword
Shall slyce doun sinne and scheild the desolat,
But should I thus with seiming schewis debord   *visions; exaggerate*
His praise so infinit, so intricat?   *complex*
        No no, deir Muse, serche not wheir is no end:
40   Onlie himself himself can comprehend.

For, all the Muses at his birth desending
Throu the cleir welkin of oure westerne clims,   *skies*
As when a firie flashe of lightning bending   *forking*
With twinkling rays glids dounward oftentyms
45 Amid the tufted plains, so they, attending   *bosky*
On his blist birth, infuse their sacred rims   *pour in; poetry*
        His spreit within, and, with ambrosiall kisses,
        In his blisd soule, they breath a heav'ne of blisses.

This done, they with a wreath of starrs haif cround   *have*
50 His tempills, which a tripill croune adorne;
With dowble bayes and laurel much renound,
They give two glorious titles new'r outworne,†   *never obsolete*
And maks his voice divinelie to resound
Our all the earth, on wings of fame still borne;   *o're*
55   O miracle! his voice lyik lightning darte,
        The golden schowrs of poleist witt and arte.   *polished; wisdom*

His Muse shall flie with sweetest eloquence
In learned layes to charme all spreits, all sences,
And, like a queene in pomp's magnificence,†
60 Sche's richest still when lairgest in expences,   *most generous*
In scarlot heir, in crimsone their, and thence
In purple robs, adorning royall prences,
        More ritche then golden Tessen's swelling cost,   *Tagus; rich store*
        With rairest jems and pretious stones imbost.   *ornamented*

65 And then anone, in arm's addrest for warr,†   *soon; prepared*
    A steill bright sword she'is bravelie brandishing;
    Heir dois she place the thundring connons, their   *cannons*
    To Mars she bids the roiring trumpets sing;
    The victor gets her lawrell for his schare,
70 That bring him more then Cresus' gold could bring;
        But now in sabel blak her self she suits   *attires*
        And magick spells divinlie she refuits.†   *counters*

    Then sanct like sits she in a secret cell,   *saint; obscure*
    And sacred phraises, sent from heavin above,†
75 Furth from her pen in plenty doeth distell,   *distill*
    Confounding all that quest'ons vaine would prove;   *try*
    And from her witt's deip tressour springs a well
    Whoes source from God's celestiall throne doth move;
        On golden channell slyds this silver streame,
80   And drouns her foes in groundles gulfs of shame.   *bottomless*

    Yea, how soev'r her self she list t'adorne   *choose*
    With diadems or coats of warlick steill,
    Or wisdom's graver suits she list have borne,   *choose to wear*
    Yet evrie thing becums her schaip so weill,
85 That still her self she seims, whoes rising morne
    Shall have no night, whoes mightie flowing Nile
        Ourflows all lands, and with her swelling wawe   *rolling tide*
        Holds hirs in peace and uthers all in awe.

    This Prince more wealth, peace, honor, greatnes brings
90 Then all that swey'd his scepter ever before,   *wielded*
    But heir since heavne him by his worth desings   *now; assigns*
    That to all times and aige shall him restore;
    Since all and evrie thing his praises sings,
    I can but lessen what all tyms makes more,
95   But in his seid rare blessings shall attend him,   *offspring*
        Which it sall pleas almightie Jove to send him.

In midst of famous Scotland dois their ly
A valey grac'd with nature, airt and care,
As fertill as the soill of Araby,
As pleasaunt as Thessalian Tempe fair,†
On which frome heavne no blustring tempests flye, *rough*
Nor zephyr blow's, but sweit and wholsome air,
Along whoes side the Ochell montans rise,
And lifts their swelling topps above the skyis. *lofty*

Doun through the midst of this fair valey glids
The chrystall Forth with glansing silver hew, *shining*
Whose roaring stream on golden channell slids *sounding; flows*
With murmur sweit in Thetis' bosume blew, *into*
Of brooks supply'id with lib'rall store besids,
Which tops of towring montans still renew,
Whoes springs the dry insatiat meids supplies, *thirsty; meads*
And moister lends to herbs, to fructs and treis.

In midst of this fair valey doth arise
A mightie mounting roche of wondrous height, *looming; rock*
On whoes ambitious bak as in the skyis *proud ridge*
A citie stands, impregnabile to sight;
A castell on his loftie crest espyis *looks upon*
The valeys rownd about the montans' hight;
Below the roche the glanncing river glids, *gleaming*
In whose cold streams hee coolls his horie sids. *venerable*

When Titan doth up to the sowth aspire, *rise in the south*
Ascending through heaven's vaults of brightest azure,
These loftie turrets seim to have desire
To view their beautei's pride whill thay have leasure;
Then sett they all the rowling flood on fire, *rolling*
Whose trembling billows show their golden treasure;
The smilling flood illustrats them with beams, *illuminates*
Whill as their beautie beautifeis her streams.

Within this paradise of all delight,
130 Thus grac'd with airts, proud wealth and Natur's care,
Shall to the world be borne that lampe of light[†]
Whoes schyning shaip yow ar beholding their;
But ah, too soone snatcht up from humane sight,
Whoes lose shall make the western-world dispair,   *loss*
135   That heavins can raise them to their former blis,
Since they have reft so great a good as this.   *carried off*

O, could hee leive, he were a worthie prence,   *live; prince*
By Nature in her ritchest wealth enrold,
And fraught with all the guifts of excellence
140 That either man could wisch or heavins unfold;
But O, too wise and too too sone taine hence,
Heavin scorns that earth so great a good should hold.   *resents*
  Albione, be war, least heavins upon the lowr,   *frown*
  Who thus untimelie cutts thy fairest flowr.

145 Then shall arise a prince of his owne kind,[†]   *family*
Borne of his dame and of his sire begot,   *mother; father*
Whoes matchles, haughtie and heroic mind   *noble*
Shows heavens assignes great empires for his lot;   *destiny*
Heir doth he marche in arms, to warr inclind,
150 Ou'r Danube, Neill, Euphrates, Ganges hote,
  And treds on all as on that fearfull here,   *lord full of fear*
  Gainst his victorious arms that dars prepare.

He, at his royall father's heigh command,[†]   *high*
This greate and weghtie chairge shall undergo,
155 For dred revenge, with warr's hote burning brand,   *torch*
Send from that angrie monarch's breist, shall thro   *sent; cast*
A thundering tempest our all sea and land,   *over*
With schame, lose, foyll, blood, ruin, wrak and wo;   *loss; trouble*
  For why his waiting slaves ar warr and death   *wherefore*
160 T'unbind his browes, knit up in cloudes of wrathe.   *relax; enclosed*

To whoes brave sone, thus sent, the Lord hath granted –[†]
If hee his thoghts hoord in that heavenlie place –   *though; keep secret*
With him and his hee sure hes covenanted   *firmly; pledged*
To pour an ocean of his plenteous grace;
165 Nor his greate syr's dominions shallbe wanted,   *Sire's; lacking*
But all, from fertill Inde to Orcades,*   *fertile*
     All shallbe his, and his victorious hand[†]
     Ou'r sea and earth all nations shall command.

And lo, that dreadfull serpent, scourge of earth,[†]
170 Whoes pride aloft him to the heavns doth rear,
Shall yeeld to his all-conquering arme, whoes worthe   *power*
From his proud head this diadem shall tear
And joyne it to his owne by right of birth,[†]
Then to his saviour's sacred tomb shall bear
175   This glorious standart, this triumphant signe[†]
     Of sinn, of death, of hell's great tameing king.   *conquering*

Nature and all her train on him attend,
Putting the golden key into his hand
Of earth and sea's ritche treasure, to the end
180 That all obey and he may all command;
Ceare, wisdom, foirsicht, virtue to him send   *care*
Fortun, fast bound with many thousand band;   *tied securely*
     Love, beauty youth strive to adorne him more,
     Then virtue, grace, and wisdom's plenteous store.   *than*

185 The twelf greate labors of that antick lord[†]   *ancient*
Was justlie praisd and magnifeit allone,   *in itself*
Yet much more worth to him sall be restord   *merit*
Then men, beasts, monsters conquerd one by one,
Wheir onlie strength, noght witt, did aide afford.   *wisdom*
190 Ou'r murdred beasts his glorie shall not shone;   *shine*
     But kings subdew't and mightie nations strong   *subdued*
     Shall to his fame and endles praise belong.

This prince shall always feill heavins gratious love,
And happie fortuns shall consort him still;   *accompany*
195 Proud conqueringe Mars still by his side shall move,   *always*
Fair Victorie shall ev'r obey his will:
His infancie, she nursing, shall remove   *progress*
To noble hopes, and his strong yeers furthfill   *expectations*
    With statlie trophes, and his aige with balms,   *trophies; comforts*
200   With crouns, with lawrells and triumphant palms.

The boundles sea shall seeme to him a brook,
Heavn threatning Alpes shall seime ane easie way;
Two horned Po shall his proud streams rebook,[†]   *rebuke*
Beholding his victorious armie stay;   *take up position*
205 His glassie cave he leaves, and cums to look   *icy*
Wheir as a thousand cisterns ev'rie day   *caverns*
    To pay their endles silver tribute hyis,   *hasten*
    Which til that time did never view the skyis.

The aiged flood cums gravelie from his cell,   *river-god; cave*
210 Doun from his head hings dangling silver tressis,   *hangs*
Frome ev'rie hair a christall spring doth fall,
Ay when he sweats a roaring steam* foorth* praissis,   *vapour; presses*
Eche sigh raise up a wave, eche groan foretell,
A fearfull inundation following passes;   *is the result*
215   His wrinkled brow's a pearly dew distelleth,
    His greennishe eis with endles tears still filleth.

The nimphs with daunsing round about him trips,
Aganes the sonne their azure mantils shone,   *against; shine*
From wave to wave the wanton fareis skips,   *nimble fairies*
220 Whole scoolls of fishe heir swims, their leaps anone,   *shoals*
Their watrie lord with ice cold schivering lips
Thus chyds his streams: 'You foolish streams alone,   *chides; merely*
    Ah, will you thus heavn's champion ganestand,   *oppose*
    When sea and earth obeis his conquiring hand?

225 Proud brooke, be calme, abate thy raging torrent,
   Gainst him whome Jove hath lovde lift not thy horne,
   Rol smothe, youe waves, lash not your swelling current   *flow quietly; dash*
   Furth at his glorious fleet, which should be borne
   On youre smooth backe, but dance an easie currant   *gentle corranto*
230 With me, your aged flood, with years not worne,   *exhausted*
     Till his victorious armie march before
     Their glistring ensing's, on our eastern shore'.   *ensigns*

   His fear'd renoune, like thundring cannons, roars   *reputation*
   In eche man's ears, through all lands, touns and tours,   *towers*
235 And tempest-like it beitts the Baltike shoars;   *strikes*
   Clouds of his wrathe, in haill's scharp stormie shours
   Tumbling throgh mightie winds, aloft still soar's,
   At whoes dreid sound all nat'ions sadlie lour's,   *shrink in fear*
     And ou'r all lands it fleis, at last it falls,   *flies*
240   And beats doun bulwarks, touns, tours, gates and walls.

   This valorous Prince, wise, cumlie, fair and neat,
   In everie thing himself shall bravelie beare;   *carry*
   His enemeis he shall no sooner threat,
   Than hee schall over-throw with schame and fear;
245 The terror of his name'sall tyrannes beat   *thrust*
   Doun from their throns, who yeelds before he warre;   *go to war*
     For Jove noght gev's him sparinglie good hap,   *sparingly; fortune*
     But always pours doun plentie in his lap.

   Thus thy greate house, thy race, thy ofspringe faire,
250 Unbred, unborne, all those and mor's enrold   *more is recorded*
   On heaven's brasse leafes, by the Almightei's cair,   *care*
   For all ensuing aiges to behold;
   Be thankfull, serve, love, praise his merceis rare,
   That in heavin's birth did first* their births unfold;
255   So thy blisd race shalbe more blessed still,
     Nor time nor age thy blesse'd seid shall kill.   *progeny*

And thou, deir countrie, with all grace contented,
That heav'ne on fertill earth can thee afford,
Let not thy mind with pride be once atteinted,   *infected*
260   For those great blessings of thy greatious Lord;
Let not fair fate's approch be so prevented,
And blise, once gevin, with shame soone bak restoered;
   But O, allace, heir my poore soule doth faint,
   O, then I fear a thankfull mynd thou's want;   *shalt lack*

265   Which, if thou do, th'Almighte's smyles shall turne[†]
To hote consumeing wrathe and coales of fire,
That shall thy intrealls, all thy bowells, burne;
Thou's feill his just sad wrathe and dreadfull ire,
For whiche thy maids and hearmles babes shall murne,   *mourn*
270   Nor shall thy plagues, warre, famien, death, retire,   *pass away*
   Till thow be wallowing in a crimsone flood,
   And dround almost in thy owne guiltie blood.

Greate Jove shall send straunge nations, farr and near,   *foreign*
Within thy native land, thee to distroy;
275   Earth's farrest ends thy widowes' plaints shal heare,[†]   *laments*
Wheir weeping aer thy mornings shall convoy   *air; mournings*
From Pole to Pole, beneath heavin's volts so cleir;   *vaults*
Echo shall sadlie soond thy sad annoy."   *suffering*
   Annoy cuts his discourse, thus wofull harted,   *concludes*
280   Wheirwith the prophetizing spreit departed.   *spirit*

Long time he silent stood, at last, againe
He thus began: "Brave Prince, in time bewarr,
Lest, when the crowne thou freilie shalt obtaine,
Thou let not sinn and vice creip in so farr
285   That Jove his endles blessings he refraine,
And thee and thyne with endles vengeance marr;
   Which if thou doe not, than thou heir hast sene,   *then*
   What hath for thee and thine prepared bene."

Thus said the Prophet, whill the Prince rejoisd
290 Those of his royall of-spring this to sie,   *thus*
In heavins so framed, by Jove so weill disposed,   *placed*
And rendring thanks to his greate majestie;
Evne then a vow hee on him selfe impoisd: *on the spot*
His kingdome once at peace, his crowne made frie,
295   Hee with ane armie great Christ's tomb wold view,
And with sterne warrs wold Sarasens persew.†

Then said he to that grave and antient syre:
"Wise, holie father, let me once be bold,
Thy blisd and happie name for to require,
300 Of whom my verie soule's content I hold."
"Great Prince," quod he, "I yeeld to your desire;
Rimour I hight, your slave and servand old;†   *am called*
My love and my last duetie to discharge,
I hither came, as you shall know at large.   *in full*

305 For the appointed time is drawing neir,
When my poore soule must leave this ruind towre;
Know then, an angell did to me appeir,
And of these revelationes gave me power,
Onlie for thee, because the Lord doeth heare
310 The wofull plaintes and groninges everie houre
Of thy still torterd land, which hea'vns surmounted,   *tortured; reached*
And mercie begd where mercie never wanted,   *lacked*

That onlie thou, selected for releife   *you in particular*
By the One-trine, eternall maiestie,   *Trinity*
315 Crost with misfortune, sorow, paine and greife,   *troubled*
For that wilde slaughter, sacralegiouslie,   *ferocious*
In Jove's sole sacred house – but that mischief   *misfortune*
Hath thy unfaind repentance freed from thee –   *genuine*
Should heir by me heav'ns endles bountie know,   *here*
320 For to remove thy cares, and confort show.

Persist thou still, then, in thy just desire,
For mightie Jove stands arm'd against thy foe's;
Now all thy bad misfortuns shall retire,
Hence shalt thou ever winn and never lose;
325 Thou frielie shalt posses a frie empire,
And such renoune, such fame and glorie goes   *proceeds*
    Of thy greate name, that thou shalt have more praise   *from*
    Then ever had a prince before thy dayes."

"Now," quod the Prince, "old father, I wald know,†
330 If theis great kings shal beautifie my name."
"No no," quod he, "but from thy loynis shal grow
One trie, whois fruict shall flurishe still with fame,
And one the bankis of silver Forth shall show   *on*
Two branches faire, for to adorne that stream,
335   Who turns and bows his crooked schoris about,   *twists; banks*
    To keip such heavne-blest treasur can* get out.   *protect; as can*

And so, fairweill." This said, throu shaples air   *formless*
Hee went away. A light cleir, bright and schining
Enlightened all the place so cleir and fair,
340 As Phebus seimd but Phebe, thence refining   *that; reducing*
His paill old beutie, spent with aige and cair.   *exhausted*
The Prince, his kneis and dasled eies inclining,   *dazzled; bending*
    Downe fals he straight, lyfe seemd to leave his statione,   *its place*
    Stroke blind with light, and dumb with admiration.

345 When he recoverd of this brain-sicke trance,   *mind-affecting*
He look't about, but could no wheir behold
The cause of such a golden rediance,
Nor anie wheir sie that grave Prophet old;
Which chang't and altred much his countenance
350 Twixt* dout and feare, yet neids from thence he wold,   *must he go*
    Finding a beaten path doun to the plane,
    That leids him wheir his horse doth yet remane.

Hee taks him straight, and doth from thence depart,
Revolving oft into his princelie mynd,   *within*
355 If by illusioun, visioune, dreame or airt,   *whether*
Or if he reft in spreit such thyngs devynd;   *imagined*
But, weying weil ech things with joyfull heart,
He nothing think[s] unpossible to find
   By mighte Jove, altho man's shallow witt
360   Can hardlie be induc'd to credet it.

Patrick Hannay (1594?–1629)

This poet's ancestors, according to a side-note in his collected volume *The Nightingale* [etc.] (London, 1622), belonged to Galloway, where the family seat was at Sorbie Tower, by Garlieston (Wigtonshire); he himself, however, hailed from Kirkdale (Kirkcudbright), on the eastern side of the River Cree. On the title-page of his *Two Elegies on the Death of Queene Anne* (London, 1619) he declared that he was an MA, but from which university is not known; in his other publications he designated himself as 'Gent.'. He may have gone to England as a young man, and may have been attached to the circle of the Queen. His poems show that he was familiar with the environs of London, where he must have become known, since several English poets contributed liminary verses to *The Nightingale*. That did not mean, however, that Hannay failed to maintain connections with his fellow Scoto-Britons. He contributed a liminary poem to the 1623 reprint of William Lithgow's *A most delectable, and true discourse*, and Lithgow recycled Hannay's poem in his *The Totall Discourse of the Rare Aduentures* (London, 1632). Verse of this kind indicates a degree of friendship and mutual respect, and there would seem to have been something of a nexus involving Hannay, Lithgow and Robert Allen, all of whom came from the south-west of Scotland. In 1620 Hannay was apparently with the Scottish forces assisting James's son-in-law, Frederick V of the Palatinate, and his *Songs and Sonnets* (London, 1622) were dedicated to Sir Andrew Gray, who commanded the Scottish soldiers in Bohemia, where Frederick had been elected king in 1618. Like his cousin Robert, Hannay was granted an estate in Ireland, and he became clerk to the Privy Council in Dublin. He is said to have drowned in 1629.

Robert Hannay observed in the 1622 volume that his cousin was a poet whose 'ingenious wit [was] for every measure, every subiects fit'. Patrick Hannay did indeed excel in a range of genres, for example: highly wrought and witty verse in the style of John Donne (*Elegies*); Ovidian narrative, enriched with influence from Ariosto, and couched in the intricate stanza used by Alexander Montgomerie in the *Cherrie and the Slae* (*The Nightingale*); a two-canto, Italianate-style, agony-filled love-dilemma, set in a Hungarian-Transylvanian Ruritania (*Sheretine and Mariana*); shrewd character-studies of men and women as potential marriage-partners (*A happy Husband*); a mixed bag of lyrics on the themes of love and religion (*Songs and Sonnets*).

A happy Husband, which declares itself a response to a popular poem by the recently murdered English courtier Sir Thomas Overbury, enjoyed particular success, and was printed separately and several times. Regrettably, on account of their length, *The Nightingale, Sheretine* and *A happy Husband* have had to be excluded from the present selection, though each has its own real merits and attractions. Stylistic influences from Sidney, Spenser, Jonson, Drayton, Donne and Montgomerie are discernible in Hannay's writing.

Hannay dedicated *A happy Husband* to Lady Margaret, daughter of the earl of Home. For *Sheretine* he addressed himself to Lucy, *née* Harington, countess of Bedford and former Lady of the Bedchamber to Queen Anne, and a lady who was celebrated for her literary patronage of many of the most prominent contemporary English poets (Lewalski 1987: 52–77). Another significant dedication is that of the entire 1622 *The Nightingale* [etc.] volume to the famous, individually rich, and very well-connected Court beauty, Frances Howard. She, the one-time lover of Henry Wriothesley, 3rd earl of Southampton (Shakespeare's patron), had by her second marriage become countess of Hertford, and soon after the earl's death (1621) she had gone on to marry Ludovick Stuart, the eldest son of James's first favourite, Esmé Stewart, thereby becoming duchess of Lennox. Hannay's series of dedications may reflect a rise in his own position among the literary Scots in the metropolis. However, if that is indeed the case, the dedication of his *Songs and Sonnets* (the final component in *The Nightingale* [etc.]) to the military figure of Sir Andrew Gray suggests a somewhat abrupt change, either of plan or of circumstances.

The second Elegie. [PH1]

Each countrey now contributes to the Thames,
Which a support of every currant clames.   *river*
Why dost thou so, sweet Thames? Is not thy sorrow
Sufficient for thy selfe, but thou must borrow?
5 Or wants thy waters worth for such a charge,   *strength; task*
As to conduct great Anne's last body'd-barge?
Or is it cause, so just and kind thou art,   *because*
Thou'lt not incroach that, wherein each hath part?   *encroach on*
Sure that's the cause, the losse is general,
10 And that last office must be helpt by all.
Yet wonder not they come not now so sweet,
As they do use, when they to solace meet.   *for pleasure*
They're not themselves, they are compounded things,
For every one his latest offring brings
15 And sends it by these brookes, unto her shrine,
Whose waters with their teares are turned brine.
Each subject's cheeke such falling drops distaine,   *leave a mark on*
As if to dew, sighes had dissolv'd the braine:
Which from their eyes still in aboundance powre,
20 Like a moist haile, or liquid pearly showre:
Which in such haste, each one another chases,
Making swift torrents in such torrid places,
Disgorging in these brookes, making them rise,   *pouring into*
So's soveraigne Thames almost feares a surprise.   *with the result*
25 Feare not, faire Queene, it is not their ambition,
But swelling sorrow, that breeds thy suspition.
Its sorrow feedes those currents and those rils,
Which thy vast channel with an ocean fils.
Which eye-bred-humor so hath chang'd thy nature,   *lacrimosity*
30 Thy fishes thinke they live not in thy water:
It, or thy taste, is alterd, for they thinke,
For thy sweet streames they briny liquor drinke.
How weari'd is thy sister, famous Forth,
Bringing sad Scotland's sorrowes from the north,

35 Who comes not out of dutie, as the rest
     Who unto Thames their carefull course adrest,   *direct*
     She comes, her equall, will not yield in teares,   *concede*
     In subjects' sorrow's, nor in countries' cares.
     Great Neptun's selfe doth feare invasive wrong,
40 Seeing her strange waves throw his waters throng,   *foreign; press*
     And causeth Triton to sound an alarme,
     To warne the sea gods in all haste to arme,
     Who, bringing billowes in brave battel-ray,   *battle-order*
     Do meane Forth's fury with their force to stay.   *hinder*
45 But, when they see her thus all wrapt in woe,
     And the sad cause of her just sorrow know,
     They lay not their defensive armes aside,
     But as a guard, her throw their gulfes do guide.   *through*
     Striving with all the pleasures of the maine,
50 This grieving-stranger-Queene to entertaine,   *foreign-born*
     Out throw their bowres of cleare transparent waves,   *bowers*
     Christaline-wainscot, pearles the bottome paves,   *wall-panelling*
     Her they conduct, and to abate her woe,
     Their sea-delights and riches all they show.
55 Which Neptune, now in love, would gladly give her
     For love, yet dares not offer least hee grieve her.   *lest*
     Who loves, and would not have his love unkind,   *seem intrusive*
     Must woe a pleasant humor, vacant minde: *affect*
     This makes him stay his sute, and strive to please,   *hold back*
60 With all the love-alurements of the seas.
     Yet all doe not so much as move one smile,
     An anxious sorrow soone discover'th guile.
     Yet hee will guard and guid her grieving streames,
     Whom at her entry in the wished Thames
65 He leaves, and vowes in discontent to mourne,
     Till fairest Forth back to the sea returne.
     Her sister her receives with kind embrace,
     Their liquid armes clasping, they interlace;
     In love so straight, they cannot be untwinde,   *close; separated*
70 They seeme both one, in body and in minde.

O happy union! labour'd long in vaine,
Reserv'd by God to James his joyfull raigne,
And Anne's. O blessed couple, so esteem'd,
By all fore-knowing Jove, that he them deem'd
75 Worthie each other, and to weare that jemme,
Blest Britaine's now united diademe.
He esteem'd none, worthy to weare't before them,
But kept it still in store, for to decore them.   *honour*
How did he suffer those two kingdoms try   *compete in*
80 All open power, and private policie;   *relations*
Yet still increased discord; others' force
Made seperation greater, su'd divorce!   *ensued*
How did one teare the other, spare no toyle,   *effort*
To bath in blood the neighbour's fertill soile!
85 Wrath, discord, malice, envy, rapine,* strife,   *robbery*
Thefts, rapes, and murderous mischieves were so rife,   *hostage-taking*
None liv'd secure, while each king did protect
The other's fugitives, for his respect,   *prestige*
Thus, looking for no rest, or end of hate,
90 But with the ruine of the adverse state.   *enemy*
God he effects it that to him alone   *brings it about*
We might ascribe the honour; and, being one,
We might love better – twixt united foes,
And separated friends, love and hate growes
95 To greatest heights – and for this end doth raise,
Using the meanes, the honour of his dayes.
Great James, the joy-presaging northrene starre,
Whose radiant light illuminates so farre,
As it doth warme, with its all-quickning-beames,   *life-giving*
100 The frozen love betwixt the Tay and Thames,
With wonder and delight drawing all hearts
And eyes, to love and see his princely parts.
And, what is strange, who hated most before   *those who*
With admiration most his worth adore,   *merit*
105 Wishing they were his subjects. He is king
Already of their hearts; the poyson'd sting

Of rancor is remoov'd; for love they call him,
And with their kingdom's ornaments install him.
Great confidence his vertous life must bring,
110 Whom such old foes love forces make their king.
Where was ere heard, of emulating foes –   *ever*
Rooted in hate, with other's overthrows   *defeats*
Such, and so long – that did their wrath appease,   *bring to peace*
And yeeld – won but by love – to right, as these?   *merely*
115 Yet doe they not repent; they finde report
Sometime is wrong'd, and may indeed come short
In commendations (yet it's rare, as here) –
For she's a woman, and by kinde will beare   *carry; nature*
More than she should – but his last subjects find
120 Themselves with Saba's queen of self-same mind,
That Fame – though saying by beliefe – had wrong'd
Two kings, not telling halfe to each had long'd;   *belonged*
For England heard not, nor could it have thought,
That Scotland's king such wonders could have wrought.
125 Long may he live, and die well, full of yeares,
And when his death shall draw us dry with teares,
On Brittaine's throne may his seed ever raigne,   *descendants*
Till Christ doe come, to judge the world, againe.
Who would have thought from the Scot-hated-Dane –
130 Whom vanquish'd England so much did disdaine,
Opprest with base succession, they did turne,
Being freed, "Lord-dane" in "lurdane" for a scorne –   *miscreant*
Who would have thought, I say, from Dane should spring
One, who from Scots and English eyes should wring   *draw*
135 Such hearty teares; must not her worth be much,   *heart-felt*
Since we doe find its love-effects prove such?
How great that love in such, such love could breed,
O, let it live for ever in her seed;
And let that love in our hearts never die,
140 But ever live to her posteritie!*
And those sweet streames, her mate and she conbinde
In love, O, let their armes be nere untwinde

From kinde imbraces; and though now their greetings
Be not so joyfull as at other meetings,
145 Yet is their love all one, they take one part,
The one joys not, the other sad at heart.
They surfeit now in sorrow, then in pleasure,
Joy then exceeds, griefe is above measure.
To honour Charles, our hope, when they met last,
150 How did they rob each meadow as they past:
Of sweets each banke a posie did bestow   *beauties*
Of fairest flowers, that on his brim did grow!   *its*
These and such like they brought from every part,
And gratulations from each subject's heart.
155 They, swell'd with pride, rising in loftly waves,   *tall*
And all the neighbour bordring banks out-braves.   *surpass*
Their fishes frolick'd, showing joy by gesture,
The waters, wantonnizing, woo'd their maister;   *sporting*
So fast their billowes 'bout his blest barge throng'd,   *around*
160 They hurt themselves oft, oft their fellowes wrong'd;
Each would be first, on others' backs some ride,
Some under others' slippry shoulders slide;
Though beat with oares, yet will they not turne backe,   *struck*
For they their humble prostrate homage make.
165 The sun then guilt each glistring-glassie-coat   *gilded*
Those marin-masquers wore, dans'd bout his boat,   *sea-masquers*
Who by the musicke measur'd not their paces,   *dance-steps*
Deaf'd with a confus'd cry from diverse places,
Of maidens, matrons, aged men, and boyes,
170 Which from each quarter made a confus'd noyse,   *direction*
Of hearty ave's, welcomming their prince,   *greetings*
Eccho, with answering tyrd, was mute still since.   *tired; thereafter*
The citie with the suburbs did appeare,
Like a large theater when he came neare:
175 Each window, wall, each turret top and steeple,
Was fild with every age, sex, sort of people,
So as some thought, who earst had never seene   *previously*

Such numbers, that the buildings all had beene
Of imagry contriv'd by cunning art.   *painted work*
180 For on the ground, the brewer in his cart,   *at ground level*
     The sculler, carman, and the baser sort   *boatman; carter*
     Seem'd strong and rudely carv'd clownes, to support   *fellows*
     The stately frame; maides, prentises and groomes,   *structure*
     Made shop-dore, window, stale, and lower roomes;   *made up; stall*
185 The batlements, house-coverings, and the leads,   *roofs*
     As tyles or slates, young boyes and girles ore-spreads.
     The middle roomes all round about the Thames,   *overlooking*
     Which ladies held, and choiser citie-dames,   *superior*
     Such tooke for spaces, which faire statues held,   *selected*
190 Where carver and the painter both exceld.
     So pure complexions these seem'd made by art,   *such perfect*
     As Nature never did the like impart
     To lovely youth – the large, low, open breast,
     Full, white, round, swelling, azure-vain'd, increast   *blue-veined*
195 The error, for they thought none living would
     Lay out such parts, for all eyes to behold.   *display*
     So curious were the colours which were showne,
     As Nature hardly could from art be knowne,
     So that they could adjudge them due to neither,
200 But participles, taking part of either.
     Yet all by voice and gesture seemed glad,
     Wonder it was to see a thing looke sad.   *melancholy*
     Now it's not so, the offrings are but teares,
     The sighes, and groanes, of Brittaine's blest-reft sheres   *happily deprived shires*
205 Are now the acclamations; these two streames,
     Compounded waters of mixt sorrow seems.
     Yet walke they hand in hand with equall pace,
     T'wards that late pleasant, but now pensive place
     Where sorrow, suted in a sable weed,
210 Doth with a mourning vaile each heart ore-spread,   *veil*
     And Phoebus, for to make the world and minde
     To weare one livery, all his beames confined,   *locked up*

Dimming each eye in darknesse of the night,
Either asham'd to mourne in open sight,
215 Or loth to alter with his brighter streames   *rays*
Our late obscured Cyntia's lesser gleames.
For her fled soule, which doth with glory shine,
Left with its lodging something that's divine,   *earthly habitation*
Which with reflection smileth on these rayes,
220 Which her bright soule now from the skies displeas.   *displays*
And these light orbes, which with such swiftnes roule   *shining bodies*
About the heavens, acquainted with her soule,
To light her corps doe set in every porch
Of the damantine heaven a starry torch,   *diamond-like*
225 Which, darkned with the moist earth's vapours,
Are her last lampes, and never dying tapers.   *candles*
Thames trembles, Forth doth feverise for feare,   *quiver*
Both roare to see their soveraigne thus appeare: *cry*
Their billowes breake their hearts against the shore,
230 Their fishes faint, yet cannot tell wherefore,
But, when they float upon the water crop,   *surface*
And see the teares from eyes and oars which drop,
They thinke them all to few, and adde their owne,
And swimme in proper waters, earst unknowne.   *their own; formerly*
235 The water-nymphes now round about her boat,
Cloath'd in sad sable, mourning habits, float;   *garments*
The hamadryads, and the silvans all,
To beare a part in this complaint they call,   *lament*
Who since her death had practis'd in their teares,   *produced*
240 Streames deep enough: none now the water fears.
They brought with them sweet camomile and rew,
Mint, spinard, marjoram, her way they strew,   *lavender; before her*
With flowers of choicest colour and of sent,
Which from the slender-weeping-stalk was rent.
245 Her exequies these nymphes together sing,   *funeral rites*
Till with this consort heaven and earth doth ring: *combined song*

Heavens, invying our waters, walkes, and woods,   *envying*
  Hath reft our joy, and plac'd her 'mongst the gods.   *have stolen*
No more our wandring waves shall wantonize,   *sport and play*
250 No more shall swelling billowes brave the skies,   *challenge*
No more shall purling zephyr curle our head,   *gentle*
No more we'l foamy-powders thereon spread,   *effervescence*
No more shall now meandrian walkes delight us,   *riverine*
No more despaire with death shall now affright us.

255 Since Heaven invying our late happie floods,   *rivers*
  Hath reft our joy, and plac'd [her] 'mongst the gods,
Wee'l take no sport now to persue the fawne,   *pleasure*
Wee'l no more tread light measures on the lawne,   *dances; grass*
Wee'l deck our heads no more with Flora's flowers,
260 Wee'l wooe no more our wooddy paramours,   *sylvan*
Wee'l beare no part hereafter with the birds,   *sing together*
Wee'l weepe for woe, and teach them waile in words.

Since Heaven envying our late happy woods,
  Hath reft our joy, and plac'd her 'mongst the gods,
265 Wee'l hide our heads within our shores and shelves,   *shallows*
Wee'l dwell in darkest cipresse groves with elves;
No more wee'l sollace in great Nephtune's hals,   *take pleasure*
No more wee'l dance at silvanes' festivals;
Because she's gone, whose glory grac'd our floods,
270 Because she's gone, who honour'd walkes and woods.

Thus sung they her along, but come to shore,   *once arrived*
Where she must leave them, they nere see her more;
They sinke to bottome, either in a swowne,   *swoon*
Or else themselves, now loathing life, to drowne.
275 The Forth and Thames, losing their so lov'd sight,
Vow yearely to renew their woes, that night.

An Epitaph.   [PH2]

Power to do ill, and practise onely good;
Humblest in heart, highest in place and blood;
Fairest, and freest from loose-desires in thought,
Pleasures to tempt, yet not distain'd in ought: *improper*
5 With anxious care, in courage nere dejected,   *never*
Though cause of joy, with no vaine-joy affected: *hilarity*
    Know, reader, whensoere these lines you scan,
    Such, and none such, but she, was our Queene Anne.

[Love frustrated.]   [PH3]

When I consider well how Cupid kinde
First did inflame my heart with loving fires,
And did remove the quiet of my minde,
And for it plac'd wake-rife, yet deare, desires;   *insomnious*
5 And how the friend I truely did affect,   *adore*
With like sincerity repaid my love,   *similar*
How we did strive each other to respect,
And no contention else did ever prove;   *experience*
How that our soules so nearely sympathiz'd,   *closely; accorded*
10 We oft did thinke and oft did dreame the same,
What one approv'd the other highly priz'd,
What one dislik'd the other's heart did blame;
    O, how thy envy, Fortune, makes me wonder,
    Whom love so joynd, thou should have kept asunder.

[Croydon.]   [PH4]

When curious Nature did her cunning trie   *expertise; apply*
In framing of this faire terrestriall round,   *ordering; globe*
Her workmanship the more to beautifie,
With chang'd varietie made it abound,
5 And oft did place a plot of fertile ground
    Fraught with delights nie to a barren soile,   *near*
    To make the best seem better by a foile.   *contrast*

Thus first were made by Thames the motley-meads,   *variegated*
Wearing the livery of the summer's queene,
10 Whose flourie robe ore them she freely spreads,   *generously*
With colours more than are in Iris seene,
And all the ground and hemme of grassie greene;   *verge*
    Whereon the silly sheepe doe fearelesse feede,   *innocent*
    While on a banke the shepheard tunes his reed.   *pipe*

15 Next shadie groves where Delia hunteth oft,   *beside*
And light-foot fairies tripping still doe haunt,   *dancing*
There mirthfull Muses raise sweet notes aloft,
And wanton birdes, their chaste loves cheerely chant;   *sporting*
There no delightfull pleasure ere doth want;   *ever; lack*
20   There Silvian with his satyres doth remaine,
    There nymphs doe love and are belov'd againe.

This place doth seeme an earthly Paradise,
Where on fit object every sense may feed,   *one*
And, fild with dainties that doe thence arise,
25 Of superfluitie helpe other's neede.
Yet no satietie that store doth breed,   *plenty*
    For, when the sense nigh surfets on delight,   *almost surfeits*
    New objects the duld-appetite doe whet.   *dulled*

This place I say doth border on a plaine,
30 Which step-dame Nature seems t'have made in scorne,
Where hungrie husbandmen have toild in vaine, *farmers*
And with the share the barren soile have shorne, *plough; turned*
Nor did they rest till rise of ruddie morne; *rosy dawn*
    Yet when was come the harvest of their hopes,
35   They for their gaine doe gather graineless crops. *fruitless*

It seemes of starv'd sterilitie the seat, *dead*
Where barren downes doe it inviron round, *surround*
Whose parched tops in summer are not wet,
And only are with snow in winter crown'd;
40 Only with barenesse they doe still abound;
    Or, if on some of them we roughnesse finde,
    It's tawnie-heath, badge of the barren rinde. *scrub; sign; bark*

In midst of these stands Croydon, cloath'd in blacke,
In a low bottome sinke of all these hills, *depression*
45 And is receipt of all the durtie wracke *repository; muck*
Which from their tops still in abundance trils; *always; drains*
The unpav'd lanes with muddie mire it fills:
    If one shower fall, or if that blessing stay, *cease*
    You may well smell, but never see your way.

50 For never doth the flowre-perfumed aire,
Which steals choice sweets from other blessed fields,
With panting breast take any resting there:
Nor of that prey a portion to it yeelds,
For those harsh hills his coming either shields, *rough; its; blocks*
55   Or else his breath, infected with their kisses, *poisoned*
    Cannot inrich it with his fragrant blisses. *delights*

And those who there inhabit, suting well   *corresponding*
With such a place, doe either nigro's seeme,   *negroes*
Or harbingers for Pluto, prince of hell,
60   Or his fire-beaters one might rightly deeme;   *stokers*
Their sight would make a soule of hell to dreame,
    Besmear'd with sut, and breathing pitchie smoake,   *soot*
    Which, save themselves, a living wight would choke.   *except for*

These, with the demi-gods still disagreeing,   *ever*
65   As vice with virtue ever is at jarre,
With all who in the pleasant woods have being
Doe undertake an everlasting warre,
Cuts downe their groves, and often doe them skarre;   *terrify*
    And in a close-pent fire their arbours burne,   *enclosed; groves*
70   While as the Muses can doe nought but mourne.

The other sylvans, with their sight affrighted,
Doe flee the place whereas these elves resort,   *fairies*
Shunning the pleasures which them erst delighted,
When they behold these groomes of Pluto's court;   *servants*
75 While they doe take their spoiles and count it sport   *treasure*
    To spoile these dainties that them so delighted,   *ravage; beauties*
    And see them with their ugly shapes affrighted.

To all proud dames I wish no greater hell,
Who doe disdaine of chastly profered love,
80 Then to that place confin'd there ever dwel;   *than*
That place their pride's dear price might justly prove;   *test*
For if, which God forbid, my deare should move   *propose*
    Me not come nie her, for to passe my troth,   *near; try my faith*
    Place her but there and I shall keepe mine oath.

[Grace to the sinner.]   [PH5]

O, how my sin-clog'd soule would soare aloft,
And scale the crystall-skie to seeke remed,   *cure*
But that foul sinne, wherewith I staine it oft,
Makes it to sinke through doubt of my misdeed.   *consciousness*
5   In scroule of guilty-conscience I reed   *transcript*
The rufull legend of my passed life,   *sorry tale; past*
The thought whereof maketh my heart to bleed,
Finding my foule offences are so rife.   *plenteous*

Feare makes me faint to finde such, and so many,
10 As there are ranked in that ragged roule;   *listed; sorry record*
Despaire doth say there was nere such in any,   *anyone*
Weeping cannot them wash nor heart condole.
God's wrath and justice sheweth to my soule,
For every sinne that must be satisfi'd,   *paid for*
15 What will become of me, with such a scroule,   *record*
Since "death the wage of sinne" is sure decreed.

Never to blooming-virgin truest mirror
Did represent beauty with more delight,
Then subtill Sathan, with affrighting-terror,
20 My guiltinesse doth shew me with despight.
What erst as trifles seemed to my sight   *first*
Now are death-worthy; my late-liking sin   *once-loved*
Is now displeasing, and would barre me quite
All hope of helpe, since such I wallowed in.

25 Hope to my heart my Saviour doth present,
With all his Passions prov'd for sinners' sake,   *undergone*
Yet none but hee that doth from heart repent,
Can use of that great satisfaction make.
I hold of him by a firme-faith must take,   *feu-farm; hold*
30 And all his sufferings to my selfe applie:
If penitence want not, or faith be weake,
Of heaven I know he cannot me denie.

But where's repentance for so foul a staine?
Why stint you, eies, continually to shower? *cease; weep*
35 The humid liquor of your moistening-raine
Doth make to sprout the faire repenting-flower.
Give teares no respite, nor no truce an houre,
And since with wandring-lookes you did offend:
With still-distilling-drops your canker skowre, *filth; cleanse*
40 With coming-care your passed scapes amend. *future discipline*

Ah, haplesse heart, why rend'st not with remorse, *wretched; split*
For quicke conceiving what the flesh hath wrought? *compunction at*
Hast thou, depraved, bent to ill thy force, *energy*
And knowes thy Maker thy most secret thought?
45 And wilt thou yet be negligent in ought
Thee may reclame, or with contrition wound?
Bleed, bleed to think that who so deare thee bought,
Thou'st crucifi'd againe, with thornes hast crown'd.

And thou, fraile flesh, shame not now to begin
50 Thee to submit to the reforming spirit;
Thinke of the by-waies thou has wandred in,
Which lead to hell and death, deserved merit.
Why art thou proud? Thou canst not heaven inherit;
Lie downe in dust, doe no workes of thine owne;
55 But what the soule commands, oh, willing heare it,
By thy obedience let its rule be knowne.

But, Lord, without thy sweet assisting grace,
I can doe nought, all my attempts are vaine;
I cannot come without thou call, alas; *unless*
60 Grant me this grace, and bring me home againe.
Let thy blest Spirit, Faith, Hope and Love remaine
Still in my soule: the flesh, the world and devil,
Deprive of power; let them no more raigne,
Or if they tempt, deliver me from evill.

65 Thou'rt not desirous that a sinner die,
But that hee may repent his sinnes and live;
Thou bidst the heavie laden come to thee,
And thou wilt ease the weight that doth him grieve.
Thou bidst him knocke, and thou wilt ope the leave   *postern*
70 Of that strict gate that leadeth unto blisse;   *strait*
Grant I repent, doe knocke, doe come, receave   *allow*
Life, lightning, entrance where no anguish is.   *enlightenment*

Lord, grant me grace my comming-daies to number,
To wisdome then I shall my heart applie;
75 Rowse me out of this lethargie and slumber,
Of sinne and slouth wherein I now doe lie.
Sinners, that seeing, soone shall draw thee nie,   *nigh*
Shunning base thoughts, their soules to thee shall raise,
And with a sweet consort shall pierce the skies,   *harmony*
80 Of thy great mercie, and eternall praise.

To Master Lithgow.   [PH6]

The double travell, Lithgow, thou hast tane,   *exertion*
One of thy feete, the other of thy brane,
Thee, with thy selfe doe make for to contend,
Whether the earth, thou'st better pac'd or pend.   *walked; written*
5 Would Malaga'es sweet liquor had thee crownd,
And not its trechry, made thy joynts unsound,   *treachery*
For Christ, King, Countrey, what thou there indur'd,
Not them alone, but therin all injur'd.   *everyone injured*
Their tort'ring racke, arresting of thy pace,   *torturing; stopping*
10 Hath barr'd our hope of the world's other face;   *denied*
Who is it sees this side so well exprest,
That with desire doth not long for the rest?
Thy travell'd countries, so described bee,

As readers thinke, they doe each region see;
15 Thy well compacted matter, ornat stile,   *assembled*
    Doth them oft in quick slyding time beguile.   *fleeting*
    Like as a maide, wandring in Flora'es boures,
    Confind to small time of few flitting houres,
    Rapt with delight of her eye-pleasing treasure,
20 Now culling this, now that flower takes such pleasure,
    That the strict time, to which she was confin'd,   *precise; restricted*
    Is all expir'd, whiles she thought halfe behind,   *still half*
    Or more remain'd: so each attracting line   *entrancing*
    Makes them forget the time they doe not tyne.   *lose*
25 But, since sweet future travell is cut short,
    Yet loose no time, now with the Muses sport,   *dally*
    That, reading of thee, after times may tell: *future ages*
    In travell, prose and verse, thou didst excell.

William Lithgow (c. 1582–c. 1645)

Of the authors featured in this anthology, Lithgow had by far the widest personal experience of the world, and his accounts of travels in Europe, around the Mediterranean, in North Africa, and in the Near East have made him famous. He may be compared with the Englishman Fynes Moryson (1566–1630), who visited many of the same countries, and both men provided literary accounts of explorations of exotic lands and peoples. The publications of Samuel Purchas (d. 1626) are likewise relevant, albeit that he preferred to stay at home and collect the tales of those more active than himself.

Lithgow's prose narratives are interspersed with poems expressing the author's reactions to what he has seen and described. Two aspects are therein displayed: on the one hand, the reporter's outward gaze of intellectual curiosity concerning the landmarks, the monuments, and the customs of foreign lands and cultures; on the other, the introspective adventurer's consideration of his personal and physical circumstances, his role as a vulnerable observer, and the memories of home which hitherto have shaped his national identity and now serve to maintain his psychological stability. The present selection from Lithgow's poetry shows both how the great outside world impinges on the mind of this early modern Scotsman, and also how Scotland appears within the imaginary of one who has travelled so far and experienced so much (van Heijnsbergen 2010).

As an author, Lithgow enjoyed popular success, with works printed at both London and Edinburgh. During the reign of James he published *A most delectable, and true discourse, of an admired and painefull peregrination from Scotland, to the most famous kingdomes in Europe, Asia and Affricke* [etc.] (London, 1614; reprinted 1616 and 1623) and *The pilgrime's farewell, to his native countrey of Scotland* [etc.] (Edinburgh, 1618), the latter consisting only of poetry. He addressed many poems to the great and the good of his day. In the 1630s and '40s further publications appeared, recycling to varying degrees material from his earlier works, and even after 1660 volumes continued to be published under his name.

Lithgow is not known to have studied at a university (cf. WL8/47–50) but his fondness for Latinisms shows that he had received at Lanark grammar school a solid grounding in the language. That he may have been something of an awkward outsider in the world of publishing may be surmised from a certain naivety in the dedications in his works, and from the fluctuating order of the names of those contributing liminary material. In 1614, for example, he secured such poems from John Murray, L.W. (unidentified), Robert Allen, William Alexander and Simion Grahame; in the 1616 reissue only Allen and Alexander appear; however, in that of 1623, Patrick Hannay, Robert Allen and John Murray were his supporters. The prefatory prose dedication in the first two editions of the *Most delectable discourse* was addressed, optimistically but feebly, 'To all Noble-minded Gentlemen, and Heroicke Spirits, in Court, Citty and Countrey', but in 1623 this was expanded to the perhaps more confident-sounding, but in reality equally unfocused, form, 'To all the Illustrious Nobles, and Generous Gentlemen, of his Maiesties most royall Court: the Honourable Earles and Lords, worshipfull Knights and Magistrates in City, County, and Shire, through all the three Kingdomes'. In the 1618 *Pilgrime's farewell*, the liminary verses were supplied by Lithgow himself, by an elusive 'Ignoto' (possibly the *nom de plume* of a contributor to *Mausoleum* (1613), the volume commemorating Prince Henry: see under Robert Allen, below), and by a mysterious 'W.R.' Shire's identification (1969: 229) of the latter with Sir Walter Ralegh seems improbable, given that the once great man in that year was in discredit after his final and unsuccessful expedition, and was in prison awaiting execution. The poems that follow in the 1618 volume were, with few exceptions, dedicated to a concatenation of notables, including the King, Prince Charles, the Archbishops of St Andrews and Glasgow, the other bishops, a group of earls, and many others. It would seem that Lithgow was not so much expecting to please individual patrons, as pitching for payment per poem.

A conspicuous element in Lithgow's writing is his pride in his Scottish, and in particular his Lanarkshire and south-west, background. The local dimension is reflected in his friends – Patrick Hannay, Robert Allen and the many others whom he names in WL8, nearly all of whom connect with the area of Clydesdale, Ayrshire, Galloway and Dumfries. Lithgow is of great and unusual interest by virtue of his degree of self-revelation, and through the circumstantial and corroborative details designed to augment the credibility of his adventures. Noticeable is the naïve power and rhetorical attraction of his writing, qualities especially praised by those who provided him with liminary verses. Lithgow's sturdy independence in confronting matters foreign and exotic is admirable, whether he be recording his trepidation at potential dangers to himself, or expressing wonderment at whatever an alien cultural tradition may have rendered venerable to its local devotees. For this poet, the metaphorical path up Parnassus was a hard slog, but he looked forward to an inspiring drink from the well of the Muses (WL3) when he got to the top.

[On Helen.]   [WL1]

A sonet made by the author upon Helen:
When hee pitched at Argo and Mycene in Sparta,   *made camp*
whence shee was ravished.

I would thy beauty, fairest of all dames,
Had never causd the jealous Greeks to move;
Thy eies from Greece to Ilion cast flames,
And burnt that Trojane with adulterat love.
5 He, captive-like, thy mercie came to prove,   *experience*
And thou, divorc'd, was ravish'd with a toy: *trifle*
Hee swore faire Helen was his dearest dove,
And thou a Paris swore for to enjoy.
Mourne may the ghosts of sometimes statelie Troy,
10 And curse that day thou saw the Phrygian coast;
Thy leacherous lust did Priam's pride destroy,
And many thousands for thy sake were lost.
      Was't Nature, Fortune, fancie, beauty, birth,
      That crossed thee so, to be a crosse on earth?   *trouble*

15 Some of thy sex, baptiz'd with thy curst name,
Crown'd with thy fate are partners in thy shame:
Helens are snakes which breed their lovers paine,
The mappes of malice, murder, and disdaine;   *patterns*
Helens are gulfes whence streames of blood do flow,
20 Rapine, deceit, treason, and overthrow.   *spoliation*
      Curst be thou hell, for hellish Helens' sakes,
      Still crossd be they that trust such stinging snakes.   *ever troubled*

[At Negroponte.]   [WL2]

A Dire, made by the Pilgrime in the Ile of Nigroponti:
When he was constrained by Greekes, to keepe centinell six daies   *sentinel*
(according to the times), who then stood in feare of two
Turkish gallies.   *galleys*

Carmina secessum scribentis, et otia quærunt
Me mare, me venti, me fera iactat hyems.

I wander in exile,
    As though my pilgrimage
Were sweete comedian scœnes of love   *joyful*
    Upon a golden stage.
5 Ah I, poore I, distress'd,
    Oft changing too and fro,
Am forc'd to sing sad obsequies
    Of this my swan-like wo,
A vagabonding guest,
10   Transported here and there,   *carried*
Led with the mercie-wanting winds   *merciless*
    Of feare, griefe, and dispaire.
Thus ever-moving I,
    To restlesse jorneyes thrald,   *bound*
15 Obtaines by Time's triumphing frownes
    A calling unrecal'd.   *vocation*
Was I preordain'd so,
    Like *tholos* ghost to stand,
Three times foure houres in twenty-foure,
20   With musket in my hand,
Ore-blasted with the stormes
    Of winter-beating snow,
And frosty-pointed hailstones hard
    On me poore wretch to blow?
25 No architecture, lo,   *shelter*
    But whirling-windy skies,

Or'd-syld with thundring claps of clouds,   *covered*
    Earth's center to surprise.
I, I, it is my fate   *alas, alas*
30   Allots this fatall crosse,   *trouble*
And reckons up in characters   *letters*
    The time of my time's losse.
My destiny is such
    Which doth predestine me,
35 To bee a mirrour of mishaps,
    A mappe of miserie.
Extremely do I live,
    Extreames are all my joy,
I finde in deep extreamities
40   Extreames, extreame annoy.
Now all alone I watch
    With Argoes' eyes and wit,   *understanding*
A cyphere twixt the Greekes and Turkes,   *nothing*
    Upon this rocke I sit.
45 A constrain'd captive I,
    Mongst incompassionate Greekes,
Bare-headed, downeward bowes my head
    And liberty still seekes.
But all my sutes are vaine,   *pleas*
50 Heaven sees my wofull state,
And makes me say: "my world's eye-sight   *knowledge*
    Is bought at too high rate."
Would God I might but live
    To see my native soyle,
55 Thrice happy in my happy wish
    To end this endlesse toyle.
Yet still when I record   *remember*
    The pleasant bankes of Clide,
Where orchards, castles, townes and woods
60   Are planted by his side,
And chiefly Lanerke, thou,
    Thy countrie's laureate lamp,   *celebrated*

In which this bruised bodie now
    Did first receive the stamp,
65 Then do I sigh and sweare
    Till death or my returne,
Still for to weare the willow wreathe   *always*
    In sable weed to mourne.
Since in this dying life
70   A life in death I take,
I'le sacrifice in spight of wrath
    These solemne vowes I make.
To thee, sweet Scotland, first
    My birth and breath I leave,   *bequeath*
75 To heaven my soule, my heart King James,
    My corps to lie in grave.
My staffe to pilgrimes I
    And pen to poets send,
My haire-cloth robe, and half-spent goods
80   To wandring wights I lend.   *men; give*
Let them dispone as though   *sort out*
    My treasure were of gold,
Which values more in purest pryse   *estimation*
    Then drosse ten thousand folde.
85 These trophies I erect
    Whilst memory remaines,
An epitomiz'd epitaph,   *concise*
    On Lithgow's restlesse paines:
My wil's enclos'd with love
90   My love with earthly blis,
My blis in substance doth consist
    To crave no more but this.
Thou first was, is, and last,
    Eternall of thy grace,
95 Protext, prolong, great Britaine's king,   *protect*
    His sonne, and royall race.

Amen.

The Epistle Dedicatorie: To the nine Pernassian Sisters,
the conservers of Helicon. [WL3]   *guardians*

You sacred Nymphes, which haunt Pernassus hill,
Where Soron flowes, and Demthis run at will,
Out from your two-topt valley shew me grace,
And on the lower listes meete mee apace.   *slopes*
5 Infuse in me the veine, I gladlie crave,   *talent*
To sing the sadde farewels my soyle must have.   *country*
And, yee Supreames, of this poore muse of mine   *Higher Beings*
As judges justlie censure this propine.   *offering*
I bring no stones from Pactole, Orient gemmes,
10 Nor bragges of Tagus, singes of golden stemmes;   *boast; boughs*
I search not Iris' square-spread clowdie winges,   *fully displayed*
Nor of the strange Herculian Hydra singes.
These franticke fansies I account as vaine: *mad*
In vulgare verse my farewels I explaine.
15 If I debord in stropiate lines, or then   *overflow; halting*
In methode faile, attache my wandring pen.   *arrest*
This veine of nature, and a mother wit,
Is more than haughtie schollers well can hit.   *refined*
So this small fondling, borne of your nine wombes,   *orphan*
20 Turns backe, and in your bosome her intombes.   *buries*
Then nurse your youngling, and repurge her veines,   *clear; talent*
And sende her backe in haste, to yeelde mee gaines.   *benefit*
In doing this, to you, and to your fame,
I consecrate my love, and her new name.

Yours, longing to bee drunke of Helicon,
William Lithgow.

To the Kinge's most excellent Majestie. [WL4]

Most mightie monarch of Great Britane's yle,
Vouchsafe to looke on this small mite I bring,
Which prostrate comes, cled in a barren style,
To thee, O kinglie poet, poets' king;
5   And if one gracious looke fall from thy face,
        O then my Muse and I finde life and grace.

Even as the sunne-shine of the new-borne day,
From Thetis' watrie trembling cave appears,
To decke the lowring leaves in fresh array,   *drooping*
10   Which sable night involves in frozen feares,   *wraps*
        And elitropian-like display their beautie,   *heliotropically*
        Unto their soveraigne, Phœbe, as bound in duetie,   *O Phœbus*

So thou, th'aurore of my prodigious night,   *dawn; great*
Lendes breath unto my long-worne wearie strife,   *tedious*
15   And from thy beames, my darknesse borrowes light,
To cheare the day of my desired life.   *brighten*
        So, great Apollo, as thou shin'st, so favour,
        That I, mongst thousands, may thy goodnessse savour.

Great pious paterne, patrone of thine owne,   *model of piety*
20   This ravisht age admires thy vertuous ways,   *deprived*
Whose princelie actes remotest partes have knowne,
And wee live happie, in thine happie dayes:
        Thy wisdome, learning, government and care,
        None can expresse their merites as they are.   *declare*
25   Long mayst thou raigne, and long may God above
Confirme thine heart, in thy great kinglie love.

The most humble and ingenochiat   *ingenuous*
farewell of William Lithgow.

[To Edinburgh.]   [WL5]

When Albion's gemme, great Britane's greatest glore,
Did leave the south this arcticke soyle to see,   *northern land*
Entred thy gates, whole miriads him before,   *crowds*
Glistring in golde, most glorious to the eye:
5   First Provost, Bailies, Counsel, Senate grave,
    Stood plac'd in ranks, their King for to receave.

In richest velvet gownes, they did salute him,
Where from his face appear'd true princelie love,   *whereupon*
And in the midst of noble troupes about him,
10   In name of all, grave Haye a speach did move.   ·   *pronounce*
    And, being horst, the Provost rode along
    With our Apollo, in that splendant throng.

What joyfull signes foorth from thy bosome sprang,
On thy faire streetes, when shin'd his glorious beames:
15   Shrill trumpets sound, drummes beat, and bells lowd rang,
The people shout: "Welcome, our royall James!"
    And when drawne near unto thy freedome's right,   *prerogative spot*
    His Highnessse stayde, and made thy Provost knight.   *stopped*

At last arriv'd at his great pallace gate,
20   There facound Nisbet, environ'd with throng,   *eloquent*
Made, in behalfe of Citie, Countrey, State,
A learned speach in ornate Latine tongue;
    And thy strong Maiden-Forte, impregnate boundes,   *unbreached walls*
    Gave out a world of shottes, strange thundring sounds.   *formidable*

25   The mustring-day drawne on, there came thy glore,   *parade-day; honour*
To see thy gallant youthes, so rich arrayde,
In pandedalian shows did shine like ore,   *intricate; gold*
And statelie they their martiall fittes displayed.   *trappings*
    With fethers, skarfs, loud drummes, and colours fleeing,   *sashes; flags flying*
30   First in the front, King James they goe a seeing.   *proceed to view*

Their salutations rent the air asunder;
And next to them, the Merchantes went in order,
Whose fire-flying volleyes, crackt like thunder,
And well conveigh'd, with sergeantes on each border.   *escorted; outer line*
35   So rul'd, so decent, and so arm'd a sight,   *ordered*
    Gave great contentment to their greatest light.   *luminary*

The worthie Trades, in rich approved rankes,
In comlie show with them they march'd along,
Whose deafning shottes resounded clowdie thankes,   *smoke-filled*
40 For our Kinge's welcome in their greatest throng.
    And in that noyse, mee thought, their honour'd fates   *actions*
    Proclaim'd that Trades maintain both crowns and states.

And more, sweet citie, thou didst feast thy Prince
Within a glasen house, with such delightes   *glazed pavilion*
45 And rare conceites, that few before or since   *exquisite devices*
Did see it paraleld in forraine sightes;
    And those fire-workes, on his birth-day at night,
    Gave to thy youthes more prayse, thy selfe more light.

All these triumphes, and moe, encrease thy fame,   *more*
50 Which, breiflie toucht, prolixity I shunne.
And for my part, great Metrapole, thy name   *capital city*
All-where I'll prayse, as twise past I have done.   *everywhere*
    And now I bidde with teares, with eyes which swell,   *overflow*
    Thee, Scotland's seate, deare Edinburgh, farewell.   *capital*

[To Etna.]   [wL6]

High standes thy toppe, but higher lookes mine eye,
High soares thy smoake, but higher my desire;
High are thy roundes, steepe, circled, as I see,   *flanks*
But higher farre this breast, whiles I aspire;
5   High mountes the furie of thy burning fire,
But higher farre my aymes transcende above;
High bendes thy force through midst of Vulcane's ire,
But higher flies my sprite with winges of love;   *spirit*
High preasse thy flames the chrystall air to move,   *press*
10   But higher farre, the scope of mine engine;   *mind*
High lyes the snow, on thy proude toppes, I prove,   *find*
But higher up ascendes my brave designe;
        Thine height cannot surpasse this clowdie frame   *layer of clouds*
        But my poore soule the highest heavens doth claime.
15   Mean-while with paine I climbe to view thy toppes,
        Thine hight makes fall from me ten thousand droppes.

Yours affectionate, William Lithgow.

[To the Clyde.]   [WL7]

How sweetlie slide the streames of silent Clyde,
And smoothlie runne, betweene two bordring bankes,
Redoubling oft his course, seems to abyde,   *doubling back*
To greete my travelles with ten thousand thankes,
5   That I, whose eyes, had view'd so manie floodes,
     Deign'd to survey his deepes and neighb'ring woods.   *depths*

Thrise famous Clyde, I thanke thee for thy greeting,
Oft have thy brethren easde me of my paine;
Two contrarie extreames we have in meeting,
10 I upward climbe, and thou fall'st doune amaine: *with force*
     I search thy spring, and thou the westerne sea.   *seek*
     So farewell flood, yet stay, and mourne with me.

Goe, steale along with speede the Hyberne shore,   *Irish*
And meete the Thames upon the Albion coast;
15 Joyne your two armes, then, sighing both, deplore
The fortunes which in Britane I have lost,
     And let the water-nymphes, and Neptune too,
     Refraine their mirth, and mourne, as rivers doe.

To thee, great Clyde, if I disclose my wronges,
20 I feare to loade thee with excesse of griefe;
Then may the ocean, bereave me of thy songes,   *deprive*
And swallow up thy plaintes and my reliefe.
     Tell onelie Isis so, and so, and so;
     Conceale the trueth, but thunder foorth my woe.

25 My bloode, sweet Clyde, claimes intrest in thy worth,
Thou in my birth, I in thy vaprous beames;   *misty light*
Thy breadth surmountes the Tweede, the Tay, the Forth,
In pleasures thou excell'st in glistering streames.
     Seeke Scotland for a fort, O then Dunbertaine,
30   That for a trophee standes at thy mouth certaine.   *secure*

Ten miles more up, thy well-built Glasgow standes,
Our second metrapole, of spirituall glore;   *chief town*
A citie deckt with people, fertill landes,
Where our great king gotte welcome, welcome's store;   *profusion*
35   Whose cathedrall and steeple threat the skies,
And nine archt bridge out ou'r thy bosome lies.

And higher up, there dwelles thy greatest wonder,
Thy chiefest patrone, glorie of thy boundes,   *lord; lands*
A noble marques, whose great vertues thunder
40 An æquivox backe to thy pleasant soundes;   *fitting reply*
    Whose greatnesse might command thine, head to foote,   *completely*
From Aricke stone, unto the Ile of Boote.

As thou alongst his palace slides in haste,
Stay, and salute his marquesadiane dame: *marchioness*
45 That matchlesse matrone, mirrour of the west,
Deignes to protect the honour of thy name.
    So, ever famous flood, yeelde them their duetie,
They are the onelie, lampes, of thy great beautie.

And now, faire-bounded streame, I yet ascende,   *fair-banked*
50 To our old Lanerke, situate on thy bankes;
And, for my sake, let Corhouse Lin disbende   *break out*
Some thundring noyse to greete that towne with thanks.
    There was I borne. Then, Clyde, for this my love,
As thou runnes by, her auncient worth approve.   *acknowledge*

55 And higher up, to climbe to Tinto Hill,
The greatest mountaine that thy boundes can see,   *lands*
There stand to circuite, and strive t'runne thy fill,   *wait to circle*
And smile upon that barron dwells by thee: *baron*
    Carmichell, thy great friende, whose famous sire,
60   In dying, left not Scotland such a squire.

In doing these requestes, I shall commende thee,
To fertile Nyle, and to the sandie Jore,
And I recorde, the Danube latelie sende thee,   *recall; sent*
A thousand greetinges from his statelie shore.
65   Thus, for thy paines, I shall augment thy glorie,
And write thy name, in time's eternall storie.
So, ever-pleasant flood, thy losse I feele,
In breathing foorth this woorde: Faire Clyde, fareweele.

[Farewell to Scotland.]   [WL8]

Tu vero, O mea tellus, et genitorum patria,
Vale: nam viro licet plurimum malis obruatur
Nullum est suavius solum, quam quod nutriuit eum.
    Eurip[ides], in *Phœnice*

To thee, O dearest soyle, these mourning lines I bring,   *country*
And with a broken bleeding breast, my sad farewell I sing.
Nowe, melting eyes, dissolve; O, windie sighes, disclose,
The airie vapoures of my griefe, sprung from my watrie woes,
5 And let my dying-day no sorrow uncontrole,   *disturb*
Since on the planets of my plaintes, I move about the Pole.
Shall I, O restlesse I, still thwarting, run this round?   *always frustrated*
Whiles resting mortalles restlesse mount, I mouldarize the ground   *rot upon*
And in my wandring long, in pleasure, paine, and greife,
10 Begges mercie of the mercielesse, of sorrow, sorrowe's cheife.
Sith after two returnes my merites are forgot,
The third shall ende, or else repaire, my long estranging lot.   *alienating fate*
Then kindlie come distresse, a figge for forraine care,
  I gladlie in extreames must walke, whiles on this masse I fare.   *earth; travel*
15 The Moorish frowning face, the Turkish awfull brow,
The Saracene and Arabe blowes, poore I, must to them bow.
These articles of woe, my monster-breeding paine,

As pendicles on my poore state, unwisht for, shall remaine. *attachments*
Thus fraught with bitter cares, I close my malcontentes, *grievances*
20 Within this kalendar of greife, to memorize my plaintes. *record*
And to that westerne soyle, where Gallus once did dwell,
To Gallowedian barrons, I impart this my farewell. *disclose*
A forraine debt I owe, brave Garlees, to thy worth,
And to my genrous Kenmure knight, more than I can sing forth.
25 To Bombee I assigne lowe homage for his love: *render*
And to Barnbarough kinde and wife, abreast whiles breath may move.
Unto the worthy Boyde, in Scotland, first in France,
I owe effectes of true good-will, a low-laid countenance.
And thou, grave Lowdon lord, I honour with the best,
30 And on the noble Eglinton my strong affections rest.
Kilmaers I admire for quicke and readie wit, *sharp; intellect*
And grave Glencairne, his father deare, on honour's top doth sit.
And to thee, gallant Rosse, well seene in forraine partes,
I sacrifice a pilgime's love amongst these noble heartes.
35 From Carlile unto Clyde, that southwest shore I knowe,
And by the way Lord Harries I remembrance duelie owe. *near that route*
In that small progresse I, surveying all the west,
Even to your houses, one by one, my lodging I adrest;
Your kindnesse I imbrac'd; as not ingrate, the same *ungrateful*
40 I memorize to future times, in eternized fame. *record*
Amongst these long goodnightes, farewell, yee poets deare,
Grave Menstrie, true Castalian fire, quicke Drummond in his spheare. *orbit*
Brave Murray, ah, is dead, Aiton supplies his plaice,
And Alen's high Pernassian veine rare poems doth embrace.
45 There's manie moe well knowne, whome I cannot explaine, *set out*
And Gordon, Semple, Maxwell too, have the Pernassian veine.
And yee colledgians all, the fruites of learning grave, *students*
To you I consecrate my love, enstalde amongst the leave. *grouped; rest*
First to you Rectors, I, and Regentes, homage make, *professors*
50 Then from your spiring breasts, brave youths, my leave I *ambitious*
humbly take.
And, Scotland, I attest, my witnesse reignes above, *swear*

In all my worlde-wide wandring ways, I kept to thee my love;
To manie forraine breastes, in these exyling dayes,
In sympathizing harmonies, I sung thine endless prayse;
55 And where thou wast not knowne, I registred thy name, *made known*
Within their annalles of renowne, to eternize thy fame. *records*
And this twise have I done, in my twise long assayes, *attempts*
And now the third time, thrise I wil thy name unconquered raise.
Yea, I will stampe thy badge, and seale it with my blood, *impress; sign*
60 And if I die in thy defence, I thinke my end is good.
So, dearest soyle, O deare, I sacrifice, now see *beloved*
Even on the altar of mine heart a spotlesse love to thee.
And Scotland, now farewell, farewell for manie yeares:
This echo of farewell brings out from mee a world of teares.

[Love known and unknown.]   **[WL9]**

To his unknowne knowne, and knowne unknown, love,
These now knowne lines an unknowne breast shall move.

Selfe-flattring I, deceiver of my selfe,
Opinion's slave, rul'd by a base conceate, *notion*
Whome ev'erie winde naufragiates on the shelf *wrecks; shallows*
Of apprehension, jealous of my state; *condition*
5   Who guides mee moste, that guide I most misknow,
Suspectes the shaddow for a substant show. *solid*

I still receive the thing I vomite out,
Conceives againe imaginarie wracke; *react; disaster*
I stable stand, and yet I stand in doubt,
10 Gives place to one, when two repulles me backe. *room; haul*
I kindle fire, and that same fire I quench,
And swim the deepes, but dare not downwarde drench. *seas; dive*

I grieve at this, prolong'd in my desire,
And I rejoyce that my delay is such;
15 I trie, and knowes my tryall may aspire,   *have expectations*
But flees the place that should this tyme avouch.   *confirm*
    In stinging smartes my sweete convertes in sowre,
    I build the hive, but dare not sucke the flowre.

Well, honney combe, since I am so faint hearted,
20 That I flee backe when thou unmaskst thy face;
Thou shalt bee gone, and I must bee decarted,   *discarded*
Such doubtfull stayes enhaunce, when wee imbrace.   *delays; are keen*
    Farewell, wee two divided are for ever,
    Yet undivided whilst our soules dissever.   *as long as*

    Thine, as I am mine,
    William Lithgow.

[A figge for the world.]   [WL10]

Now, hauing seene most part of thy selfe glore,   *self-glorification*
Great kingdomes, ilands, stately courts, rich townes,
Most gorgeous showes, pomp-glory, deck't renownes,   *robed honours*
Herbagious fields, the pelage-beating shore,   *ocean-repelling*
5 Propitious princes, prelats, potent crownes,   *benevolent*
Smoake-shadow'd times, curst churles, misers, clownes,   *obscure*
Impregnat forts, devalling floods, and more,   *untaken; waterfalls*
Earth-gazing heights, vale-curling plaines in store,   *towering; curving*
Court-rysing honours, throwen in envie's frownes,   *Dissolution; awarded*
10 Worme-vestur'd works, enamild arts, wit's lore,   *silk-clad; prettified*
Masse-marbled mansions, minerals, coyned ore,   *ponderous; coinage*
State-superficiall showes, swift-gliding moones: *ceremonial; fleeting*
    I loath thy sight. Pale streames staine watry eyne,   *eyes*
    Whose glorious shades evanish, no more seene.   *fade away*

❧ ❧ ❧

15 So world, farewell, since I'me included now	*shut in*
Within a lesser world, so times allow,	*circumstances*
In a sequestrat house, incloystred fast,	*secure; shut off*
For many a cloyster, I have seene and past.	
And yet no monke I am, much lesse a priest,	
20 Nor bald Chartuzian, although now I feast	*Carthusian*
Within their roome; for that unworthy race	*house; lowly*
Made way to me, as worthy of the place.	*deserving*
Yet I'me religious, mine order I'le expresse,	*declare*
Brave sprits, and honest men, false in distresse.	*through misery*
25 The worke, the founder, I admire: what than?	
The like good deed was never done by man.	*similar*
Nor all the merits Italy and Spaine	
And Rome can forge, shall match this deed againe.	
Well may his ghost be pleas'd, to heare each day	
30 Such sacrifice of prayers, that make way	
To pierce the highest clouds. O soule most blest,	
That both in earth and heaven finds praise and rest!	
But I may thanke the Spaniard, not my Fortune,	
That drove me here, yet both have beene importune;	*demanding*
35 Shee strumpet-like, still fickle, false, and blind,	*ever*
Growes deafe and dumbe, when reason sutes to finde.	*pleads; understand*
Away, thou wicked weird, away, curst frownes,	*fate*
That man's desert subverts, regards base clownes,	*undermines; rewards*
And welcome, Spaniard, with thy tortring rack,	
40 And cruell torments, fatall in my wracke.	*ruin*
They can no paine inflict, no imposition,	*sentence*
So holy is their holy Inquisition:	
Nor yet suspect a friend for deadly fo,	
Nor rack a man to try how matters go;	*stretch on rack*
45 Me thinkes this rack, compos'd of plankes and ropes,	
Was by the divell devis'd, confirm'd by Popes;	
Such tiranny is strange to pagan blood,	*foreign*
For hell it selfe can not be halfe so rude.	*cruel*

Thus was I cross'd, and now made for a nones   *persecuted; while*

50   To live – poore living man – on dead man's bones.

Then welcome, shadow of eternall pleasure,   *fore-sight*

The charter of my house, is heavenly treasure,   *promised wealth*

Where, hating of this world, the world to come

I still may looke for; ther's the totall somme.   *entire thing*

55   I am content with my poore lazar lot,   *wretch's*

Heavens may recall, what's here on earth forgot:

I must not clayme desert, reward, respects,

The weake one stumbles, where the great neglects.

A patient minde shall undergoe my fate,

60   In changing thoughts, I cannot change my state,   *condition*

And if I had ten worlds, more than this one,

The grave is all I'le get, when I am gone.

The monarch, sheepheard, mighty men, and meane,   *lowly*

When dead, have one resemblance, judg'd by heaven:

65   No difference is made: like deed, like doome:

All rot, all turne in dust, all must consume.

And can I better live, then learne to die,

That, dying, I may live eternally.

Robert Allen (fl. 1613–25)

With the exception of an essay by Shire (1974), almost no attention has been paid to the place of Allen (or Alen/Allan/Allane/Allyne) in the literary history of Scotland. Nonetheless, though his voice is that of a minor poet, it is a distinctive one within the Jacobean Parnassus. Liminary contributions by Allen appear in the printed volumes of William Lithgow and Patrick Hannay, and several other poems by him are found transcribed in EUL MS Laing.III.436, which is a collection of Jacobean and Caroline lyric verse, both English and Scottish. It is possible, as Shire has claimed, that still more items in that manuscript may, unrecognised, be his.

The first known poem by Allen is a couplet (RAL1) published in *Mausoleum* (Edinburgh, 1613), the collective memorial volume inspired by the death (6 November 1612) of Prince Henry. Other contributors included Walter Quin, William Drummond, Hugh Holland (in Latin), George Wither, George Chapman, William Rowley, and the anonymous 'Ignoto' (according to Laing (1825: vi), supposed by some to be Sir Walter Ralegh). This volume therefore illustrates the contacts and cooperation between poets from the two nations, and shows that Allen was considered a worthy associate of such distinguished company. Allen's first independent publication (which includes RAL2) celebrated the marriage (14 February 1613) of Princess Elizabeth and Frederick V, Elector of the Palatinate: *Teares of Joy, at the happy departure from Great Britaine, of the two Paragons of the Christian world . . . Prince and Princesse Palatines* [etc.].

Despite his friendships in England, Allen remained proud of his Scottish background, and in the general dedication-poem of *Teares of Joy*, addressed to Sir Thomas Erskine, 'Captaine of His Majestie's Guards', he mentions that his 'simple Muse . . . liv'd obscurely on the banke of Clide'. The link to Lanarkshire and its principal river is confirmed in another poem, known only in manuscript (RAL5). It is not surprising therefore that Allen should be named in a farewell poem by another Clydesdale man, William Lithgow (WL8/44). Given that in 1614 Allen addressed Lithgow as 'deere friend, Countriman, and Condisciple' (RAL3), the two men may have overlapped at school in Lanark, or perhaps had had the same teacher. Significantly, of those who provided liminary verses to Lithgow's *Most delectable discourse*, it is only Allen whose name occurs in all three early editions (1614, '16 and '23) –

a detail suggestive of a strong friendship. It seems that Lithgow and Allen – together with Patrick Hannay and not improbably some of the further associates named in WL8 – comprise a literary and social coterie with roots in Lanarkshire and the south-west of Scotland; this coterie would later have acquired a London dimension.

Allen structures RAL5 on a search for his father's supposedly lost sword. This image should be understood in the light of a 'father's sword' motif encountered in a sonnet by an earlier poet of the west of Scotland, Alexander Montgomerie (Parkinson 2000: I, 108). Allen tells that, in his attempts to recover the paternal heirloom, he began by studying philosophy. However, since, like Lithgow, he does not seem to have enrolled at the nearby University of Glasgow, the philosophy is likely to have been gained from life rather than the library. At any rate, the hopeful young man must have found stoicism a disappointment, for, failing to find the sword in places where tranquillity of mind is cultivated, he betakes himself to scenes of active life in London, where he investigates the worlds of finance, shipbuilding and politics. From none of these can he get any satisfaction. Disappointed, he departs to fight in the Netherlands against Spain, but even in that course of life his quest is unsuccessful. Finally, and in desperation, he tries his luck at Court, where he is disgusted to find himself reduced to the level of the hypocritical courtiers who shed their coats with every season.

Sartorial imagery is even more strongly present in RAL6, in which the poet's immutable jerkin is ironically commended for seeing him through a period of some three years, while the Court is criticised for its frequent changes of habiliment. Allen's vein of satire may perhaps stem from a reserve regarding the eirenic policy of the King, which was directed towards keeping the country out of Continental wars (cf. RAL7). The poet may have thought along different lines, preferring to gird on his father's blade; but whether he himself perished by the sword is unknown.

[On Prince Henry.]   [RAL1]

I liv'd three kingdomes' hope, foes' terror, parents' life,
I di'de their dearest losse, their joy, their endlesse griefe.

❧

To Fredericke, Prince Palatine of Rhine, Duke of Bavaria, etc.   [RAL2]

Great off-spring of a high Imperiall race   *descent*
And now allyed with a Royall kinde,   *dynasty*
Whose worth exceeds thy years, whose glorious place   *position*
Is more then matched by a generous minde,
5   Whose outward grace, and inward gifts are such,
      As highest veines cannot expresse too much.   *talents*

Yet neither doth thy race, nor place, nor worth,
Nor these rare parts of body, and of minde,
Nor all thy merits, halfe so much set forth   *constitute*
10 Thy happinesse, as being now combin'd
      In love and life with one whose vertues shall
      Adde new renowne to race and place, and all.

Great *Cæsar*-maker, thou whose powerfull vote,   *Elector*
Can raise a subject to the Imperiall hight;
15 Thou canst make Emperours, and hast thou not
In creating an Empresse equall might?
      Expresse it then upon thy better halfe,   *employ*
      And, in advancing her, raise up thy selfe,
      That, both together gracing *Cæsar's* chaire,   *throne*
20   Thy sonne may bee *Arch-sewer* to his sire.

To my deere Friend, Countriman, and Condisciple,   *fellow pupil*
       William Lithgow.   [RAL3]

Rest, noble spirits, in your native soiles,   *stay; minds*
Whose high-bred thoughts on deare-bought sights are bent,
Renowned Lithgow by his brave attempt
Hath eas'd your bodies of a world of toyles.

5   Not like to some, who wrongfully retaine
God's rarest giftes within themselves ingrost,   *hoarded*
But what thou hast attain'd with care and cost,   *expense*
Thou yeelds it gratis to the world againe.   *freely*

Upon the bankes of wonder-breeding Clide,
10   To these designes thy heart did first assent;   *plans*
One way, indeede, to give thy selfe content,
But more to satisfie a worlde beside.

Thy first attempt in excellence of worth
Beyond the reach of my conceit's confinde,
15   But this thy second pilgrimage of minde,
Where all thy paines are to the world set forth,
    In subiect, frame, in methode, phrase, and stile,   *structure*
    May match the most unmatched in this ile: *outstanding*
    But this renownes thee most, t'have still possest   *makes famous*
20   A constant heart, within a wandring brest.

In Imaginem. [RAL4]

[On Hannay's image]

T'expresse the author's face, brasse, inke and art
Have done their best, but for his better part,
The Grecian *Philomel* in English tongue,
Marian, A Husband, Elegies well sung,

5 Have given a touch – as in a clowdie night   *indication*
Obscured Phœbe shewes her vailed light,
And at some turns, where clouds doe ill cohere,   *moments; open*
With full beames shines out from her silver sphere,
So are his shaded passages of wit,   *painted*

10 Where birds doe speake, and women in a fit.   *passion*
Who could so well have told faire Marian's wrong,
Or taught the Athenian bird a London song,
As he to whom the depth of love is knowne,
And carving others can cut out his owne?   *delineating*

15   Which in some part is here so well exprest,
     None but himselfe can represent the rest.

Father's Sourde. [RAL5]

Lowe upon Clyde, my father crossed at foorde;
His trustie sourde into the revir ffell;
The streames was ranke, the windes were at discord,   *strong*
And tossed the strugelinge mettall non can tell   *weapon*

5 Upon what coast, how farr, or whare about: *bank*
But lost it is, and I must find it out.

Ane universall searche I undertooke,
And first at scooles I plummed the sacred weell.   *explored; well*
The Learned Sisters told me I mistooke,

10 For gownes and sourdes togither cannot dwell;
Philosophie taught me for to beare the greeff,
But for the loss no airt culd yeeld releeff.   *theory*

To London nixt, from Ratliff to the Strande,
Both lawfull and forbiden pairtes I rainge;   *traverse*
15 They asked me what I lacked. My strainge demande
Meade Cheapsyde mute, amased the whole Exchainge;
Off peace, of warrs, of traphik there was worde,   *commerce*
But all were silent when I named a swourde

To warrs I went, and served the States for gaine,   *pay*
20 God knowes but small, yet free from hurt or foile;   *defeat*
The Lombard proved ane greater foe then Spaine,
While I was yet alive it took my spoile;   *rewards*
Longe monthes, short pay, hard bed, harder boord   *accommodation*
Meade me returne without my father's sourd.

25 To Court I come. What hope to find it heir,
Whare useles iron disdanefullie is throwen
O[n] dwarffes and pages? If the hilts be deare,   *handles*
The hingers riche, the blade may pase unknowen.   *hangers; untested*
My father's hunge in leather plaine, ungilt:
30 A surer edge, thocht not so proude ane hilt.   *sharper; fancy*

Lyk Cadmus, sent from his father to repeat   *seek*
His ravisht sister, hopeinge nothing less,
After strainge fortounes in a forrane seat   *land*
At last turned serpent, such is my success.
35 From sourd, from soyle, from father's sight estrainged,
Into a snakeinge courteir I am chainged,   *slippery*
    Where, serpent-lyke, it may fall to my lott,
    That on[c]e a yeare I may renew my coat.

Allan's Jerkin. [RAL6]

The lamp of heaven that measures out the yeare
Hath three tymes chainged the nature of the tyme, *season*
The winter's spent and doth no more apeire, *exhausted*
The springe's expyred, and summer past his prime;
5   And since men chainge with chainge of tyme, it's strainge –
Tyme chaingeinge thryce – that I can never chainge.

While baseless groomes in cuntrie or at Court *male servants*
I[n] lightest suites are to the skin cut out,
And everie slave must with the seasoun sort, *correspond*
10 I still my winter's burden beare about;
   And lyk a wreath, seeke of some cold disease, *ill from*
   In midle of July in a jerkin freize.

Yet thocht I cannot to the tyme be suited, *matched*
Me thinkes the tyme doth suit itself to me: *fit*
15 The plesant floures are from the ground upruted,
Brount up and gone; the fertile earthe we see *burnt*
   For want of raine all withered, wan and drie,
   Lyk old December lookes, and so doe I.

But since my jerkine is so drie and bare
20 That feare therof withhold the raine so longe, *deter*
Least it suld suck up all that heavin can spare,
I'le not be guiltie of so great a wronge.
   Coat, thow salt off, to let the warld have raine;
   When all is wett, coat, thow sal't on againe.

25 And yet, poore freze, thocht thow be drie and old, *grogram*
Thy use to me hath bein exceedinge great:
First thow was proofe against the pearseinge cold,
Now thow resists the force of Phebus' heat.
   Wilt thow but last an uther winter's spite, *harshness*
30   I'le bury the, and on thy grave I'le write:

   Heare lyes a coat, that patient owercomer *survivor*
   Off two* sharp winters, and a burning sumer.

Upon the lait King James.   [RAL7]

He that keept peace at home, meade peace abroade,
Left peace to all, rests now in peace with God.

Sir Robert Kerr, Earl of Ancram (1578–1654)

This poet must be distinguished from his cousin, contemporary and namesake, the dashing and scandal-ridden courtier Sir Robert Kerr/Carr, the favourite of King James, raised to Viscount Rochester (1611) and Earl of Somerset (1613).

The poet Kerr was Groom of the Bedchamber in the household of Prince Henry, and after the latter's death, Gentleman of the Bedchamber to Prince Charles. He was well known to John Donne, who addressed several letters to him (Laing 1875: ii, 507–16). For '[his] own recreation' he made versifications of ten psalms, and in April 1624 sent them to his son, then in Paris (where he may have coincided with George Lauder); several of Kerr's psalms were done from the neo-Latin paraphrases of George Buchanan. His sonnet on the solitary life (RK2) was written at Court in December 1624, when arrangements were being finalised for the marriage of Charles to Princess Henrietta Maria of France. On Charles's visit to Edinburgh in 1633, Kerr, a staunch royalist, was elevated to Earl of Ancram. After the execution of the king (1649) the poet retired to the Low Countries, where he died in obscurity. His son, following his marriage (1630) to Lady Anne Kerr, 3rd Countess of Lothian, in 1631 became 1st Earl of Lothian in his own right. He later supported the party of the National Covenant.

In a letter to William Drummond, Kerr expressed diffidence about his own poetic talents. His sonnet, which in its bracing frankness owes something to the style of the Metaphysicals, is interesting as an expression of the neo-Stoicism which exerted a strong influence on the minds of contemporary minds both in Britain and in Europe (Allan 2000), and which clearly affected this poet who was closely associated with the Court.

Psalme I. [RK1]

The man is blest whom no lewd counsell can   *impious gathering*
Intice to turne from the right path aside,
Nor sit with the ill-naturd scornfull man,
Nor in the way of sinners will abyde;
5 But on God's law doth studye day and night,
  And takes great care how he may keep it right.

He shall be like a goodlye tree that grows
Neare to a river, where no sumer's heate,
Nor winter with his eager frosts and snows,
10 Doth scorch the leaves, nor yet the branches beate;
  Nor doth the owner's greedy hope deceave,
  But yeelds him as much fruit as he can crave.

With the ungodlye it shall not be so,
Because they doe neglect the Lord's command.
15 Looke how a whirling wind the dust doth blow,
Or how the chaff from out the corne is fan'd;   *winnowed*
  So shall the Lord them utterly deface,   *overwhelm*
  That where they have beene none can shew the place.

And when the Judge shall in the clouds appeare
20 To give true judgment upon good and bad,
The godly may looke up with joyfull cheere,
But the ungodly fearfully and sad;
  For he that all our secret thoughts doth view,
  Will give each one according to his due.

In praise of a solitary life. [RK2]

Sweet solitary life, lovely dumb joy,   *quiet*
That need'st no warnings how to grow more wise
By other men's mishaps, nor the annoy
Which from sore wrongs done to one's self doth rise;   *great*
5 The morning's second mansion, truth's first friend,   *residence*
Never acquainted with the world's vain broils;
Where the whole day to our own use we spend,   *benefit*
And our dear time no fierce ambition spoils;   *valuable*
Most happy state, that never tak'st revenge
10 For injuries received, nor do'st fear
The Court's great earthquake, the griev'd truth of change,   *painful*
Nor none of falshood's savoury lyes do'st hear;   *pleasing*
    Nor know'st hope's sweet disease, that charms our sense,
    Nor it's sad cure, dear-bought experience.

George Lauder (1603–1670)

Lauder's development is that of a Scoto-British poet who became a Scoto-British European. The present anthology contains only poems by him written in the Jacobean age, though he continued writing poetry into the reign of Charles II. Around 1625 he took the important step of joining the army, and left Britain in connection with the hapless campaign on the Ile de Ré led by the King's favourite, George Villiers, Duke of Buckingham. His subsequent work arises from and reflects his military experience on the Continent, his reaction to political developments in Britain, and his contacts with prominent Protestants and intellectuals in the Netherlands – whether Dutch, French, German, English or Scottish.

Two years after graduating from Edinburgh University, Lauder published *The Pope's New-Years Gift* (St Andrews, 1622), consisting of translations and imitations of neo-Latin anti-Catholic and anti-Papal satires, mostly the work of Italian writers of the Renaissance. This first collection, after undergoing revision and anglicisation, reappeared at London in the following year, under the title of *The Anatomie of the Romane Clergie*. Between these two publications, Lauder, in a farewell poem (GL1) tinged with neo-Stoicism, took his leave of his family and his home province of Lothian. He profoundly admired William Drummond of Hawthornden, and through such contact it is possible that he could have encountered Ben Jonson on the latter's visit to Scotland. The young Lauder was attracted to the incisive and witty manner characteristic of the Roman epigrammatist Martial. There is some irony in the fact that the writings of Italian Catholic poets (e.g. Petrarch, Sannazaro, Lelio Capilupi) should have furnished material to a fervent Scottish Protestant, and that the young, smartly up-to-date and ambitious poet should choose as his models humanists who lived and wrote a century or more earlier (GL2). Whereas George Buchanan and others had criticised the Roman Catholic Church in neo-Latin verse admired by the learned throughout Europe, Lauder opted for the vernacular, in which he combined Classical-style epigram and neo-Latin mannerisms within his lively vein of Protestant satire.

Once Lauder had moved to London, he embarked on the search for patronage, and he clearly familiarised himself with the style of metropolitan poets, such as Robert Ayton. In 1624 he is found in Paris, perhaps in connection with the negotiations for the marriage of Prince Charles to Henrietta

Maria; when there, he may have overlapped with William Kerr (son of the poet Sir Robert). Lauder's one known amatory lyric (GL4) is said to have been composed in the French capital. With its well-turned but somewhat cynical stanzas, it points the way ahead to the style often designated as 'Caroline'.

[Farewell to home.]   [GL1]

Launcht from my native shore, forth in the world's great maine,	*ocean*
No stormy blast of Fortune's frownes shall drive me home againe;	
For patience is my shippe, though silly-like, yet strong,	*seeming weak*
Whose plankes are proofe of Envie's shot, and bide both	*survive*
scorne and wrong;	

5 Foresight my compasse is, sweete pleasure is my carde,   *sextant*
  Skill steeres the sterne, and all my hopes as anchors are prepared.
  Thus fraughted with desire farre distant shores to see,   *laden*
  Scotland farewell, I goe to seeke what is ordain'd for me.
  The world my country is, through which I'le wandring go,
10 And think my home where ere I come, the heavens commaund me so;
  The Articke snowey hils, or Affrick's sun-burnt sand,
  I'le thinke them as my home-bred haunts and as my native land.
  For with the savage wild in concord I can live,
  And have as great content when poore as Crœsus' rent could give.   *riches*
15 I scorne the idol Wealth, which all the world adores:
  To worship Earth's unworthy drosse a worthy mind abhorres.
  Yet if it be my chance, or fates haue so conspir'd
  To powre a showre of Tagus' ore on me that least desir'd;
  And if I cannot shunne, but must of force be rich,
20 What then? that scurvy stamped pelfe cannot my mind bewitch,
  Nor yet withdraw my thoughts, or force affection so,
  As to forget my Arete, my soule's sweet mistris: no.
  Might I have Midas' wish, and all the Lidian's store,   *wealth*
  My minde to me an empire is, whose worth I value more;
25 And when the time shall come, if so it be decreed,

In which that unexpected wealth is heaped on my head,
I'le give the world to know how little I regard it,
And raise my ruin'd friends with it whom Fortune hath discardit.
If I reserve a share, my selfe to entertaine,   *support*
30 In honest state I crave no more, the surest lot is meane.   *safest; small*
The treasure I esteeme is closed in my brest,
More worth to me then all the gold within the miser's chest;
And that no time, nor theefe, nor tyrant can bereave,   *steal*
In having that I have enough, and for no losse can grieve.
35 Let Fortune's minions laugh, who have no God but gold,   *darlings*
And let the World say what it will, thus Lauder is resolv'd.
And therefore I will go, that happy lot to find,   *fate*
Which was at my nativity by heavens to me assign'd.
Farwell then, famous shire, where first I saw this light,
40 Great Brittain's garden, Louthiane, I must foregoe thy sight.
Farwell, my worthy Sire, the honor of thy race,   *family*
Whose shining glory doth eclips thy grandsire's with disgrace;
Heavens make the happy here, and grant thee Nestor's yeares,
Then give the life's eternall joyes above the roling sphæres.
45 Farwell, my loving Dame, from out whose fertill wombe,   *mother*
This body free from all the markes of Nature's scorne did come;
Long may thou live in joy, and long enjoy thy mate,
To sympathise with him in all, health, honors, happy fate.
Farwell, fraternall twigs that from one stocke do spring,   *shoots; trunk*
50 All happinesse befall you here, that earthly blisse can bring;
And when of honor's load you wish to be releev'd,
Heavens put that period to your dayes when least you can be griev'd.   *end*
Farwell, deare virgin dove, whom as my life I love,
Sweet sister, whom I wish both faire and fortunate to prove,
55 Heavens grant thy wishes all, but that, by all the rest,
A happy husband for thy mate to make thy fortunes blest,
That like two turtles then, thou faithfull to thy pheere,   *doves; mate*
And he, as kind as thou art true, may hold thee alwayes deere.
Farwell, my loving friends, whom either love or blood
60 Binds me to love and honour still, and to affect your good.   *desire*

Since no great meanes I have your favours to requite,   *return*
Accept my zeale, I wish you well, and to your foes' despight.
And thou, O faire, farwell, well may thou faire, farwell,   *prosper*
It's only thee I grieve to leave, whose want I'le ever feele:
65 The heavens upon thy head powre out their joyes and blisses,
And grant the glad accomplishment of all thy choycest wishes.
Let Fortune do her best to please thee evermore,
And wondring Earth admire thy worth, whose like was nere before.
Though I, Earth's wandring guest, a vagabond do stray,
70 And must, alas, forgoe thy face, fates call me so away,
Yet Time shall trie the truth of my affection to thee,
And in my song I'le praise thee so, that all the world shall woe thee.
Againe, faire faire, farwell! though last on thee I call,
Yet thou art first into my thought, both first and last in all;
75 And if I ever chance those northerne coasts to see,
And find thee, as I never doubt, of this same minde to be,
With thee I'le anchor then, and leave the stormy maine,
And for thy sake henceforth I vow, nere to launch forth againe.

The Epitaph of Alexander the sixth,* by Sanazer. [GL2]

Fortasse nescis cuius hic tumulus fiet, adsta viator, etc.
Stay, passenger, a space, thy wearied limbes to ease,   *wait*
Perhaps thou know'st not who lies here intomb'd; stay, if you please.
'Tis not great Philip's sonne, that all the world subdu'd,
But Alexander, filthie Pope, in bloodshed all embru'd.   *stained*
5 Great kingdomes he o'rethrew, and cities turn'd to nought,
All to advance his bastard brood a world of mischiefe brought.
This land with fire and sword he utterly destroid,
And to subvert God's lawes and man's, his care he all employ'd
That he more freely might – O, filthie to be told! –
10 Incestuously enjoy the child his lust begot of old.

Yet he, for all this, sate and rul'd proudly the papall sea   *see*
Elev'n yeares, as great Pope and head, in sole supremacie.
Speake not of cruell kings, old tyrants do not name,
Caligula came short of him, and Heliogablus' shame.
15 The rest for modestie I cannot well declare,
Suppose the worst, set on thy way, I wish thee well to fare.   *prosper*

An addition by the translator. [GL3]

There is a monster strange begot of late,
Betwixt a begging frier and a nun,
Whose subtiltie hath troubled Europe's state,   *order*
And, sowing jarres, all princes hath undone.   *conflicts*
5 His shaveling followers do him deifie,   *tonsured*
As he were God, and lord of sea and land:
For he – but stay there – most impetuously,   *stop; arrogantly*
For supreme power and highest seate doth stand.   *position; insist*
Of this vile stocke a filthy race is sprong,
10 Which over-rules the land of Italy,
And in new Rome hath sway'd the scepter long,   *modern*
By witchcraft, incest, and foule sodomie.
Some call him Pope, some father of the saints,
Some say he is Christ's Vicar, left behind;
15 The knave himselfe most arrogantly vaunts,   *boasts*
That he in heaven can loose, in hell can bind,
Such is the power he hath the world throughout,
With triple crowne when he in chaire doth sit.   *throne*
Kings, emperours and great monarkes all about
20 Most humbly come to kisse his foote, as fit.   *appropriate*
This monster now in Europe doth command,
And to the Inds his putent power's extended,   *disgusting*
So that no king nor prince dare once withstand
The torrent of his wrath when he's offended.

25 This prelate's pride I cannot all declare,
Nor gorgeous pompe, which daily doth increase,
With cardinals, who kings' companions are,
Whom to enrich, poore princes' states decrease.   *are depleted*
When hel's great monarch ended hath his life,
30 The cardinals convent to chuse another,   *convene*
Whose holy meetings oft are mar'd with strife,
Which to appease, they take some frier brother.
This done, they carrie him through all the towne,
High mounted on priests' shoulders, magnifi'd,
35 Then in a chaire unbottom'd set him downe,   *with no seat*
Where his humanitie is search'd and tride –   *investigated*
Because an English wench them once beguild,[†]
Who, in disguise, unto the Popedome came,
And with a frier the holy see defil'd,
40 Having a child, to Rome's eternall shame.
On solemne dayes, when he his masse would make,
Two cardinals do carrie up his traine;
The multitude attends him at the backe,
Till he be set in state, they throng amaine;
45 And while in pompe he sitteth in his chaire,
They bring him wine and consecrated bread;
Such is his pride, he will not do it bare,
Lest some mischance befall his mitred head.
Many strange tricks this hell-hound he devises,
50 Setting his neighbours all at great debate:
To warre and armes all princes he entices,
That he may live in a more quiet state.
If any prince this demidivell offend,[†]   *half-devil*
Or wrong his servants in the lightest sort,
55 Incontinent his bloud-hounds he will send,   *immediately*
Friers disguis'd, and make his life pay for't,
And then give pardon to the murderer,
And as a saint him canonise, as right: *fitting*
Men must adore the bloudie furtherer   *perpetrator*
60 Of his damn'd plots, which even his soule delight.[†]

What shall we say? but pray the God of peace,
Soone to confound this Antichrist of Rome,
Whose rage and mischiefe is not like to ceasse,
Against th'Annointed, till he get his doome: *before*
65 To go to hell with all his companie,
There to remaine in that abhorred place,
And suffer tortures everlastingly,
Without all future hope of after grace.   *pardon*

The unconstant lover.   [GL4]

What an asse is he,
Waits a woman's leisure
    For a moment's pleasure,
And may chance to be
5   Gulld at last, and leese her   *cheated; lose*
    For his constancie.

If I chance to sie
On that's fair, I love her,   *one*
    Till I sie ane other
10 Is more faire than shee;
    For I am a lover
    At my libertie.

If I fancie one,
And that one could love me
15   But with frowne, to prove me,   *only; test*
Fair-well, I am gone;
    Shee shall never move me,
    I can ly alone.

If I chance to choose
20   One that can love no man,
     Shee is butt a woman;
  And though shee refuse,
     There are others commone   *aplenty*
     No such coynes use.

25   Shall I sigh and die
  If a wench denie me,
     Or, that shee may trie me,
  Suffer patiently?
     Noe! noe face can tye me
30   Slave to crewelltie.

Shall the pricking thorne
Be my dounie pillow,
     And each idle fellowe
Laugh my head to scorne?
35   Noe! I'le weare the willowe
     Ere I wear the horne.

For a fading rose,
Quhich perhaps is stayned,
     Shall I be constrained
40   Sweeter flours to lose?
     Noe! the sweat restrained   *essence re-distilled*
     Smells best in my nose.

Evrie day I change,
And at once love manie,   *at the same time*
45   But not ty'd to anie,
For I love to range;
     And, if one can stay me,   *detain*
     I shall think it strange.

Love is all my life
50 For it holds me doeing, *active*
Yet my love and woeing
Is not for a wife;
Noe! 'tis good eshewing *avoiding*
Mariage, jarrs, and stryfe. *rows*

55 Love's a play to me,
Quhich my laughter moveth, *evokes*
And most pleasing proveth
In varietie;
He's an asse that loveth
60 With most constancie.

NOTES

Simion Grahame

SG1

Text: *Passionate Sparke*, 1604, sig. C2v.

Source: based on Giovanni Battista Guarini (1538–1612), composer of madrigals, and famous for his tragicomedy *Il Pastor fido* (1585). Variation in line-length and stanza-form is typical of the madrigal genre.

11: A pun on 'bee', both noun and verb.

SG2

Text: *Passionate Sparke*, 1604, sig. C3–D2v.

An address to the united kingdoms, reflecting Grahame's celebratory attitude of 1604.

1: The poet adopts the position of Apollo, surrounded by the Muses, in order to sing James's praise.

3: Apollo metamorphosed the nymph Castalia into the fountain on Mount Parnassus.

8: Such is the prestige of the island of Britain that all the Muses reverence it.

10: The 'subject' is Britain.

13: nyne-voyced – as sung by the nine Muses together.

17: The Phœnix, unique among birds, generates its own successor.

20: barren branch – the Virgin Queen Elizabeth, recently dead.

22: James's children add to the glory of his laurels.

30 Not only potent in arms, but also through the army.

34: The Latin line, *Parcere prostratis scit nobilis ira leonis* [the wrath of the noble lion knows to spare the prostrate] is quoted by several Scottish poets; in heraldry, a red lion rampant appears on the shield of the Scottish king.

52–53: Cimmeria – in Homer, a land of fog and darkness, near hell, the abode of Pluto.

53: presage* – emended from *preflage*.

67: The trope of Britain's isolation is Classical (cf. Virgil, Eclogue I, 66); live* – emended from *liues*.

74: This anticipates a famous chiasmic line (294) in Drummond's *Forth Feasting*.

76: On James's return from Denmark (1590), witches allegedly tried to drown him.

79–84: The language here recalls depictions of Christ's harrowing of hell.

82: James is the personification of rigour, in punishing the evildoers.

89: A pun on heaven and haven.

103: 'Apollo' addresses the English at their most eager anticipation of James's arrival.

127–32: This refers to the chroniclers of hitherto unhappy political history.

142: on – supplied for metrical reasons.

144: Momus – the personification of sharp criticism.

150: Historians who misrepresent James will finally win eternal contempt.

173: Curiously, Grahame omits to mention Prince Charles, born on 19 November 1600.

177: troopes – the nine orders of angels. The motif of the heavenly host makes an effective conclusion to a poem which opens with the 'laureat troopes' of the Muses.

178: compear – a Scottish legal term.

SG3

(a): Text: *Passionate Sparke*, 1604, sig. D3.

Title: A farewell poem (*syntaktikon*), written from an unspecified foreign location.

4: The swan was reputed to sing before its death.

25–28: Grahame leaves Scotland in an angry and defiant mood.

(b): Text: *Anatomie of Humors*, 1609, sig. T4–T4v.

The new title shows that Grahame is in his Italian exile, but nostalgic for home. The change of metre, from hexameter couplets to hexameter plus heptameter ('poulter's measure'), associates this version with the genre of the dier (cf. Verweij 2013).

15–17: The kingdoms are Scotland, England and Ireland.

20: Perhaps a reference to the armies of the Ottoman sultan, then threatening Europe.

SG4

Text: *Passionate Sparke*, 1604, sig. D4–E3.

Title: A *passionado* is a poem recording the author's sufferings.

1: Phaëton – driver of the chariot of the sun.

2: Cinthia – the moon.

12: Eccho – turned into stone, she retained the power of speech.

31: The coarse garb of the penitent.

42: Anagrams, as here of 'Simion Grahame', were a contemporary craze.

65: A reference to avalanches.

86: He bears the sign of the Cross on his breast, and crosses his arms as in devotional representations of Christ as the Man of Sorrows.

117: All my understanding has been acquired by dear-bought personal experience.

138: A reference to tobacco.

150: cf. Psalm 51:17.

SG5

Text: *Passionate Sparke*, 1604, sig. E3v.

13: The first 'I' in this line is a pun on 'Ay', as an expression of lament.

14: The repetition of the opening line is a formal correlative to the moral idea voiced in SG4/48.

SG6

Text: *Passionate Sparke*, 1604, sig. E4–F1v.

Title: The word *estate* has various senses: the poem focuses on the true nature or condition of what passes for honour in the ranks of human society.

Motto: Proverbial.

1: cf. Ecclesiastes 3:1–15.

41: Sodom – cf. Genesis 19.

SG7

Text: *Passionate Sparke*, 1604, sig. F2–F3.

Title: The poet speaks with the hard-won insight of someone contemplating the proximity of death. In the version in the *Anatomie of Humors* (1609) a Latin motto from Psalm 114:3 was prefixed:

Circundederunt me dolores mortis, & pericula inferni invenerunt me.
[The sorrows of death have compassed me: and the perils of hell
have found me.] (Douay Bible). This psalm is said at the beginning
of the Vigil of the Office of the Dead and as an antiphon at mass on
Septuagesima Sunday.

24: cf. Job 1:21; for emphasis repeated in the following stanza.

54: cf. Luke 23:46 (cf. Psalm 31:5) – the last words of Christ on the Cross.

SG8

Text: *Anatomie of Humors*, 1609, sig. D3–D3v.

1–6: The first stanza of this powerful poem uses ideas from Psalm 1.

4: cf. Jeremiah 22:23.

18: cf. Matthew 26:49.

SG9

Text: *Anatomie of Humors*, 1609, sig. K1–K2v.

12: Circe – legendary temptress and magician.

14: Aurora – the Dawn.

23–24: The lady pleats her hair, turning it into chains.

29, 31: The lady's teeth, and lips.

45: Syrens with their song lured sailors to their death.

52: The peacock's tail-feathers seem to display eyes.

55–56: The delusive attractions of art conquer the intelligence naturally
inherent in the human mind.

65: The conquest of love overcomes the victor in battles.

James Cockburne

JC1

Text: *Gabriel's Salutation*, 1605, sig. A2.

Title: This prefatory sonnet follows a prose dedication to Lady Skirling.

8: cf. Psalm 25:6.

12: cf. Psalm 51:17.

13: Cockburne directs his prayer to all three Persons of the Trinity.

JC2

Text: *Gabriel's Salutation*, 1605, sig. A2v.

Title: This pair of sonnets immediately precedes the main poem (JC3).
They combine the genres of dedication to a patron, religious devotion, and love-epistle.

6: Cockburne contemns philosophy that is not explicitly Christian.

12: Clearly, books of poems were not treated by everyone with care and respect.

17: Somewhat boldly, the poet compares Lady Skirling to Mary, mother of Jesus.

20: cf. 1 Corinthians 9:19.

24: Christ was conceived of Mary by the Holy Spirit (cf. Luke 1:35).

25: Before the world was created, Christ had already consented to incarnation for the redemption of mankind.

26: Since Adam, the first man, was created from the earth, so Christ, becoming man, covers His divinity with the coarse element.

27: The three Persons of the Trinity.

28: In a venerable pun, the Fall of man, attributed to Eve (*Eva*), was restored through Mary (cf. the prayer, *Ave Maria* [Hail Mary]).

JC3

Text: *Gabriel's Salutation*, 1605, sig. A3–B3.

Title: For the Annunciation to Mary, cf. Luke 1:26–38. JC has expanded and dramatised the story, in particular by supplying God's speeches and by making many picturesque additions to the Biblical account.

6: The disobedience of Adam, husband of Eve, caused the Fall of mankind.

19–20: The descendants of Jacob include the community of believers in Christ.

23–25: cf. Genesis 3:15.

27: The twelve tribes of Israel.

43: Æolus controlled the winds.

46: Titan – here, the sun.

57–63: Christ, Son of God, was begotten before all worlds, and His fate after incarnation is already fully known in advance.

71–84: The physical details stress the femininity of Mary (whom Lady Skirling resembles).

85–98: By tradition (also in art) Mary is reading the Bible at the moment of Gabriel's arrival, and in particular the story of how the nation of Israel came out of Egypt (cf. Exodus 3–14). In this case, Mary has a printed Bible, equipped with illustrations. The Geneva Bible has a woodcut showing the crossing of the Red Sea, with the Egyptian army in pursuit.

95: Arke – cf. Genesis 8. In medieval historiography, the first age of mankind ended with the Flood.

97: cf. Genesis 21. Abraham's readiness to sacrifice Isaac foreshadows the God the Father's treatment of His Son.

107: A heavenly light shone upon Mary (cf. Luke 1:35).

112: cf. Luke 2:14.

118–19: The angel's use of Latin evokes the language of theology and liturgy; Christ, as man, redeems the first man, Adam (cf. John 1:29).

137: cf. Judges 11:34–39.

138: Sehon was king of the Amorites (cf. Numbers 21:29).

141–54: Mary repudiates the patterns of early modern courtly life.

168: Bethleem – emended from *Bethlem* for metrical reasons; mirth – *myrrh* is meant (cf. Matthew 2:11).

172: The night of the Nativity.

176: The poet includes all the company of Heaven.

193: cf. Matthew 2:1–10.

194: The reference is to the sun.

199–200: The Sibyl and the Oracle of Delphi, being pagan, shall lose all power.

203: The name 'Emmanuel' means 'God with us'.

204–24: These three stanzas, modelled on Isaiah 9:6, consist of a catalogue of commonly known names, emblems, symbols, images and antitypes of, or for, Christ, e.g.: rock of rain (Isaiah 48:21); cornerstone (Psalm 118:22); rod of Jesse (Isaiah 11:1); Silo[am] (cf. John 9:7); Ark (cf. Genesis 6–10); alpha (and omega) (cf. John 6:48; Revelation 1:8); well of life (cf. Proverbs 10:11); serpent (cf. John 3:14); bread from heaven (cf. Exodus 16:15)

224: cf. Luke 11:27.

236: promise – cf. Genesis 9:8–17.

239: cf. Psalm 51:7.

249: The dove is a figuration of the Holy Spirit (cf. John 1:32).

260–89: This section, in a new six-line stanza, versifies the *Magnificat* or Song of Mary (cf. Luke 1:46–55). The five stanzas may suggest the Five Joys of the Blessed Virgin (of which the Annunciation is the first). The refrain, ending on *lullabie*, accentuates the human aspect of the scene, perhaps recalling something of the spirituality informing many medieval carols.

279: God's promise was spoken to Eve, but as an antitype she prefigured Mary (cf. Genesis 3:16).

280: cf. Genesis 22.

281: cf. 1 Samuel 18:23.

286: In art, the crowned Mary is often depicted in Heaven alongside the Trinity.

Walter Quin

WQ1

Text: *Sertum poeticum* (1600), sig. C2v.

Title: Anagrams were very popular at the time, and 'Elisabeth Stewart' transforms into 'A blist sweet heart'.

2: Elizabeth (b. 1596), daughter of James and Anne, was named after the Queen whom James intended to succeed.

13: The king over all is God Himself.

WQ2

Text: Edinburgh, NLS, Hawthornden MS 2065, fols. 44–45.

Title: Alexander and his wife married in 1601. The MS gives only their initials.

The MS is copied in the hand of William Drummond, who was a close friend of Alexander, and possessed a copy of Quin's *Sertum poeticum*.

1: Alexander was twenty-three or twenty-four at the time of his marriage. See Reid, *ODNB*.

2: Janet Erskine was a daughter of Sir William Erskine, known as the Parson of Campsie.

6: Hymen – the god of marriages.

12: O* – emended from *Of*. The MS gives only the beginning of the refrain here and in the subsequent stanzas.

19: Phœbus (Apollo) – the sun, and god of poetry; the sisters nine are the Muses.

35: The belt, or 'zone of Venus', is the symbol of sexual access.

37: Juno – chief goddess, and patron of Hymen.

38: Cupid – god of sexual attraction, and son of Venus, goddess of love.

45–46: The bride, after only a short struggle, will soon win by submitting.

WQ3

Text: *Lachrimae lachrimarum* (1612), sig. C1.

Title: The death of the Scottish-born Prince Henry was keenly felt and dutifully recorded by both Scottish and English poets, and especially by those who, like Quin and Sir David Murray, had been attached to the Prince's household.

WQ4

Text: *The Memorie* (1619), sig. F1v.

Title: Bernard Stewart died in 1508 in the house of Sir James Forrester at Corstorphine, then a village west of Edinburgh. Stewart's arrival in Scotland, and his death, had been celebrated and lamented in poems by William Dunbar.

1–4: Publius Cornelius Scipio Africanus, the victor over Carthage in the Second Punic War, later felt insulted by an ungrateful Rome, and died at his villa in the obscure hamlet of Linternum, north of Naples (193 BC).

7: Quin is alone in saying that France showed a lack of gratitude to Stewart for his military successes in Italy.

WQ5

Text: *The Memorie* (1619), sig. F1v. This poem is a specimen of a sonnet in couplets.

1: Bernard Stewart was descended from the Stewarts of Darnley, and thus related to James and Charles. One of the poems in *The Memorie* was an account of the Lords of Aubigny, descended from the earls of Lennox.

5–6: Stewart acted as ambassador of France to Scotland, during the Wars of the Roses, when Scotland (the thistle) was mostly aligned with France. In his role of bringing reconciliation to the royal families of Scotland and England, Stewart is a foreshadowing of King James.

Elizabeth Melville

EM1

Text: *Ane Godlie Dreame* (Edinburgh, 1603), sig. C1v–C2.

Title: As with many a religious lyric, the poet indicates the proper tune.

This poem is a *contrafactum* of the Elizabethan song 'Farewell, dear love', which was set to music by Robert Jones in *The First Book of Songs and Airs* (London, 1600).The secular song was used comically in *Twelfth Night* (II, iii, 98–107): cf. Duffin 2004: 138–39, who reproduces the text of Jones's original. Melville has used considerable freedom in her recasting of the English song. An anglicised version of her Scots-language poem was issued at Edinburgh by her printer, Robert Charteris, in 1604, and, together with the *Godlie Dreame* was thereafter frequently reissued.

13–14: The poet orders worldly pleasures ('showes') to go away from her, but she herself is fully prepared to go away from the wickedness of the world. The 'her' of line 14 is the world as a seductress.

Robert Ayton

RAY1

Text: London, BL Additional MS 10308, fols. 9–9v.

Title: Supplied by Gullans, who (p. 259) dates the poem to 1600.

This lyric communicates a subtly ironic message by using much of the traditional diction of amatory poetry in an untraditional argument – namely, that while the poet entirely realises that it would be to his good that he should break with his beloved, the pain caused by the lady's unyielding denial of his silent suit prevents him from saying that word of farewell. The poem therefore displays an unromantic clash between reason and passion, and, as in certain lyrics by Donne, the novelty resides largely in the intellectualised coolness of tone.

RAY2

Text: London, BL Additional MS 10308, fol. 19.

Title: Imported by Gullans from London BL Additional MS 28622, fols. 36–36v. Gullans (p. 259), dates the sonnet to 1600–1605.

1–2: Margaret Leslie was the daughter of Patrick, first Lord Lindores (in Fife, by the tidal Firth of Tay). In 1609 she married John Drummond, second baron Maderty (by Crieff, in Perthshire).

RAY3

Text: London, BL Additional MS 10308, fol. 10v.

Title: Supplied by Gullans, who (p. 279) dates the sonnet to 1600–1605.

1–2: The poet contemns the idea that he, as a lover, might be expected to violate his noble nature and his freedom of choice, for the sake of immediate personal and material advantage. This sonnet must have been admired, since it survives in four manuscripts. Two of the latter employ spellings that contain Scots features. The poem has also been attributed to William Fowler (in Gullans' view, without justification).

RAY4

Text: London, BL Additional MS 10308, fol. 19.

Title: Supplied by Gullans, who (p. 259) dates the sonnet to 1600–1605.

1: The River Tweed divides Scotland from England. In March 1603 James crossed it on his way to London, and the poem was presumably composed shortly thereafter. The opening words echo those of a sonnet by James on Lady Cicely Weems (Craigie ed. 1958: 118).

13: The heart of King Robert Bruce was buried in Melrose Abbey, by the Tweed. The poet fancifully imagines that a high tide from the sea will carry up to the royal shrine Tweed's tidings of James's crossing of the river.

RAY5

Text: London, BL Additional MS 10308, fol. 21.

Title: The sonnet relates to the Gunpowder Plot, of 1605.

1: Gullans emends ms 'zealous' to 'jealous': the god Mars (Mavors) is jealous of the power of the earthly Mars, who is James himself.

9: Pluto – god of the underworld.

11: The thundering god is Zeus.

14: Laurel leaves give protection against thunder, but, once woven into a wreath, is the tribute traditionally given to poets.

RAY6

Text: Craig, *Poetical Recreations* (Edinburgh, 1609), sig. B4v.

Title: This is Ayton's reply to Craig's sonnet (AC9), on the preceding page of *Poetical Recreations*.

2: The rhyme here suggests a pun on 'main' (the sea).

9–10: Ayton, supposedly in a sad mood, declines Craig's invitation to write fancifully.

13: A humorous allusion to the water which gushed out of the rock, when struck by Moses (cf. Numbers 20:11). The tears of Craig will cure the depression of his fellow poet.

RAY7

Text: Edinburgh, EUL MS Laing.III.436, pp. 19–20.

Title: This is technically not an epistle to the poet's mistress, but a declaration in which he refers to her in the third person. In the course of the poem, the speaker changes from helpless captive to cynically aggressive victim.

Gullans offers no date for the poem. See Verweij 2016: 251–55.

9: Perhaps a reference to phosphorus.

RAY8

Text: London, BL MS Additional 10308, fol. 5v.

Title: Supplied by Gullans.

11–12: cf. Psalm 58:4–5.

15–18: When burnt, damp wood may emit a hissing sound. Vulcan – god of fire and blacksmith of the gods.

RAY9

Text: London, BL MS Additional 10308, fol. 21v.

Title: Prince Henry died on 6 November 1612.

1: The (unique) Phœnix bird was (re)born from the ashes of its predecessor, as Charles has succeeded his elder brother.

Alexander Craig of Rosecraig

AC1

Text: *Essayes*, 1604, sig. A1v.

Title: By venerable convention, an author might well address his book. Craig, however, suggests the importance of adapting style to audience – especially where the Court is involved.

1, 5: Dædalus made waxen wings to allow himself and his son Icarus to fly, warning the latter of the fatal dangers of misuse.

The Latin lines quoted here are taken from Giovanni Pontano/Pontanus (d. 1503), *Parthenopeus*, I, 6, 1–4. Craig's choice of quotation shows his alignment with the famous neo-Latin poet in declaring a love of homeland. Despite the ostensible modesty expressed in the Italian's lines, Craig's use of them amounts to a discreet self-paid compliment.

AC2

Text: *Essayes*, 1604, sig. B1–B4v.

Title: Craig's task in this epistle is the delicate one of simultaneously praising and advising the monarch, navigating between grovelling humility and impertinent authority.

1–4: James has succeeded in pacifying church and state in Scotland.

10: cf. Horace, *Carmina* I, iv, 13–14.

11: Elizabeth's crowns were those of England, Ireland and France.

12: James was Elizabeth's closest relation in the male line.

17: cf. Genesis 8:13–18.

20: brook* – emended from *breok*.

31: This line may imply that there is a lengthy gap in Craig's writing of poetry.

34: The critic Aristarchus judged even Homer harshly.

36: In this line 'for' spoils the metre, and may be an intrusion.

39: James saw his role as that of peace-maker.

41–46: Periander, tyrant of Corinth, was one of the Seven Sages of Greece.

47–48: Xenophon gave an idealised account of the virtues of the Persian king Cyrus.

49–50: The Greek poet Aratus gave advice to King Philip of Macedonia.

51: AC refers to theologian-philosophers, such as the 'Angelic Doctor' Thomas Aquinas and the 'Divine Doctor' Johannes van Ruysbroeck.

57: Momus was famous for criticising the gods; Rhamnusia was the goddess of divine retribution.

59–60: The Roman Emperor Otho preferred to commit suicide (AD 69), than that the state be ruined.

61–62: Diocletian famously abdicated as Roman Emperor (AD 305).

63–64: Dionysius I, tyrant of Sicily, invited Damocles to rule, but hung a fatal sword above the latter's head, causing him to wish to be excused from monarchy.

71: Ariston, general of the Aetolians, in the face of an invasion of the territory of the Achaeans, insisted that the two peoples were still in a state of peace.

73: The Roman Emperor Vespasian was admired for his personal virtues.

79: Priam, in the *Iliad*, was king of Troy.

82: Ucalegon and Antenor were prominent figures in Troy.

83: Macedo refers to Alexander the Great, king of Macedon; he was rumoured to be descended from a god.

84: Parmenio and his son Philotas were soldiers in the army of Alexander the Great.

88: Robert Cecil, 1st Earl of Salisbury, chief political adviser under Elizabeth, and ready to be so again under James.

90: In *The Republic*, Plato wrote that the best government is that of a philosopher king.

95: Jove (Jupiter) – the chief god, and wielder of thunderbolts.

98: A pig teaching wisdom to the goddess Minerva – proverbial.

104: Despite its capital letter in the original, *Kate* here is probably not a generic female servant (as in many early poems), but rather a form of *kit*, a milk-based gruel.

109–14: The Persian Emperor deigned to accept water from the hands of the poor man Sinetas: cf. William Painter, *Palace of Pleasure* (London, 1575), 9th novel.

121–24: Macedo here is Alexander the Great, asserting himself to be the son of a god and not of King Philip, and thereby bringing disgrace upon the latter.

127–28: The wealthy Athenian Timon wasted all his money on favourites and ended as a misanthrope.

137: The Ancient Athenians had deserted their former allies, the Phocians, for the sake of peace with their foe, Philip of Macedon. Craig may be hinting that James might desert the Scots for the sake of alliances with Continental powers.

141–48: Pompey generously appointed Serapio to an honourable ceremonial position: James is urged to do something similar.

151–52: In the context of the war between Dionysius I and Carthage for control of Sicily, a woman of Himera famously preferred the known tyrant to an unknown replacement who would be worse.

159: Plato, *Republic*, IX.

161: cf. Plutarch, *Moralia*, IV, 46.

165–66: After killing his brother, and in order to demonstrate that he was not drunk, Cambyses II, Emperor of Persia, gave order to kill the son of Prexaspes, a court official.

167–68: Alexander the Great had the corrupt courtier Vetronius Turinus smoked to death.

169–71: Alexander, in a rage, killed Clytus, then deeply regretted his action. James, now king of England, is urged not to punish anyone who should praise the royal family of Scotland.

175: Pausanias, spurned and humiliated, killed King Philip of Macedon, his former lover.

178: Demetrius, king of Macedon and conqueror of Athens, was stung into good behaviour through the reproaches of an old woman.

183–88: In AD 695, Leontios deposed Emperor Justinian II, and had the latter's nose cut off. In 705 Justinian was restored, and took revenge.

191–92: Lycurgus of Sparta pardoned Alcander, who had stabbed him in one eye.

193–94: 12* – emended from *13*. The Roman Emperor Vitellius was famous for gluttony and cruelty.

200: Philip II of Macedon, conqueror of much of Greece.

201–04: Agathocles (d. 289 BC) – tyrant of Syracuse and king of Sicily.

209–12: Draco devised a famously harsh law-code for Athens; Solon reformed the laws.

213–14: Herodotus quotes Pindar(us) on kingship in *Histories*, III, 38.

217: Kinges* – emended from *Kinkes*.

221–22: The Oracle of Delphi expressed approval of Lycurgus, king of Sparta, in his reforms.

231: Vexores, king of Egypt, and Tanais, king of the Scythians, extended their countries at the expense of their respective neighbours: cf. Trogus, *Histories*, abridged Justinus, trans. Arthur Golding (London, 1578), I, i.

233: Ninus, the legendary Emperor of Assyria, was famed for his conquests.

243: Musæus of Athens was famous for his religious poetry.

247: From the viewpoint of Scotland, 'transalpine' here may refer to England, and to the famous dramatists in London; 'home-bred' would then refer to the Scottish poets.

248: Cothurns – buskins worn by actors in Ancient Greek tragedy.

249: Homer, significantly, was regarded by the Greeks as their greatest poet.

252: After the assassination of Julius Cæsar, Cicero delivered fourteen famous speeches (*Philippicae*) against Mark Antony, but which were lavish in their praise of Octavian, the future Emperor Augustus. After the death of Elizabeth, Craig will modestly offer James seven glowing tributes.

AC3

Text: *Essayes*, 1604, sig. C1v–C2v.

Title: The poem is supposedly the speech of a personified Scotland, but it becomes also the appeal of all Scots. Verweij (2013: 301) identifies this poem as a dier.

1–12: The Greek fabulist Æsop was accused of temple-sacrilege at Delphi and was killed by being thrown from a cliff. Solon, the impartial law-giver of Athens, was told that his son had died, in order that he should show grief at the loss of a family member. The violent tears shed by the two men prefigure those of Scotland, when deprived of the king.

13–14: Rebecca helped Jacob so that he, and not his brother Esau, should be blessed by his dying father Isaac (cf. Genesis 27).

19–20: Elizabeth Tudor died on 24 March 1603.

23: Diana and Apollo were children of Zeus and Leto, and correspond to the moon and sun respectively.

24: And all the inappropriate motions of the English cause pain to the Scottish sun (i.e. James).

25: Phœbus – Apollo, the sun, i.e. James.

26: The Cimmerians lived in obscurity, north of the known Classical world.

29–30: Symbols of lost valuable national attributes.

35–40: The Trojan Paris, while still a shepherd ignorant of his royal descent, married Œnone, but abandoned her for Helen. England is the new concubine (*pellex*) of Paris (i.e. James).

42: Craig hints that James may add the Low Countries, France and Aquitania to his dominions.

43: Legend had it that Brutus founded London as 'New Troy'.

44: James may leave London to revive in person the English claim to the throne of France.

49–50: Plato's affection for Xenocrates prevented him from rejecting the interpretations of his philosophy made by the younger man.

57: Rufus – untraced.

59: Epaminondas, a famous Theban general, invaded the Peloponnese and established hegemony over Sparta; the poet hopes that James, after invading and conquering in Europe, will not forget his native country.

61: The philosopher Democritus would prefer to discover one truth than to be king of Persia.

63: England now rejoices in possessing James, Scotland's living crown jewel.

70–72: In Sallust's account of the Jugurthine War (112–106 BC) between Rome and the Numidians, Hiempsal sat himself next to his brother Adherbal, thereby excluding the more popular Jugurtha from the place of honour.

73–74: Virgil (Maro) has Dido, at her banquet for the Trojans, sitting between Æneas and Ascanius (Cupid in disguise).

76–78: James, in London, illuminates his kingdoms from the south, like the sun at noon.

82: Anglo-Saxon 'England' was comprised of a heptarchy of seven separate kingdoms.

85: The originally Trojan Romans, who had arrived in Italy from the Tyrian (Phœnician) colony of Carthage, eventually intermarried with the native Italic Sabines.

86: The two Jewish kingdoms of Israel and Judah came to be joined together.

AC4

Text: *Essayes*, 1604, sig. C4–C4v.

Title: Eliazabeth is the form given for the dead Queen's name. Verweij (2013: 301) identifies this poem as a dier.

3–4: At the Battle of Marathon, Cynegirus lost both hands detaining a Persian vessel, and then tried to continue doing the same by the use of his teeth.

5: The northern Thracians were allies of the Trojans against the Greeks.

6–10: James with his wife, two sons and daughter are compensation for the loss of one (Elizabeth).

7–8: Elizabeth sees consolation in her living successor, just as Anchises did in Æneas.

12: Achates was the faithful attendant of Æneas; here Elizabeth's Secretary Robert Cecil is meant.

16: The kingdom united is like a second Eden, at the beginning of a new world.

19–20: Sardanapalus, Dionysius of Syracuse, and Nero were notorious tyrants – unlike James.

22: James is a second David, as king, poet, peace-maker and beloved of God.

23: The pupil is James, the widow Elizabeth.

24: In a peaceful country, a rush bush suffices to hold in the cow (proverb).

25: The three lions *passant* of England, are now at peace with the lion *rampant* of Scotland.

26: The patriotic poet has the Scottish heraldic emblem, the thistle, protecting the red (Lancastrian) and white (Yorkist) roses of pre-Tudor England.

27–30: The crosses of St Andrew and St George are combined in the new British flag.

29: The British flags hold even the violence of the sea (Neptune) in control.

34: Thetis, a sea nymph, was one of the Nereids; the merman Triton was the son of Poseidon/Neptune, god of the sea.

35: Galloglasses were Scottish mercenary soldiers, who fought in Ireland against the Tudor conquest.

AC5

Text: *Essayes*, 1604, sig. E3–F1.

This poem purports to be Craig's letter from London to a beloved lady back in Scotland, but it is actually Craig's message to a personified Scotland. He protests that the imposing sights of his new environment are powerless to cancel out his affectionate memories of his homeland. Craig combines the genre of the versified love-epistle with a public statement of his predicament, caught between ancient attachments and contemporary circumstances. It is typical that he begins with an elaborate Classical allusion (from Plutarch's *Life* of Themistocles).

1–30: Craig is both the Petrarchan lover whose heart is metaphorically burning with love for his *inamorata*, but also someone who has followed the King to London and there witnessed a historical scene of genuine conflagration.

23–26: On 4 June 1561, lightning struck the tall spire of the Old St Paul's Cathedral in London, causing it to collapse in flames; despite the concern of Elizabeth, and later of James, it was never reconstructed. The entire church would later be destroyed in the Great Fire of 1666.

31–42: Obscure. There is no known connection between Farnham (Surrey) and its castle, with the medieval romance of Sir Launfal (Lamuel/Lambwell), nor with Guinevere, said to have drowned there.

43–45: In Geoffrey of Monmouth, Merlin had Stonehenge transported from Ireland and erected on its present site.

51–54: Rosamund Clifford was a mistress of King Henry II, who retained her concealed in a labyrinth at Woodstock (Oxfordshire), where she met her death (cf. Samuel Daniel's 1592 poem, 'The Complaint of Rosamond'), with which Craig was familiar.

63–68: Craig's smoking might not have pleased James, given the latter's *Counterblaste to Tobacco*.

66: Aconite is a plant well known for being poisonous.

71–72: Diana – virgin goddess of the hunt and of the moon; the lover of Orion, she was tricked into killing him with an arrow, when he was swimming.

73: Bacchus – god of wine. 'Celtic wine' is from France, as opposed to that from Iberia.

75: Craig compares his lines to an Ancient Greek temple of philosophical sobriety.

76: Helicon was an alternative to Mount Parnassus as home of the Muses.

82: A reference to the seven kingdoms (heptarchy) of Anglo-Saxon times.

85: The composition-style of the lady's message gives rise to anxiety about her state of health.

95–98: James's arrival in London in 1603 coincided with an outbreak of plague, and he published official measures to cope with the emergency.

107–12: In January 1558 the French recovered Calais, which had been ruled by England for two centuries.

116: Petrarch's love for Laura continued unabated even after her death.

AC6

Text: *Essayes*, 1604, sig. F2.

This is the first of two sonnets, with which Craig rounds off his collection.

1–8: Attalus III, king of Pergamon, lacking an heir, resigned his kingdom to the Romans, as seeming most suitable.

12–14: Craig, as poet, claims kinship with James, since, in offering his own work, he follows the instructions for poets promulgated by the king in his *Reulis and Cautelis* (1584).

AC7

Text: *Essayes*, 1604, sig. F2v.

After Craig's fanciful impulse of generosity in AC6, the moment for direct request has come.

1–4: Anacreon wrote complimentary poems to his patron, Polycrates of Samos, who rewarded him with five talents of gold; these caused the poet such sleepless worry that he returned them to the king.

9–10: A citharede was a professional musician, accompanying songs in praise of a kingly or noble patron. Craig may be thinking of Philoxenus of Cythera at the court of Dionysius I, tyrant of Sicily.

11–14: Craig promises to sing James's praises, for a consideration.

14: The setting of the sun in the West.

Motto: from Horace, *Carmina*, 3.30:6. In this poem Craig may be imparting to Horace's words – normally translating as 'I shall not perish entirely' – a slightly more pointed sense.

AC8

Text: *Amorose Songes* (1606), sig. K4–K5v.

Title: The two names evoke the idiom of Classical pastoral. Craig's poem belongs with the many imitations of Christopher Marlowe's famous 1599 lyric 'The Passionate Shepherd to his Love' ('Come live with me, and be my love'), though it is more than twice as long as the model. Lesbia's answer is an imitation of the many replies to Marlowe, such as that of Sir Walter Ralegh: 'If all the world and love were young', and, in its five stanzas, is of equal length.

4: Vesta – goddess of fire; Neptune of the sea.

10: Several species of dianthus were known as gillyflowers.

13: Flora – goddess of the flowers.

15: Daphne, chased by Apollo, was transformed into a laurel tree; a laurel garland was the prize at the Pythian Games, in honour of Apollo, and became the decoration appropriate to the poet; here the garland is imaged as Daphne's hair.

24: buildings* – emended from *buddings*.

31: The River Deveron (formerly Dovern) flows into the Moray Firth at Banff, Craig's home town.

41: The Nereids were sea nymphs, descended from Nereus and Doris.

49–51: Apollo – the sun; his sister Cynthia – the moon.

52: A *tugurium* was a humble shepherd's hut.

AC9

Text: *Poetical Recreations* (1609), sig. B4.

Title: Craig and Ayton had overlapped as students at Edinburgh University. This sonnet is answered by that of Ayton (RAY6).

1: Craig compares Ayton, with his fluent verses, to a quick-moving horse.

6: *Basia* – a frequent title for neo-Latin poems expressing love or friendship, cf. Ayton's *Basia: sive strena Cal. Ian. ad Iacobum Hayum equitem illustrissimum* [Kisses, or New Year's Gift to James Hay, that most excellent knight] (London, 1605), Ayton's only poem printed independently under his own name. Craig would clearly like to see Ayton publish more than only this one work. The pun on *basia* and *bass* (i.e. 'low-pitched') implies that 'higher notes' must refer to verse in the vernacular.

10: The Cimmerians were a northern people dwelling in darkness.

11: There is presumably a pun on *If Æthon* and *If Phæthon*. Phæthon failed to control the chariot of his father Helios (the sun). However, in another myth, Phæthon is the name of one of the four horses in the *quadriga* of Eos (the dawn): this seems to be the version in Craig's mind.

AC10

Text: *Poetical Recreations* (1609), sig. C1v.

Title: The identity of Craig's friend (if there actually was one) is unknown.

1: The Ancient Iranian prophet Zoroaster did not rule over an island. The opening words imitate those of a sonnet by King James: 'Fair famous isle, where Agathocles rang' (Craigie 1955–58: II, 118, 241), where the reference is to Sicily, with a pun on the name Cecily [Wemyss].

2–4: Bactria is a region of Central Asia north of the Hindu Kush; its capital was Bactra (now Balkh), in modern Afghanistan. Artaspe is unknown as the name of a city, but the form may be an attempt at Zariaspa – either an older name for Bactra/Balkh (cf. Strabo: XI, xi, 2), or another city in Bactria, said to be the birthplace of Zoroaster.

5–6: Gether, the third son of Aram (cf. Genesis 10:23), was according to Flavius Josephus (I, vii) the ancestor of the Bactrians (cf. Lodge 1602: 11).

7–12: Craig exploits the motif of the world-upside-down.

12: A witty adaptation of a repeated response in the Litany.

AC11

Text: *Poetical Recreations* (1609), sig. D1.

Title: This poem reveals Craig's dissatisfaction with life at Court.

AC12

Text: *Poetical Recreations* (1609), sig. D2.

Title: This poem is an answer to the previous one.

AC13

Text: *Poetical Recreations* (1609), sig. D3v.

Title: John Graham, 3rd Earl of Montrose (1548–1608). From 1603 he was the commissioner in Scotland for the absent James, and was given a lavish state funeral in Edinburgh.

1–2: Rhadamanthus, Æacus and Minos were judges of the dead, before the entry of souls to Elysium or Tartarus.

6: Montrose had wielded James's sceptre in Scotland, and now in death will wield that of Minos.

AC14

Text: *Muses' Welcome* (1618), pp. 99–103.

Two poems were presented to James on his visit on 22 May 1617 to Kinnaird Castle (in Perthshire): the first in Latin, by John Leech, the second in English, by Craig.

3: James, here addressed, wears the crowns of Scotland, England and Ireland.

11: Astræa – goddess of justice and purity.

19: James, having conquered, can raise others to the status of kings.

29–30: The bridge over the River Tay at Perth was many times destroyed by the flooding river; though repaired in 1616, it would succumb again five years later.

40: cf. 1 Samuel 20:11–17.

56: Thracian banquets were characterised by an abundance of meat and bread, accompanied by sports (cf. Athenaeus, *Deipnosophistae*, I, 27).

61–62: See Herodotus on the tributes offered to Darius (*Histories*, III, 88–96).

71: In Ancient Greece, Tamii were entrusted with the treasure belonging to temples.

84: *Ave Cæsar* [Hail, Caesar] was said by those about to die in the Roman arena.

97: Turbo – untraced.

101: James had experienced the severe cold of Norway when on his marriage journey from Oslo to Copenhagen (1589–90); Scythia was a mountainous region of central Eurasia, north of Iran.

103: The kings of England still claimed to be kings of France, then troubled by wars of religion.

113–28: cf. Genesis 49:29–50:26.

129: Nestor, king of Pylos, in his great old age took part in the Trojan War.

139–46: cf. Job 5:23–27, Psalm 122:7; Babel is the antithesis of Jerusalem, and the 'man of sin' is Satan.

150–72: This final passage is inspired by, and expands upon, Psalm 61:6–7.

158: In addition to the early death of Prince Henry, James and Anne had already lost four children as infants and suffered two miscarriages.

AC15

Text: *Poeticall Recreations* (1623), sig. C2.

Title: The identity of the troublesome boor, if he actually existed, is unknown; it is more likely that the poem simply derives from Craig's reading about the illustrious neo-Latin poet Jacopo Sannazaro (1458–1530).

3–6: Philibert Aurantius, a general of Emperor Charles V, was in 1530 responsible for destroying the villa at Mergellina, by Naples, which was the beloved residence of Sannazaro. The poet on his deathbed forgave him, on hearing that Aurantius had been killed in military action.

15: Charon was the boatman who ferried the dead over the river Styx to the Underworld.

13–18: This curse is deliberately hyperbolic.

AC16

Text: *Poeticall Recreations* (1623), sig. D3v-D4v.

Title: Satire is here figured as a flying [*Volans*] messenger, bringing the urgent news to all sections of society that ideals are in truth subverted by corrupt and sordid realities. The poet's use of the brusque imperatives 'Goe' in the first line and of 'Tell' in many subsequent lines, and of a similar rhetorical method, consisting of a lofty survey of widespread immoralities, suggests influence from Sir Walter Ralegh's famous lyric 'The Lie'. The latter circulated in manuscript from 1595 onwards and many replies were composed to it (May 1989: 61, 125). Craig puts flesh, as it were, on Ralegh's satirical skeleton, but he does not develop the memorable defiance contained in the Englishman's 'give the lie' refrain.

14: These tyrants will oppress their immediate families, before they begin to practise on society at large.

21: In the play *Heauton timorumenos* [The Self-Tormentor] by the Roman dramatist Terence, Chremes is a niggard who spoils things for others.

32: The dictionaries offer no meaning for *scalerigs*, though the context within the poem implies something purchasable and consumable. On that assumption, a derivation may be hazarded from *scaly* [hard, shell-like] + *rigs* [backs], possibly indicating some shell-fish delicacy; a further punning link with *scelerate* [cf. Fr. *scélérat* = villain(ous)] would increase the negative connotations.

50: cf. Matthew 25:22–23.

60: Damon and Pythias were famous for their friendship.

Sir David Murray

DM1

Text: *Sophonisba*, 1611, sig. E5. This is the final sonnet (numbered 22) in *Cælia*.

Title: Flavius Belisarius (d. 565) was a general under Emperor Justinian I (the Great), and reconquered much of the lost Western Roman Empire. According to legend, at the orders of the Emperor he was accused of corruption, blinded, and forced to beg for alms. Within the context of *Cælia*, and through the voice of Belisarius, Murray implies a comparison with his own situation, in which, after failing to win the love of his lady-love, he is reduced to begging for sympathy.

DM2

Text: *Sophonisba*, 1611, sig. E5v.

Title: This is one of a pair of sonnets by Murray in praise of John Murray, occurring towards the end of the 1611 volume, to which John had provided a liminary sonnet. This interesting but somewhat elusive poet was identified by Shire (1969: 181–86) as an associate and poet-disciple of Alexander Montgomerie's, and as the poet who died in London on 11 April 1615, while in disfavour with the King. John Murray's death would be lamented in verse not only by his cousin, David, but also in a sonnet by William Alexander to William Drummond, and in Latin epitaphs by Robert Ayton and John Dunbar. On John Murray and his family connections, see Verweij 2011: 158–60. The poet's cousin John is to be distinguished from Murray's brother John, who, after years spent as minister in Leith (*Fasti*, I, 165), retired in his last years to Murray's estate at Gorthy.

5–6: Ambrosia was to the Ancient Greeks the food of the gods, as nectar was their drink.

10: Icarus flew too near the sun, where his waxen wings melted with fatal consequences.

DM3

Text: *Sophonisba*, 1611, sig. E7.

Title: Lady Cecilia/Cecily Wemyss, daughter of Sir John Wemyss, in 1599 married William Murray, son of Sir John Murray, later (1606) created first earl of Tullibardine (in Perthshire). The latter was a childhood friend of James Murray of Tibbermuir, who compiled the poetic miscellany CUL MS Kk.5.30, discussed by Verweij (2011: 158–60; 2013: 210–17). Cecily Wemyss must have died around late 1603, for William Murray married his second wife in September 1604. William (d. 1626) succeeded as second earl in 1613. King James, in earlier days, had also written a sonnet in praise of Cecily Wemyss (Craigie 1955–58: II, 118, 240–01).

2: The conflict between Rome and Carthage provides the background to DM's *Sophonisba*.

3: Murray's sonnet was presumably written shortly after 1603.

12: The unique Phœnix renewed itself by self-immolation.

DM4

Text: *Sophonisba*, 1611, sig. E8v.

Title: Adam Murray was another cousin of David Murray (see DM2), and was also a poet, since his pen will have given immortality to his fame (cf. line 9).

DM5

Text: *CIV Psalme*, 1615, sig. π2.

Title: The Biblical King David was traditionally the prophet–author of the Psalms, and King James had a life-long interest in rendering the holy texts in vernacular verse. His paraphrase of Psalm 104 appeared in his first publication, *Essayes of a Prentise* (1584), and he completed versions of a further 29 psalms (Craigie 1955–58: I, 85–88; II, xi–xxii). A dedication to the 'sacred Majestie' of James was therefore tactful on Murray's part.

DM6

Text: *CIV Psalme*, 1615, sig. π3–4v.

Title: Murray, like King James, favoured for psalm-translation the more literary style of rendering rather than the plain 'ballad stanza' associated with the versions of Sternhold and Hopkins. Murray's version of Psalm 104 is in almost every respect superior to that of James (1584), and especially in the happy correspondence achieved between units of content and of stanza. Whereas James is the more literal of the two poets and omits nothing of consequence, Murray is prepared to leave some details untranslated, and unlike the King, he introduces references to Classical mythology. The resulting version is therefore unsuited to devotional use, though it makes for a good poem. *The Psalmes of King David translated by King James* (Oxford, 1631) was, despite its title, largely the work of Sir William Alexander; the version of Psalm 104 contained therein is not the King's 1584 attempt, but a dull rendering, divided into three parts, extending to 130 eight-line stanzas, and reverting to plain 'ballad-type' metre.

9: Æolus – the controller of the winds.

48: For James, the rocks were inhabited by 'Alpin ratts'; the Authorised Version has 'conies'.

52: Thetis – a sea-nymph.

57: The Biblical text contains no crocodiles.

William Alexander

WA1

Text: *Aurora* (1604), sig. M2v–M3.

Title: This is the tenth song and the final poem in *Aurora*. The paradoxes and rationality of the lyric make an interesting and untypical conclusion to a sonnet sequence charting the course of an infatuation.

5: The sexualised imagery implies that the speaking persona has been ravished by love, has been made pregnant therewith, and is now desirous of deeper experience.

9: cf. Cicero: *nunquam minus solus* [never less alone].

13: The reference is to Eros, the god of love and desire.

16: Hymen, god of marriages, was regularly portrayed with a burning torch.

19–24: Paris, son of King Priam of Troy (in Phrygia), was, as a baby, exposed, but grew to become a shepherd on Mount Ida. He was asked to determine which of three goddesses was the most beautiful: Juno/Hera, Minerva/Athena or Venus/Aphrodite. He opted for the latter, a decision which ultimately led to the Trojan War and his own death.

26: The dispute between the goddesses was over the possession of a golden apple. Alexander declares that he, in the place of Paris, would have awarded the prize to Juno/Hera, sister of the chief god, Jupiter/Zeus.

31–36: As the dove is the bird of Venus, so is the peacock that of Juno. Argos, with his hundred eyes, was tasked by Juno with guarding the heifer Io.

43–48: Alexander, on the point of marrying a lady who will promise to obey him, is content to surrender for the sake of the new relationship; this is somewhat different from many sonnet sequences, which are often focused on exclusively erotic attraction, under the aegis of Venus and Cupid.

WA2

Text: *Monarchicke Tragedies* (1604), sig. L1–L1v (at end, following Dd4v).

Title: James crossed into Berwick on 6 April 1603 and arrived in London on 7 May.

1–7: This poem was printed at the end of Alexander's four verse-tragedies, and the horror-stories of the past are contrasted with the jubilation (and expense) of the present occasion.

10: Though the poet concedes the admirable qualities of the famous heroes of old, he has lost his admiration for the violence used by them in their conquests.

21: James, like an unpolluted ocean, has absorbed all the honour of past heroes, pouring in from all rivers of praise.

25–30: James conquers in peace, not in war.

WA3

Text: *Poems by William Drummond of Hawthorne-denne* (1616), sig. Q3v.

Title: Alexis and Damon are pastoral names for Alexander and Drummond respectively. The strong friendship between the two poets is reflected in the presence of a liminary sonnet by Alexander (*alias* Parthenius) in the 1616 volume, and by the placing of WA3 as the final item therein.

5–8: The pastoral genre requires that the two poets be shepherds. The reference to the Ochil hills, close to Stirling and Menstrie, anchors the pastoral conventions within the Scottish reality.

7: Bodotria is the River Forth, which flows by Stirling, not far from Menstrie, and on to Edinburgh.

9–10: Alexander, as a shepherd, has gone like a vagabond, straying abroad (i.e. England) to try his luck amidst foreign (i.e. non-Scottish) shepherds (i.e. poets).

11–12: Drummond, who has stayed at home, is best able to estimate the value of his friend's wide experiences, since he understands perfectly the other's mind.

Alexander Gardyne

AG1

Text: *Garden* (1609), sig. A3v.

Title: It seems typical of Gardyne that he should ingratiate the reader by admitting his limitations, but he is also justifying himself through asserting the value of plain and truthful speaking.

10: distich's last – emended from *distich' lasts*. Evidently, the poet sometimes found it hard to complete a couplet.

AG2

Text: *Garden* (1609), sig. B1.

Title: James's arms appears as an emblem above the title of the sonnet.

2: Referring to the thrones of Scotland, England and Ireland.

8–12: Gardyne, as lawyer, emphasises the legitimacy of James's right of succession (even to France).

13–14: Heraldic beasts stand for James's new kingdoms: leopards/lions for England, lilies for France, and the harp for Ireland.

AG3

Text: *Garden* (1609), sig. B1v.

Title: Gardyne emphasises that God has determined that James should rule in Britain. In October 1604, James assumed the title of 'King of Great Britain', which, despite being rejected as inappropriate in England, was enforced in Scotland.

7: James's inauguration has brought about the perfection and end of time.

9: Bellona – the goddess of war.

12: Bonfires were associated with Midsummer, and were also signals of important events.

AG4

Text: *Garden* (1609), sig. B2.

Title: The assassination attempt on King James (the Gunpowder Plot), took place on 5 November 1605. This is the first of two sonnets under the same title.

2: A reference to David, king of Israel, whose psalms addressed praise to God.

AG5

Text: *Garden* (1609), sig. B3.

Title: David Cunningham was Bishop of Aberdeen 1577–1600 and Chancellor of King's College. He baptised Prince Henry (1594), and reconciled the Catholic Earl of Huntly with the King.

1: This line recalls James's words on Alexander Montgomerie: 'the prince
of poets in our land' (ed. Craigie, STS, II, 107).

6: Cunningham is compared to the Biblical King David.

7: These Church Fathers were respectively bishops of Carthage, Milan
and Hippo.

17: The comparison is to such a sign as the rainbow (cf. Genesis 9:13),
which will protect the city against the approach of any danger.

19: cf. Psalm 45:1.

AG6

Text: *Garden* (1609), sig. C4.

Title: A prayer for fair weather has since 1549 been included in the
English Book of Common Prayer, though nothing similar made it
into the Scottish Book of Common Order. The Kirk, however, permitted impromptu prayer for good weather, if the circumstances so
demanded.

1: *Cunctipotent* – Gardyne was fond of such latinate terms; not recorded
in *DSL*.

5–6: The Atonement of Christ protects mankind from a second over-
whelming disaster, like that of the Great Flood in the time of Noah
(cf. Genesis 6–9).

8–9: Gardyne prays that God will send again the manna from heaven,
which fed the Israelites while wandering in the desert (cf. Exodus
16:11–36).

AG7

Text: *Garden* (1609), sig. G4.

Title: This poem, structured as a catalogue, exploits the rhetorical
devices of anaphora and insistent alliteration in its pessimistic
vision.

5: Belial – the devil, responsible for maintaining the fires of hell.

AG8

Text: *Garden* (1609), sig. I4v.

Title: An anguished cry from the heart of a sinner to himself, expressed
with overpowering alliteration.

AG9

Text: *Garden* (1609), sig. K1v–K2.

Title: Like not a few others before him, the older poet Gardyne regrets the non-serious, and now dispersed, scribblings of his early life; were it possible, he would withdraw them, or write them anew in a spirit of moral seriousness and leaving no room for the exercise of the fanciful imagination. Alas, the effect of the new and stern aesthetic is shown all too clearly in his two *Theatres.*

AG10

Text: *Characters and Essayes* (1625), sig. C2v–C3.

Title: This is number 27 of fifty character-sketches. The genre of Theophrastan-type characters was then popular – cf. John Barclay's *Icon animarum* (1614) and John Earle's *Microcosmographia* (1628). In this poem, Gardyne makes much use of the devices of alliteration, phrasal parallelism, and chiasmus. As the invective intensifies, the poet slips back and forth from the regularity of iambic pentameter into a four-stress quasi-dactylic rhythm.

36: In his religious doubt, the atheist becomes the personification of despair.

William Drummond

WD1

Text: *Poems* (1616), sig. K1–L1.

Title: The first edition (1613) gave the form 'Meliades'; in 1614 it became 'Mœliades'.

3: *Poems* (1616) was the first edition to supply the following marginal note: †*The name which in these verses is given Prince Henrie, is that which he himself in the challenges of his martiall sports, and mascarads, was wont to use, Mœliades, Prince of the Isles, which in anagramme maketh Miles a Deo.*† There was a craze for anagrams around this time.

13: destines – according to the *OED*, Drummond is the last person to use this disyllabic form.

17: Ganges is a symbol of extreme remoteness.

18: Cypress is a symbol of mourning; Hymen – the god of marriage.

25–26: The moon has now obscured the light of the sun, the lover of the earth.

39–46: Prince Henry has died before he could wage war against the Ottomans, whose empire stretched from the Danube (Ister) valley to the Caspian Sea.

45: The red planet represents Mars, the god of war.

47: Charles III, duke of Bourbon, commanded the forces of Emperor Charles V at the sack of Rome (1527), in which Bourbon was killed. Henry IV, the first Bourbon king of France, had very recently (1610) been killed.

49–50: The great deeds which Henry would have performed, would have been written in the stars, for the edification of future generations.

57: A future poet would improve the flight of Fame, by telling of Henry's deeds – thereby following the example of Homer, who celebrated Ancient heroes.

58: Cicero (*Somnium Scipionis*, v) refers to the legendary deafness of those who dwell beside the cataracts of the Nile.

61–64: As once Ancient Troy, the Roman Catholic empire of Spain, controlling both domains of the sun/Titan (i.e. the east and west Indies), dreads the young hero.

69: sweet – there may be an associative pun on Latin *mel* (honey) and the first syllable of Mœliades.

70: The island of Thule, in the far north, and the River Hydaspes, in the Punjab, mark the extremities of the known world.

71–73: Prince Henry was born at Stirling (1594), by the winding River Forth.

77: *Cyclades* here refers to the islands in the estuary of the Forth.

79–80: The Clyde flows over several famous waterfalls.

83: Atlas, the Titan tasked with holding up the heavens, is situated in the extreme west of the Ancient world, and said to be king of Mauretania. His tears on the death of Mœliades are the source of many flooding rivers.

93–94: The shepherd Alexis refers to Sir William Alexander, whose home at Menstrie was situated close to the River Devon. Alexander's *Elegie* on Prince Henry appeared in 1612. For the motif of the instrument hung in grief on a tree, cf. Psalm 137:2.

97–98: The fount of Aganippe was in Bœotia, at the foot of Mount

Helicon; the Vale of Tempe, in Thessaly, was famous in its association with Apollo and the Muses.

106: Delos, a supposedly floating island in the Cyclades and famous as
the birthplace of Apollo, is envious of Britain.

107–10: The Acidalian archers are Cupids, associates of Venus, who was
wont to bathe in the fountain Acidale; Venus mourned the death of
her beloved Adonis. To Venus, Henry is a second Adonis, and even a
second Mars, the god of war and her lover.

113–14: Unlike the extremely remote Thule and Hydaspes, these
European rivers indicate countries where Henry might have come
and made alliances (Portugal, the Palatinate, France). A few lines
later, the same rivers bewail Henry's death.

117–18: The similarity in wording to that of lines 113–14 indicates the
seriousness of the loss of Henry to his father's European ambitions.

122: The anemone, narcissus and hyacinth flowers represent respectively
Adonis, Narcissus and Hyacinthus.

129: The flower helenium is said to have sprung from Helen's tears.

130–33: The palm and myrtle trees carry positive connotations; myrrh,
cypress and fir connote sadness.

134: The song of the sirens was believed to lure men to their death.

139–40: Iris was daughter of the cloud-nymph Electra, and goddess of
the rainbow.

147–48: The *Primum mobile* [First mover] was the outermost sphere
surrounding the earth, and which imparted motion to the spheres
below.

151: Boreas – god of the north wind.

161: The sun and moon communicate with each other through their
looking.

168: Men, down in their earthly and mutable world, are mad to suppose
that they can challenge the immutable gods.

180: The soul of Mœliades, now in heaven, enjoys the Beatific Vision of
God.

183: Narcissus fell in love with his own reflection. The reference here is to
the one God, of whom (cf. 'him', line 180) everything reflects the glory.

185: Magic mirrors, in which the future can be descried, are a common

motif in romance literature and elsewhere; here the glass is the face
of the heavens, reflecting the divine plan.

191: Boötes – a constellation, turning round the North Pole.

WD2

Text: *Teares on the Death of Meliades* (1613), sig. B2.

This epitaph-sonnet is printed within borders resembling those of a
tombstone, with much black above and around the poem. It occurs
in the prints of 1613 and 1614, but is absent from *Poems* 1616. The
two versions exhibit interesting and significant differences: most
obviously, lines 3 and 4 in 1613 are in the wrong rhyme-order, since
the intended scheme was clearly that of the Scottish-type interlaced
sonnet (*ababbcbccdcdee*). The error was corrected in 1614, when
several other stylistic improvements were also introduced; the poet
also took the chance to remove his first-person presence from the
poem. The lines to which no change had to be applied are by far the
most successful.

(a)

1: The opening words – 'Stay, passenger' [Latin: *adsta viator*] – figure as
a standard rhetorical formula in many Renaissance poems, in which
the reader is invited to behold the tomb and contemplate the merits
(or demerits) of the person commemorated.

7: spirit – here monosyllabic.

13: Cadiz and India symbolise the western and eastern extremities of the
Ancient world.

(b)

Text: *Teares on the Death of Moeliades* (1614), sig. B3.

Comparison of the two versions reveals the poet's meticulous attention
to detail, as he made the images clearer and the rhythm smoother,
and adjusted the body of the sonnet to the natural three-quatrain
structure basic to the genre. This version also appears in *Mausoleum*
(Edinburgh, 1613), p. 4: cf. Kastner, ed. (1913: xlix–l). Drummond's
decision to exclude the sonnet from *Poems* (1616) suggests that, even
as revised, it did not yet reach his high standard; it did, however,
resurface in the posthumous (1656) print of his poems (p. 78).

9–10: amaranthus – the everlasting flower; sweet flower – the hyacinth.

WD3

Text: *Poems* (1616), sig. A3v.

1: The sublunary (i.e. earthly) world is subject to change.

9–10: The day lily is the typical symbol of transience (cf. Jonson, 'The Noble Nature'), but the colour purple is rather associated with the pansy ('love-in-idleness').

WD4

Text: *Poems* (1616), sig. A4v.

1: The reference is to Plato and his philosophical work *Timæus*, which tells of the creation of the world and of souls.

5: The 'mansions blinde' are the dross of physical human bodies, into which pure souls are poured.

WD5

Text: *Poems* (1616), sig. B1.

3: Tethys, wife of Oceanus, was a Titan and sea nymph.

4: The stars circling the North Pole are seen as nymphs.

5: Cynthia – the moon.

6: Latmos is a ridge of mountains by the coast of western Anatolia.

11: Proteus – god of seas, rivers, the ocean and all that changes.

WD6

Text: *Poems* (1616), sig. C2.

Title: Madrigal verse, often written to be sung, can exhibit considerable variety in length of lines, rhyme scheme, and in stanza pattern.

1: The term *dedale* is from Dædalus, the designer of the legendary labyrinth on Crete.

2: The silkworm eats leaves and winds itself in a cocoon of silk.

WD7

Text: *Poems* (1616), sig. C3.

9: The rhetorical figure of correction through contradiction (*epanorthosis*), though contrived, has the function of emphasis.

13: The lady's attractions, by inspiring deep love in the poet, make it impossible for him to think that he could increase the love which he feels, even were such a thing to be possible.

WD8

Text: *Poems* (1616), sig. C4.

1: Taurus (Bull) is the second zodiacal sign (after Aries), relating to a month of late Spring, from April to May.

7: See the note to WD1/122, above.

9: In a pun, the lamb, with its sound of 'baa', seems to be bewailing something.

WD9

Text: *Poems* (1616), sig. D2. Another madrigal.

1: The town of Idalion, in Cyprus, is associated with Aphrodite (Venus) and her beloved Adonis.

5–6: Roses, of which the thorns are said to have drawn blood from the feet of Aphrodite, as she hastened to the dying Adonis.

8: The Graces were minor female deities, in some accounts descended from Aphrodite.

14: Just as Hyacinth died in the arms of his lover, the god Apollo, so the poet wants to die in the hand of his mistress.

WD10

Text: *Poems* (1616), sig. D3.

4: The Phœnician city of Tyre gave its name to the highly-prized purplish-red dye produced from the murex sea-snail.

5: those shining lights – his lady's eyes.

8: The legendary musician and poet Orpheus was born in Thrace, in northern Greece; he had the power to charm all animate or inanimate things.

13: Time, the cruel tyrant, destroys beauty.

WD11

Text: *Poems* (1616), sig. E3.

1–4: The wavelets of the Forth, which flows past Edinburgh, are here cast in the role of a lover, trying to kiss the boat in which the perfect lady is crossing the river.

14: Although the only wind consists of the lover's sighs, the waters swell up, as the river competes with the open sea in their passionate desire to kiss the boat.

WD12

Text: *Poems* (1616), sig. F2.

In this sonnet the poet in winter contemplates the scene of his summer-season protestations. Everything that then was beautiful and pleasant is now changed, except for the still purling spring, into which the poet weeps, as he had done earlier, when happy in his love.

WD13

Text: *Poems* (1616), sig. G3.

The sonnet articulates the poet's intense grief over his mistress, now dead.

WD14

Text: *Poems* (1616), sig. G3v.

In this sonnet the dead mistress has become a saint looking down from heaven.

12: By tradition, a pyramid was the appropriate monument for a great ruler.

13–14: Laurels are symbols of triumph; the purple-coloured myrtle was sacred to Venus.

WD15

Text: *Poems* (1616), sig. G4–H2.

This song rhymes in couplets, but is constructed in units of three lines, consisting of one trimeter line followed by two in pentameter, giving a technically intricate pattern of continual variety.

1: Damon is a generic pastoral name – in this case for a shepherd mourning his dead beloved.

5: The prison is the tomb of the beloved.

12: The echoic pun in this line intensifies the grief felt by Damon.

23: In the past, the beloved never showed Damon any favour.

25: Damon is the unfortunate one.

53: The ring which has lost its stone is like an eye gone blind.

79–80: Occurring at a near-central position in the work, this couplet, formally unique in consisting of two consecutive trimeter lines, inevitably captures the attention of the reader, even as it encapsulates the entire message of the poem.

87: Pan – god of wild nature, of shepherds and their flocks.

89–90: Jove (Jupiter), the chief god, dealt death with his sceptre.

97: Zephyrus was the gentle, fructifying wind of springtime.

117: Hybla (in Sicily), where bees produced famous honey, produces here only bitterness.

123: The shepherd Argus, with his hundred eyes, was appointed guardian of Jove's beloved Io, who had been metamorphosed into a white heifer.

124: Another device of intensification, conjoining the ideas of quiet and perpetuity, with tears dropping as if from a still.

129: Helen's tears gave rise to helenium flowers (cf. WD1/129).

WD16

Text: *Poems* (1616), L4v.

This sonnet makes an interesting comparison with that of Robert Kerr (RK2).

4: The eternal love refers to God.

9: Zephyr – the west wind.

WD17

Text: *Forth Feasting* (Edinburgh, 1617), sig. A1–B4v.

Motto (on titlepage): *Flumina senserunt ipsa, quid esset amor* [The rivers themselves felt what love is.] – Ovid, *Amores*, 3.6.24.

1: The opening of the poem consists of the first words of the personified River Forth, as if of a god aroused from slumber. The sudden noise is that of the welcome given to King James.

16: The river remembers the king's previous residence in Edinburgh.

17: James is hailed as god and man, appropriately heralded by a star in the east (cf. Matthew 2:2).

24: Helen's brothers were Castor and Pollux, transformed by Zeus into the constellation Gemini; they were invoked by sailors seeking favourable winds.

25: The phœnix, ever renewed by self-immolation, had its home in Arabia. One of James's early works was the tragedy of 'Phœnix' (1584), on his then favourite, Esmé Stewart, 1st duke of Lennox (d. 1583).

26–29: Memphis is in Egypt, by the Nile, close to the temple at Saqqara dedicated to the god Serapis.

30: Mygdonia was the name of a region of Grecian Thrace, and of another in northern Mesopotamia. Of neither is a connection with Serapis recorded, nor is either likely to have supplied any stone carved in Memphis.

32: Apollo, the sun god, admired the song of the Phœnix.

36: India in particular was famous as a source of rubies.

37–38: Jove/Zeus is said by Pindar to have rained down golden showers when the blue-eyed Pallas Athene sprang from his temples.

39: The hours of day, personified as the Horae, should never complete the garment that they are weaving, and so bring the day to an end.

43: Arion of Corinth was a famous poet and lyre-player, who, having been thrown into the sea, was saved by a dolphin charmed by his playing.

49–62: A list of Scottish (Albanian) rivers, of which the modern names are: Tay, Tyne (East Lothian), Don, Dee, Spey, Naver (Sutherland), Ness, Leven (Dumbartonshire), Ken, Ayr, Doon, Urr, Nith, Clyde, Tweed, Annan, Liddel, Esk (Black and White); Lomond and Ryan are lochs, Solway a firth.

51: From the Grampian Mountains and the Ochil hills flow many tributaries of the Forth; these do not need to be named separately.

75: King James entered England on 6 April 1603, *en route* to London.

76: Another case of *epanorthosis* – cf. WD7/9.

77: sighs* - emended from *sights*.

81–82: Ceres was the goddess of agriculture, crops and fertility. Her daughter Proserpine was carried off by Pluto, the god of the underworld, and only restored to the earth for six months of each year.

89: Naiads were water-nymphs who inhabited fountains and streams; Napaeæ inhabited pools in wooded valleys.

95: Tithonus, a prince of Troy, was loved by Eos (goddess of the dawn); although made immortal, he continued subject to the ageing process.

104–06: Hydaspes, in modern Pakistan, was famous for its pearls; Indian Ganges received the offerings of the faithful, and was first to see the sunrise; Acheloüs was the god of a river in western Greece, often depicted with the head of a bull.

107: The Elysian fields were the lands of the blessed dead.

108: The sight of the king made eclipsed everything else.

111: Hecla is a volcano in Iceland; Quincy/Quinsay (i.e. Kinsai) is a lake in China, mentioned by Marco Polo.

117: Sisters – the three Fates, responsible for the thread of man's destiny.

124: Halcyon days were those in winter when no storms could occur.

125: diadems – the crowns of two kingdoms.

128: The opposition is that between (deserving) Virtue and (undeserving) Fortune.

134: Fortune, goddess of chance, was often depicted veiled, and with her famous wheel; Drummond implies that good fortune will never desert the king.

135–40: James was passionately fond of hunting.

145–78: Drummond sketches James's intellectual achievements in (*inter alia*) divinity, cosmology, astronomy, astrology, meteorology, psychology, government, justice, music and poetry.

163: Just as Atlas had to support the heaven, so James the kingdom.

164: spare the humble – cf. SG2/34.

168–72: The fountain in the Pierian groves was sacred to the Muses and source of poetic inspiration. James's 1584 poem *Uranie* (the heavenly Muse) was a translation from Du Bartas. The walls of Thebes were built by the music of Amphion, son of Zeus. Arion's playing charmed a dolphin and saved his life. Orpheus overcame Pluto by his music and almost brought his wife Eurydice back to the land of the living.

175–78: Apollo and the Muses, habitually resident on Mount Helicon or in the Vale of Tempe, lose their own language, in marvelling at the poetry produced in Britain. Virgil described Britain as 'divided from the world' in Eclogue I, 66.

182: By 1617 there was little resistance in Scotland to James's policies.

184: Phaethon foolishly tried to drive his father's chariot of the sun. The reference is presumably to the assassinated rulers William of Orange (1584), Henry III of France (1589), Henry IV of France (1610). Recently dead from natural causes were Charles IX of Sweden (1611), and Emperor Rudolf II (1612).

193: The spheres are those of the Old World and the transatlantic New.

195–201: The Bear, Arcturus, Leo and Orion are constellations; Artemis/ Diana, sister of Apollo, is the Virgin Huntress.

200: Zeus struck Phaethon from the chariot of the sun; he fell into the River Eridanos, by legend associated with the Po, in Italy.

217: cf. Isaiah 2:4.

223: The green locks of Ceres are the leaves of the growing crops.

225: Pan was the god of the wild woods; Pales, of shepherds.

226: Piracy has been suppressed.

227: The Palladium was a statue of Pallas Athene, protectrix of Troy, then of Rome.

233–34: Three peoples notoriously difficult to reduce to subjection: the Scythians, in Asia, the Gaditans, in southern Spain, and those of Aurora (i.e. the dawn), in the Far East.

248: The earth was viewed, Pole to Pole, as having seven distinct climatic zones.

250: The three rivers Thames, Liffey and Tay denote the three kingdoms ruled by James.

252: All that the planet (Earth) will see in one year.

255–84: The similarity of structure and wording in these three paragraphs mark them as an emotional high-point within the poem.

261: Astræa, the virgin goddess of justice, abandoned the wicked world of men for life in heaven; now she keeps her sword upright, and her scales in balance.

263: The god Saturn was associated with time and with agriculture, and with an early Golden Age.

273: cf. Isaiah 11:6.

276: Weather-vanes, atop church-steeples.

279: Hyperion is a Titan, and here stands for the sun, which sees the area of James's influence spread through the world.

280–84: The country ruled by James is symbolised by the heraldic lion rampant (Scotland) and the Tudor rose (England); foreign powers are symbolised by the rivers Iber (Spain), Tiber (the Papacy), and Rhine (the Palatinate, of which the Elector had married (1613) Princess Elizabeth, the 'hence-brought beams').

291–92: While still in his mother's womb, James miraculously survived the murder of Rizzio (1566); more recently he survived the Gowrie Conspiracy (1600) and the Gunpowder Plot (1605).

295–300: Among the peoples impacting on British history were the Picts, Danes and Normans. Brutus/Brute of Troy is the legendary eponymous first king of Britain.

312: To Virgil, the age of Augustus inaugurated a period of blissful peace (Eclogue IV).

313–15: The reign of James will surpass that of other famous British kings, from Arthur onwards.

316: Edward III founded the Order of the Garter (1348).

318: The Idalian star is the planet Venus.

319–20: Proteus was both a god of the sea, and a prophet.

322–34: The British settlement in America, with Jamestown (1607) as its focal point, adds to James's glory. The new colony lies further west than the Fortunate Isles of Ancient legend, or the Somers Islands (now Bermuda), settled in 1609.

328: Jamestown stands on the James River, in Virginia.

330: The Sibyls prophesied the peace, coming under Augustus (cf. line 312).

336: cf. the proverb: *finis coronat opus* [the end crowns the work].

343–47: The sun, in the course of a year, observes everything above and below it, including the constellations of the Greater and Lesser Bear, circling the North Pole, and witnesses the advent of Auster, the warm wet south-west wind of autumn.

355: The poet may be thinking of Edinburgh Castle, on its great rock.

357: The Scottish rivers, though they may meander, all flow directly into the sea, the home of Thetis – unlike, for example, the Isis, which flows into the Thames.

358: Nestor, king of Pylos, was famously old when taking part in the Trojan War.

359–60: The Titan Cronos (Saturn to the Romans) devoured his own children and was overthrown by his son Zeus, and imprisoned in Tartarus. However, he is also associated with the Golden Age (cf. line 263), and the presence of Saturn (grim, but bound) in Scotland betokens a time of prosperity for the country.

361–62: Zeus, in the form of a swan, made love to Leda, queen of Sparta; Pasiphaë, queen of Crete, was impregnated by a white bull sent by Poseidon, and gave birth to the Minotaur. The poet doubtless has in mind the aboriginal British white cattle, as praised by Hector Boece (*Chronicle of Scotland*, trans. John Bellenden (Edinburgh, 1540?), Introduction, chap. X).

364: The beautiful shepherd Endymion was loved by the goddess Selene, the moon.

368: Perhaps a reference to the kestrel, which has long wings and hovers.

371: The Paniskoi dwelt in forests, like satyrs, and were followers of Pan. Pomona was a wood-nymph and goddess of fruit. The maiden followers of the sea-nymph Thetis bring amber from the northern island Thule.

373: Triton was a son of Poseidon, god of the sea, and often portrayed as one of many mermen, who harvest the sea as if shepherds.

375–78: Seres, a land in the Far East, was most famous for its silks; Erythrea (Eritrea) was noted as a source of gem-stones. In the New World, Argentina, by the River Plate, produced an abundance of silver, and Peru of gold. Antarctic parrots (whichever bird species is meant) are from the southern hemisphere in general, rather than from Antarctica; exotic feathers are from Ethiopia. Saba (Yemen) was celebrated as the source of incense and fragrant spices.

383–84: At Oxford the Thames is known as the Isis. On the occasion of the royal visit to Edinburgh, the university (originally the 'Tounis College') was renamed 'King James's College', which would have added an academic dimension to the competition between the two rivers and countries.

387–90: Isis, despite being comparable with Seine (France) and Rhine (Holy Roman Empire), is outclassed by Forth, which has the greatest, since the longest, claim upon James's affection.

391–98: The Thames chides James for indulging in a romantic dalliance with the Forth.

400: wore* – emended from *The Muses' Welcome* (1618). In 1617: were.

405: The Hours [Horae] were goddesses of the seasons, and responsible for keeping the record of passing time.

WD18

Text: *Flowres of Sion* (1623), p. 23.

Title: adopted from Kastner.

The sonnet owes much to the neo-Stoical philosophy, combined with Christianity, which was widespread at the time, and which clearly appealed to the bookish Drummond.

8: Earthly passions are to be converted into citizens of the heavenly regions.

WD19

Text: *Flowres of Sion* (1630), p. 104.

King James died on 27 March 1625 and was buried on 7 May in Westminster Abbey.

1–4: David, Solomon, Numa (advised by the minor goddess Egeria), Augustus and Constantine (son of Helena, finder of the True Cross) were famous kings or emperors, enjoying divine approval.

6: After his contest with Marsyas, Apollo was borne heavenwards by a swan; the dead James will similarly have been transported – as in Rubens's painting of the Apotheosis of King James (1634).

8: The fame of James extends to all points of the compass.

11: Niobe's children were all killed, which made her a famous figure of mourning; all the remaining virtues become like her.

13–14: According to the poets, the first age of man was golden, and the best; the last age was that of iron, and was the worst.

WD20

Text: Edinburgh, NLS, Hawthornden MS 2062, fol. 9 (a discarded draft is at fol. 28). Reprinted in Kastner II, 236, who notes (p. 397) that it is based on madrigal by Giovanni Battista Guarini (1538–1612).

William Mure

WM1

Text: Edinburgh, EUL MS La. III. 454, fol. 14v.

Title: Supplied. In the MS the heading is merely 'Sonett'. In the poet's hand, the page is dated 1616. It is not clear whether the poet's muse is an earthly beloved, a personification of his inspiration (as in WM4/1–5), or the Holy Spirit.

1–4: Mure gives as standard reasons for writing poetry fame, innate talent, and personal ambition.

9–12: Three different poetic styles lend themselves respectively to the topics of the lady's quality (elegiac), beauty (lyric), and excellence (heroic).

WM2

Text: Edinburgh, EUL, MS La. III. 453, fols. 37–38.

Title: Supplied. Extracted from Book II of *Dido and Æneas*. Lines 301–42 are Mure's addition to the Classical story.

The background: After the sack of Troy, Æneas and his men, driven by the winds, eventually arrive at Dido's city of Carthage, in North Africa; there they are welcomed, and the hero becomes enamoured of the queen. When they are out on a hunting party, a storm, raised by Juno, forces them to take shelter in a cave, where their love is consummated.

298: The goddess Juno, always hostile to Æneas, caused the storm to prevent his journeying on to Rome.

300: Fairies are often associated with mountain-tops.

306–10: Typically, the hero's will is conquered via the senses, and Dido is cast as the seductress.

318: The beautiful song of the Sirens lured mariners to their watery grave.

323: The blinded boy is Cupid, god of sexual attraction.

WM3

Text: Edinburgh, EUL, MS La. III. 453, fols. 44–46.

Title: Supplied. Extracted from Book II of *Dido and Æneas*. Lines 589–658 are Mure's addition.

The background: Despite the firm love between Æneas and Dido, the gods inform the Trojan hero that his destination is to found a new dynasty at Rome. Reluctantly, he accepts that he must leave Carthage, and in secret begins to make preparations to depart.

619: The cave is that of WM2.

648: Dido's colouring is not artificial, but derives from a combination of love and modesty.

679: Dido was being pressurised by the Berber king Iarbas.

695: Thund'rer – Jupiter, the chief god.

WM4

Text: *Muses' Welcome* (1618), pp. 271–74.

Title: The title adds that the occasion of the poem was 'on Moonday the xxviii of July', 1617. Since Mure's seat of Rowallan, near Kilmarnock, was close by Hamilton, it was natural for him to be invited to compose this poem of welcome to the King, who by that stage of his tour had already begun to head back to England.

4: Mure's poetry before this date had been often on the theme of love (i.e. Venus and Cupid).

7–10: James excels even Apollo, the god of the sun, who ruled over the Muses.

13: The triple sceptre is that of Scotland, England and Ireland.

20: Many exorbitant contemporary prophecies of James spoke of him as the conqueror of continents.

21: Bellona – goddess of war.

41: A clutch of Ancient conquerors: Julius Cæsar, Trajan, Pompey, Alexander the Great.

52–54: Mure is presumably alluding to the King's ongoing interest in liturgical reform, and perhaps the innovations brought in after the General Assembly held at Aberdeen in August 1616. These changes alienated many of James's Scottish subjects.

57–60: A reference to the Gunpowder Plot (1605).

61–62: cf. Joshua 15:13–14.

63: envy'd* – emended from *envyd'd*.

77–78: Religious conflicts in the Low Countries, France, and Savoy – the latter at the hands of Spanish forces.

79: The salmon plays an important role in the legend of St Kentigern of Glasgow, and is featured on the town's coat of arms. When James announced his intention of visiting Scotland, he put it down to a 'salmon-like instinct' to return to the place of his original. Appropriately, James was presented with a gilt cup in the shape of a salmon, when he passed through Glasgow on his progress.

104–08: Mure refers to the Hamilton family and their closeness to, and service of, the Scottish royal family.

Patrick Gordon

PG1

Text: *The famous historie* (1615), sig. F2v–G2.

Title: Supplied.

Background: Bruce and Douglas join forces. Bruce discourses on the misery of Scotland under John Balliol, who has become a vassal of Edward I of England. Bruce begins his campaign of conquest. When hunting down a mighty and dangerous wolf, Bruce finds himself on a towering rock, where he loses the wolf but encounters an aged hermit, who turns out to be Thomas the Rhymer. Prophecies attributed to Thomas were well known, and several had been printed in *The Whole Prophesie of Scotland* (1603): see MacDonald 2013.

130: The moon is the queen of the night.

151: sicles* – emended from *siclee*.

153: The Prince is Robert (the) Bruce.

154: Diana, goddess of the hunt, here stands for the moon.

168: The reference is to the murder (1306) by Bruce of John III Comyn, Lord of Badenoch and a Guardian of Scotland, in the Greyfriars church at Dumfries.

173: The entire country pays the price for Bruce's sacrilegious crime and their own sins.

199–200: The apparatus not only shows the movements on earth, but also those in the heavens, in which each planet has its 'house'.

201: †*The diurnall motion of the sphers. Their naturall motion is shawed lykewayes* [shown in the same way,] *beginning at the moone.*†

203: The Primum Mobile, in the Ptolemaic system of astronomy, is the outermost of the several spheres around the earth, and sets those below it in motion.

214: †*To witt, Jupiter.*†

232: virtue* – emended from *virture.*

243–48: God conceives in advance what is later to happen in the physical universe; in particular, Bruce's descendants will become defenders of the Church.

255–56: The reference is to constellations, with their pagan names.

257: †*The Prophet'is Prayse.*†

263–64: The prophet's eyes are dark like the light of the moon, shining down on the earth, but he longs for illumination from the heavenly sunshine from above.

265: †*Heir follow the constellations about the polls, alooding* [alluding] *to the kings discendit of the Bruce.*†

268: God is the unique (sole) figure of majesty, but also, as the sun (sol), of light.

273: The rampant lion is the heraldic beast of the king of Scots.

273: †*Constellation: Hercules holds a lion bound in chayns, alluding to King Robert holding the Scots' arms.*†

279–80: This alludes to the acceptance of Bruce as king in Scotland, and doubtless also hints at that of James in England.

281: †*Constellation: Jason in the schip Argus. David Bruce* [1329–71] *that sailit to France, wheir he stayit nyne ʒeirs induring the warrs against the Baleoll ayded by England, but when he returnit he brought home peace allu—* [the subsequent words are lacking].†

287–88: Jason was the hero who sailed to Colchis with the Argonauts to capture the Golden Fleece; he married the king's daughter, the magician Medea.

289: †*Constellation: Auriga draweth a cotch* [coach] *full of gallent youths.*†

296: †Robert Stewart the 1., of whom the kingis of that name discended.†

297: Gordon passes over Robert II (1371–90). Robert III (1390–1406) is said to have wept for the sad fate of his eldest son, David, Duke of Rothesay.

299: Swans – unclear: perhaps a reference to the constellation in the Milky Way, deriving its name from Cygnus, the lover of Phaethon.

304: †*Constellation: Zepheus a-weeping for Andromada* [a] *Swane and a eagils one ether hand of him alluding to Robert the 3 [1390–1406].*† Andromeda was the daughter of Cepheus and Cassiopœia of Ethiopia; chained to a rock as prey for a monster, she was rescued by Perseus.

305: James I (1406–37).

308: †*Constellations: Perseus releives the vergin Andromadœ, ind*[icat]*ing James the first, who institute the colledge of justice.*† The College of Justice was actually founded under James V (1532). The reference is rather to the suppression of the tyrannical Albany Stewarts by James I, in the early fifteenth century.

311: †*Medusa's head.*† Medusa was a female monster, with snakes for hair; killed by Perseus.

313: †*Constellatione: Chiron the centaur with a lance holds a wolf by the nek alooding to James the 2, a zelous reformer of sinne and wyce.*† Chiron was the tutor of the young Achilles. The wolf is an emblem of lawlessness.

318–20: The poet's words on the renewal of religion presumably relate to James's foundation (1429) of the Charterhouse, *Val virtutis*, [Vale of Virtue], at Perth.

321: †*Heir the prophet taks occasion to intreat* [insert] *a litel of the beginning of the Hammiltouns.*† On the origins and early rise of the Hamilton family, see Borthwick, *ODNB*.

329: †*Sir James Hamiltoun, that mareit King James the 2. his doghter.*†

331–33: The family of the Hamiltons is the garland with which the gods will ever decorate the temples of the royal family.

334: †*King James 6.*† James, at the time of Gordon's writing, was the flower at the end of the genealogical stem.

337: The worthy prince here is James II. James, 1st Lord Hamilton, became the (second) husband of Mary Stewart, countess of Arran and sister of James III. †*King James the 4. send Hammilton Erll of Arran with ane armie with the Danish king whom he reastablist in his kingdom and after returned to his countrey with great glorie.*† This was James Hamilton, 1st earl of Arran (c. 1475–1529), who was sent with a navy to assist King Hans of Denmark, uncle of James IV, in suppressing a rebellion on the part of the Swedes: see Greig, *ODNB*.

346: Thetis – a sea-nymph, one of the Nereids.

353–54: Hamilton's campaign will restore the king of Denmark to his throne.

361: †*The Erll of Arran, Protector of Scotland in Queene Mare'is minoritie, whom the King of France maid Duge of Chastelraut.*† This was James, Lord Hamilton, 2nd earl of Arran (c. 1519–1575), Duke of Châtelherault in France: see Merriman, *ODNB*.

365: The king of France styled himself 'Most Christian'.

377–84: With this flattering stanza Gordon ends the prophet's digression on the Hamiltons.

385: James III (1460–1488) is seen as the constellation Serpentarius (i.e. Ophiucus, the serpent-bearer); his favourites are the base-born snakes in his hand.

385: †*Constellacion: A serpent in either hand of Serpentarius: alloding to King James the 3. Reuld by Chochrins and the Dasie, who lik serpentes poisoned the land with vice, the cause of his fall.*† The snakes in the hand of James III (1460–88) are his favourite Thomas Cochrane and Dasie, alleged to be the king's catamite.

393: †*Constellation.* [Arcturus] *Induc*[ating] *an archer marching to fight on fut. James the 4., who flighting on fut was sleane in Flouden Field.*† The archer is James IV (1488–1513), killed at Flodden.

401: †*Constellatione Bootes is a man strong and powerful: James the 5* [1513–42].†

405: †*Constellatione Cassiopea is a quein setting in a chyre* [chair]: *Quein Marie, dowager of France. Berenici's crinis or* [illegible], *cald the garland of hear* [hair].† Mary Queen of Scots (1542–1567). Berenice II, Ptolomaic queen of Egypt, is said to have dedicated locks of her hair to Aphrodite/Venus; the hair, transported to the heavens, became the constellation known as *Coma Berenices*. This stanza refers briefly to James V and to his daughter Mary, but Gordon seems laconic in his comment on the latter.

PG2

Text: *The famous historie* (1615), sig. G2.

The single stanzas between the various books of Gordon's poem give summaries of the respective following matter. Spenser did similarly in the *Faerie Queene*.

1: †*Constellatione: the north and south crownes of Polophiax before him* an[d] *after: allading* [alluding] *to James the 6., who joynd the north and south crounes of Britane.*† 'Polophylax' was introduced by the Protestant clergyman and celestial cartographer Petrus Plancius in 1592, as the name of a southern constellation; however, the name was abandoned six years later.

4: James and Anne had three living children, but Prince Henry died on 6 November 1612.

PG3

Text: *The famous historie* (1615), sig. G2v–H2v.

Title: Supplied.

4: i-wish – the print has 'I wish', but the archaising adverb *iwis* seems to be intended.

8: o're* – emended from *o'ra*.

9: †*The north and south crowns: corona borealis, corona australis.*†

12: Titan – the sun.

25: †*God'es wonderfull love showin to him in his so many and notabile delyveries from treson.*†

50: James's triple crown (of Scotland, England and Ireland) is a Protestant counterpart to that of the Pope: significantly, James's head adorns the crown, not vice versa.

52: †*Sol* [the sun], *monarch of the north, and prince of poets.*†

59: †*His eloquence compaird to a queene.*† This leads to the use of both him and her for James.

63: The River Tagus (Portuguese: Tejo) was famed for bearing golden ore.

65: †*His wark cald the Battell of Lepanto.*†

67: cannons – emended from *connons.*

70: Crœsus was the fabulously rich king of Lydia.

72: †*His book against Magik.*† The reference is to James's *Daemonologie* (Edinburgh, 1597).

74: †*His answer to that book sett furth in the nam of Bellarmine.*† This is either James's *Triplici nodo, triplex cuneus* [A triple wedge for a triple knot] (1608) or his *Premonition to Christian Princes* (1609), both being contributions to the controversy stirred up by the Oath of Allegiance of 1606, to which the Pope's reply was composed by Cardinal Bellarmine.

91: Heaven rewards James according to his virtue by assigning him everything that will make his fame eternal.

97: The valley of the River Forth.

99: Araby – *Felix Arabia* (i.e. modern Yemen).

100: †*The description of Stirling, the birth-place of Prince Henrie.*† The Vale of Tempe, in Thessaly, is conventionally cited by poets as the most famously beautiful landscape in all Ancient Greece.

103: The Ochils are a range of hills, north of the Forth, and extending east from Stirling.

108: Thetis – a sea nymph.

111: The source of the Forth lies in the lower Grampian mountains.

114: The castle and town of Stirling are built on a rocky outcrop.

124–28: The towers seek their reflection in the water, and when lit by the sun turn the river to gold.

131: †*Constellation: Antinous, a must rear* [most rare] *and beutifull youth, alooding to Prince Henrie.*† Henry was born in Stirling Castle on 19 February 1594. Antinous was the favourite of Emperor Hadrian.

133: Prince Henry died on 6 November 1612, aged 18.

143: Albion – the united kingdom.

145: †*Constellation: Orion, marching in arms our a river, and a heir* [chief] *under his foot, alooding to Charlis, Prince of Waillis, acording to the propheseis.*† Charles was proclaimed Prince of Wales on 4 November 1616. Orion was a famous hunter.

150: The rivers suggest the future empire of Charles, who will have conquered the Holy Roman Emperor (Danube/Vienna) and matched
Alexander the Great (Nile, Ganges).

153: †*Hee as generall under his father.*†

161: †*The vearsis following ar translated out of the Propheseis.*† Gordon is
referring to such texts in *The Whole Prophesie of Scotland* (1603) – cf.
MacDonald (2013).

166: The empire of Charles will extend from India to Orkney; Orcades*
– emended from *Occades*.

167: †*Agreing with the Propheseis.*† cf. line 161.

169: †*Hiedra, alluding to the greate Turk.*† The Ottomans were a real
threat to central Europe. The Lernæan Hydra was a many-headed
serpentine monster, killed by Hercules as the second of his Twelve
Labours.

173: †*Corona australis, corona borealis* [Southern crown, northern
crown].†

175: †*Crux* [The Cross of Christ].† Gordon presents James here as a
crusader who, after defeating the Turks, will carry to Jerusalem the
Cross, with which Christ defeated sin and death and harrowed hell.

182: James's virtues mean that Fortune and her vicissitudes are entirely
powerless.

185: †*Hercules' twelf labors.*† The Ancient Greek hero Hercules performed twelve great tasks.

187: him – i.e. James.

197–200: Gordon uses the motif here of the Three Ages of Man.

203: †*A digression discriving the river Po.*† The label of 'two horned'
may be indebted to Revelations 13:11, and refer to the river emerging
from the earth at its Alpine source. The Po, here personified, is so
impressed by the victorious arrival of Charles as to instruct his
waters to cease their normal flow.

207: This refers to the silvery colour of the icy water gushing down from
the Alps.

209–11: The silver hair of the aged hermit is an image for waterfalls.

212: steam* – emended from *steams*; foorth* – emended from *foorrh*.

221: lord – i.e. the River Po.

229: There is a pun on *currant* and *corranto* (a dance).

232: The Po envisages Charles's forces on the eastern side of the Adriatic, fighting with the Ottoman forces.

254: first* – emended from *frost*.

265: †*Propheceis*.† Bruce is warned for himself against the possibility of pride, and also of future danger for the entire country: by implication, therefore, he should be a conqueror in the manner of James and Charles.

275: †*Glaidsmoor*.† In the Whole Prophesie of Scotland (cf. PG3/161), a battle at Gladsmoor, in connection with Bruce, is obscurely predicted by Bertlington and Waldhave, who both refer to Thomas the Rhymer.

282–88: This warning, given to Bruce, is discreetly aimed at James and Charles.

296: †*He deit onperformd this vow, whar for he send his heart to the holie ground*.† Bruce was not the only medieval king to die before a vow of crusade-pilgrimage to Jerusalem could be performed.

302: †*This was Thomas Rymour, ane old prophet who died about six months after this time*.† Sir Thomas de Ercildoune (thirteenth century) is remembered as the Thomas the Rhymer of medieval romance and from ballad. Prophecies attributed to him were printed in 1603 (cf. note to PG3/161).

307–14: The angelic source of the prophecies guarantees that they have been communicated from the Trinity, and not from any devil or witch.

316–20: This refers again (cf. PG1/168) to Bruce's murder of Comyn in the church of the Greyfriars at Dumfries, but conveniently makes clear that Jove (i.e. God) has forgiven the sacrilege.

329–36: †*King Robert hade a base [bastard] soone that was Erll of Ros, of whom is descended the two famous families of Clakmanan and Erthe [Airth], both surnemid Bruce*.† The name of Bruce would be 'beautified' via the two noble branches of the Bruce family, established on either side of the Forth, near Stirling. The direct line of the royal Bruce family was fated to cease, but the noble line continued to flourish as a result of the dynastic marriage union with the Stewart family.

336: can* – emended from *con*. Stirling Castle, by the Forth, was traditionally used as a safe residence for children of the royal family.

340: The brightness of the sun is reduced to that of the moon.

350: Twixt* – emended from *Tiuxt*.

358–59: cf. Luke 1:37.

360: After this visionary episode, the narrative returns to the business of knightly combat.

Patrick Hannay

PH1

Text: *Two Elegies* (1619), sig. C1–D2.

Title: Hannay's poem, which is witty in the style of the English Metaphysicals, is indebted both to the elegies of Donne and to the masque-pageants of Jonson; there is also clear influence from Drummond's *Mœliades* (WD1) and *Forth Feasting* (WD17).

1: Both England and Scotland answer the general appeal for support made by the Thames.

6: Anne died at Hampton Court on 2 March 1619, whence her body was brought by barge to lie in state in Somerset House, in the City of London. On 13 May the body was transported to Westminster, for burial in the Abbey.

13: The rivers are no longer pure water, but mixed with briny tears.

24: The Thames is the 'sovereign' of each brook.

33: As the two countries join in mourning, so the Thames and Forth mingle their tears.

35–38: Hannay insists on the Scottish river having equal status with the English.

39: Neptune is alarmed at the invasion of his waters by a stranger.

41: Triton, son of Poseidon, was, with his conch-shell, the messenger of the sea.

52: The bower of the Queen (Forth) is panelled with chrystal (water) and floored with pearls.

67: The embracing of the sister-rivers is a pretty piece of mannerism.

85: rapine* – emended from *rapiny*.

91: him – i.e. James.

110: Love forces the old foes to make him (James) their king.

118: The woman here is the personified Report/Fame (Latin: *Fama*).

117–24: In the past, Fame has wronged the kings of both Scotland and

England, by giving only half·an account to each about either, with that half purporting to be the whole truth. Just as the Queen of Sheba discovers the full truth of Solomon's greatness (cf. 2 Chronicles 9:1–9), so England is discovering that of James.

129–32: The Danes conquered Anglo-Saxon England, and, though hated, became kingly overlords, replacing the native royal family; as soon as the English were again free, they contemned the Danes as miscreants (*lurdanes*).

133–36: Hannay recalls that Queen Anne was of the royal house of Denmark.

140: Posteritie* – emended from *Pesteritie*.

141–43: The union of the rivers (i.e. countries) is likened to the physical union of lovers – initially happy, but on this new occasion sad.

149: After the death of Prince Henry, Charles became the heir apparent. The honour now given to Charles recalls that given to James, at his first entry into London.

150–54: The rivers strip the prettiest flowers from their respective banks.

155–56: The two rivers, in their pride, overflow their banks.

158: The master is Prince Charles, who accompanied the dead Queen from Hampton Court in the funerary barge. James was not present, on account of his own illness.

173–202: This description of the city shows life in gladness imitating art, with scenes which surpass those of Nature. From line 203, the mood is utterly transformed.

200: In grammar, participles belong to two categories, of verbs and adjectives.

201–02: The surprise is that a scene that seemed so glad could actually be the opposite.

207: Thames and Forth, like characters in a masque, are figured walking hand in hand, as mourners.

211: Phœbus, the sun, dims his light, in sign of his sorrow.

217–20: The dead Queen's soul shines down from Heaven, with a radiance reflected in the water.

226: The heavenly bodies become the funerary candles round the dead queen.

237: Hamadryads were linked with trees; Sylvans were followers of Silvanus, god of the woods.

247–70: This stanzaic choral lament is not typographically distinguished in the layout of the original print.

253: Meander was to the Ancient Greeks both god and river.

256: 'her' – supplied for metrical reasons in the recurring refrain.

259: Flora – the Roman goddess of flowers and the spring.

PH2

Text: *Two Elegies* (1619), sig. D3.

Title: A final verdict on the Queen, in phrases of neat contrasts, as in a concise epitaph on a tomb.

PH3

Text: *The Nightingale* [etc.] (1622), pp. 237–38. Title: Supplied.

PH4

Text: *The Nightingale* [etc.] (1622), pp. 240–44. Title: supplied. The original title is 'Song VIII'.

7: It is possible that Hannay has in mind a place such as the banks of the Thames at Twickenham, where Lucy, Countess of Bedford had her residence and held her *salon* between 1608 and 1617. The Countess's garden was described as a 'True Paradise' by Donne, in his 'Twicknam Garden'.

9: Persephone was queen of the summer.

11: Iris was both rainbow and messenger of the gods.

15: Delia – a name of the hunting goddess, Diana.

20: Silvanus – god of the woods, where satyrs resorted.

30: Nature was only a step-mother to this ugly place.

43: Croydon neighbours neither Thames nor Twickenham, but in the quasi-Spenserian allegory the geographical symbolism serves to point a moral.

59: Pluto – god of the underworld.

68–69: The reference is to charcoal-burners.

71: The sylvans are the various inhabitants of the woods.

PH5

Text: *The Nightingale* [etc.] (1622), pp. 245–49. Title: Supplied. The original title is 'Song IX'.

16: cf. Romans 6:23.

27–28: Christ was the only possible atoner for human sin.

29: This would seem to refer to the theological dogma of election, seen as a fixed legal contract between the soul and God, and which can be relied upon to hold.

39: The drops are distilled in a still, which is unceasing (still).

48: Human sin causes the Passion of Christ to be repeated.

61: cf. 1 Corinthians 13:13.

62: cf. Ephesians 2:1–3.

65: cf. Ezekiel 18:23.

67–68: cf. Matthew 11:28–30.

69–70: cf. Matthew 7:8; 13–14.

69: The leaf is one small section of a large door.

73–74: cf. Psalm 90:12.

PH6

Text: Lithgow, *A Most delectable and true discourse* (1623), sig. A4.

Title: The title of Master normally implies a graduate.

5–8: Lithgow was imprisoned and tortured at Malaga.

10–12: Lithgow had planned to describe the other side of the world.

15–24: Hannay describes a 'page-turner', impossible to put down.

William Lithgow

WL1

Text: *A Most delectable, and true discourse* (1614), sig. T3v.

Title: Supplied. Helen was the wife of Menelaus, king of Sparta and brother of Agamemnon of Mycenae, king of Argos. Paris eloped with her to Troy, thereby causing war between Trojans and Greeks.

3: Ilium – another name for Troy.

10: Phrygia was a kingdom of Asia Minor.

11: Priam – king of Troy, and father of Paris.

WL2

Text: *A Most delectable, and true discourse* (1614, sig. A1v–A2). The copy is defective, and after line 62 the edition of 1623 is followed (pp. 67–68).

Title: Supplied. A 'dier' is a poem with personal and often melancholy content; on the genre, see Verweij (2013). See also AC3, 4. Negroponte is today known as Chalcis/Chalkida. Lithgow is forced to act as look-out for the Greeks, who are fearful of a naval attack by Turks.

Motto: from Ovid, *Tristia*, I, I, 41–42 [Poems require quiet retreat and leisure on the part of the author; I am tossed by sea, storms, and untamed winter.].

1–8: This is reminiscent of Simion Grahame (cf. SG3 and SG5).

18: The comparison is to someone standing in an Ancient *tholos* [circular-shaped temple] awaiting the message from an oracle.

42: Argus had a hundred eyes, and was famous as a watchman.

57–64: Lithgow never forgets the pleasures of his home region, by the River Clyde.

67–68: The wearing of a willow wreath or of black (sable) clothing is a sign of mourning.

81–84: Lithgow, in this quasi-testament, contrasts the lasting value of his virtuous life and of his poetry, with the useless attraction of gold.

96: After the death of Prince Henry (1612) Charles was James's only sur-viving son.

WL3

Text: *The pilgrime's farewell* (1618), sig. [A2].

Title: This epistle introducing Lithgow's volume is addressed to the Muses.

2: Soron, Demthis – untraced.

3: Parnassus had a double peak.

9: Pactolus, a river in Lydia (western Anatolia), was famous for its golden sands.

10: The Tagus was also famous for its golden ore; a golden bough was carried by Æneas on his descent to the underworld (*Æneid*, vi).

11: Iris was goddess of the rainbow, with many-coloured wings, like the spread sails of a ship.

12: Hercules killed the hundred-headed monster, Hydra.

17–19: It seems typical of Lithgow, to rate natural talent higher than book-learning. The 'fondling' is his own verse.

WL4

Text: *The pilgrime's farewell* (1618), sig. [A4].

Title: The poem is both epistle and dedication.

2: small mite – cf. Mark 12:42–44; Luke 21:2–4. Like the poor widow in the Bible, Lithgow implies that he is a social outsider.

8: Thetis was a sea-nymph and leader of the Nereids. In Greece, several sea-caves are associated with her.

11: Certain flowers, like the sunflower, turn to follow the sun.

WL5

Text: *The pilgrime's farewell* (1618), sig. E3v–E4.

Title: Supplied. Lithgow's header runs: 'The Pilgrime's Farewell to Edinburgh: Dedicate to the Right Worshipfull, Sir William Nisbet of Deane, Knight, Lord Provost, etc., and to the rest, the right worthie Baylies and grave Magistrates of Edinburgh.' There were four baillies (magistrates) in Edinburgh, under the Provost. In casting himself as a pilgrim, Lithgow may owe something to Simion Grahame. Lithgow records the ceremonies at James's arrival in Edinburgh on 16 May 1617, and gives the impression that he witnessed the event (cf. lines 41, 51–54). However, his chronology is problematic. His departure from Scotland on his second pilgrimage (cf. line 52) occurred in 1612; he was climbing Etna in 1615 (cf. WL6); and on 18 September 1617 he was returning to the Clyde (cf. WL7); he left on his third pilgrimage in 1619. Even had Lithgow been present at the arrival of James, he would, on social grounds, very possibly not have been invited to be a contributor to either *Nostodia* (1617) or to the *Muses' Welcome* (1618), which collected the speeches of the burgh officials and the verses of the learned.

3: In a normal Royal Entry, the sovereign would first arrive at the West Bow, and then make his way, via the Grassmarket, up to the Castle Hill. Thereafter, he would proceed to enter the burgh again through the Overbow, which faced the Castle. The poet may be thinking of both gates.

5: The Senate consisted of the judges of the College of Justice (founded 1532).

10–11: John Hay, the Town Clerk, gave a speech to welcome James to Edinburgh. That done, the Provost may have been invited to mount, in order to accompany the King on his progress along the streets.

12: 'Our Apollo' is King James himself.

13–14: These lines appear to be addressed to Edinburgh itself.

17–18: The 'freedom' of Edinburgh was by tradition awarded at the Mercat Cross on the High Street, by St Giles' church. This spot, where royal proclamations were made, was the appropriate place for the King to knight the Provost, who thereby became the first 'Lord Provost'. The procession would then ride along the High Street and leave Edinburgh via the Netherbow, thereafter riding down the Canongate to the Abbey.

19: This was the entry to the enclosure surrounding and protecting Holyrood Palace.

20: 'Facound Nisbet' – presumably Patrick Nisbet, whose welcome speech (in English) is included in the *Muses' Welcome*.

21: Beginning around 1606, the burgh of Edinburgh begins to be referred to as a city.

23: Edinburgh Castle was traditionally known as 'Maidens' Castle' (*Castellum Puellarum*).

25: The parading would have taken place on the flat ground around Holyrood Palace.

37–42: The Town Council consisted of Merchants and Trades; the democratic Lithgow especially praises the latter.

44: Even on 16 May, the day of James's arrival, a glass pavilion would have been a wise precaution in Edinburgh.

45: A conceit was a fancy dessert dish, often involving an artistic creation made with sugar.

47: This is odd, or perhaps a merely vague allusion to something that Lithgow had himself not personally seen. James's birthday was 24 July.

54: The poet's leave-taking from Edinburgh is pure literary convention, since he would seem to have been abroad on the occasion of the event which he has just celebrated.

WL6

Text: *The pilgrime's farewell* (1618), sig. F1.

Title: Supplied. Lithgow's header runs: 'A Sonnet, made by the Author, being upon Mount Ætna in Sicilia, An. 1615. And on the second day thereafter arriving at Messina, he found two of his Countrey Gentlemen, David Seton, of the House of Perbroith [in Fife], and Matthew Douglas, now presentlie at Courte: to whome he presented the same, they being at that instant time some 40. Miles from thence.' In the version of 1623, Lithgow remembered a different list of the countrymen whom he met at Messina (on 16 August 1615), and there is no longer any trace of David Seton. The sonnet turns on the contrast between heights physical (Etna) and metaphysical (the soul). The antitheses are enlivened in the final lines by the realistic reference to the sweat dripping from the poet during his ascent. William Fowler also wrote a sonnet ostensibly on Etna (cf. Meikle et al, 1914–40: I, 269), but his somewhat trite Petrarchan amatory contrasts of fire and chill lack Lithgow's actuality.

7: Vulcan – god of fire.

WL7

Text: *The pilgrime's farewell* (1618), sig. G2v–G3v.

Title: Supplied. Lithgow's header runs: 'The Pilgrime, entring into the Mouth of Clyde, from Rossay, to view Dunbartane Castle, and Loch Lowmond, anno 1617, Septemb[er] 18, he saluted his native river with these Verses'. Lithgow is returning by water from his second long 'pilgrimage', and, via Rothesay and Loch Lomond, approaching his family seat, near Lanark, along the River Clyde. Immediately before this item in the *Pilgrime's farewell*, he had written of his escape from ship-wreck between Arran and Rothesay on 9 September, but now the mood changes to one of happy expectation.

15: The personification of the two rivers is reminiscent of Patrick Hannay (cf. PH1).

23: Isis, the Egyptian moon goddess, is associated with the Nile, but here with the Thames.

25: This seems to owe a debt to Drummond's *Forth Feasting*, 389–90.

27: Lithgow's assessment of the relative breadth of the Clyde is a measure of his local patriotism.

29: Dumbarton Castle, on its eminence, is a prominent landmark on the lower Clyde.

32: Scotland's two traditional ecclesiastical provinces are those of St Andrews and Glasgow.

33: 'City', as applied to Glasgow, is used informally.

36: The bridge in Glasgow, begun in 1611 and completed in 1624, had only seven (or eight) arches according to the English traveller, Sir William Brereton, writing in 1636 (Hume Brown 1891: 133, 152).

39: The reference is to the residence of the Marquess of Hamilton.

42: Aricke Stone is some sixteen miles upstream from Lanark, and Lithgow elsewhere calls the stretch from there down to Dumbarton 'The Paradise of Scotland': *Lithgow's Nineteen Years Travels* [etc.] (London, 1682), p. 472. Bute is an island in the wider Clyde estuary.

43: Hamilton Palace was less than one mile distant from the Clyde.

50–52: As Lithgow reaches his birthplace, he introduces a possessive 'our'. Corhouse Linn is an impressive waterfall on the Clyde, below Corra (Corhouse) Castle, and close to Lanark.

55: Tinto Hill is a prominent local landmark, round which flows the Clyde.

58–60: Sir James Carmichael (1579–1672) was baron of Hyndford, near Lanark: under Charles I appointed sheriff-principal of Lanarkshire, senator of the College of Justice, and Privy-Councillor.

62–63: Jore – unclear: Lithgow may be thinking of the Jordan, the Euphrates, or even the Indus; if a river nearer home is intended, could that be the Loire?

67: The 'losse' is that of the poet, in leaving the favourite river of his homeland.

WL8

Text: *The pilgrime's farewell* (1618), sig. H3v–H4v.

Title: Supplied. Lithgow's header runs: 'An Elegie, containing the Pilgrime's most humble Farewell to his native and never conquered Kingdome of Scotland.' This 'Elegie' – or dier (cf. WL2) – is to be understood as the words to be spoken by Lithgow, when he will set out on his third journey.

Motto: Only fragments of Euripides's play *Phœnix* have survived (here in Latin translation). [Farewell indeed to you, O my country, and homeland of my ancestors. For, though a man be overwhelmed by misfortunes, nothing is sweeter but only this, that it has nourished him.]

1: Lithgow again somewhat resembles Simion Grahame.

8–9: The poet contrasts the advancement of those who seem to make no effort, with his own lack of success; 'mouldarize' is a *hapax legomenon*: the poet turns mouldy upon the earth.

15–16: On his earlier journeys Lithgow had suffered at the hands of such peoples.

21: Gallus (Galdus) was a legendary king of Galloway.

23: Alexander Stewart became the first Lord Garlies in 1607, and in 1623 would become the 1st Earl of Galloway; the castle is close to Newton Stewart (Wigtonshire).

24: Kenmure castle, close to New Galloway (Kirkcudbright) was since the thirteenth century owned by the Gordon of Lochinvar family; Sir Robert would become a baronet in 1626.

25: Bombie, just over a mile east of the burgh of Kirkcudbright, was the seat of the MacLellan family; since 1582, however, it had been abandoned in favour of a new tower-house within the burgh. Sir Robert MacLellan was a courtier under kings James and Charles, and would become Lord Kirkcudbright in 1633.

26: Barnbarroch House, near Kippford (Kirkcudbright) was the residence of the Vaus family. Lithgow would have met Sir John Vaus, who was a gentleman of the chamber to James. His wife was Margaret MacDowall of Garthland (Wigtonshire).

27: Robert, 7th Lord Boyd of Kilmarnock (Ayrshire) (d. 1628) studied at the University of Saumur, in France.

29: Sir Hugh Campbell of Loudoun (Ayrshire) (d. 1622) – made a Lord of Parliament by James in 1601.

30: In 1612 Alexander Seton (d. 1661) succeeded his cousin Hugh Montgomerie, and became Montgomerie, 6th Earl of Eglinton; the ancestral seat was close to Kilwinning, in north Ayrshire.

31: William, Lord Kilmaurs (d. 1630) – the eldest son of the 7th Earl of Glencairn, but survived his father only by a few months.

32: James Cunningham, 7th Earl of Glencairn (d. 1630) – a Privy Councillor to James, and a Commissioner for the Union with England.

33: James, 6th Lord Ross of Halkhead (Renfrewshire) (d. 1633); in 1621 he became an opponent of James's Five Articles of Perth.

36: Lord Herries of Terregles (by Dumfries) – a cousin of Robert Maxwell, 9th Lord Maxwell.

42: William Alexander of Menstrie; William Drummond of Hawthornden.

43: Lithgow refers to the poets John Murray and Sir Robert Ayton.

44: On Lithgow's fellow Clydesdaler, Robert Allen, see below in this anthology.

46: Gordon may be a member of the family of Lochinvar (cf. line 24). Semple is probably Sir John Semple of Beltrees (Renfrewshire) (d. 1626). Maxwell is perhaps a relative or descendant of John Maxwell (d. 1606) of Southbar (Renfrewshire), who compiled a manuscript collection of poetry (cf. Bawcutt 1990: 60); alternatively, in view of the reference to Carlisle, it could be to Lord Herries of Terregles (cf. line 36).

47: The reference is perhaps to university students, with whom the poet wishes to associate himself.

51: God is Lithgow's witness.

56: Lithgow is an enthusiastic ambassador for his country.

59: Pilgrims normally carried such authenticated documents with them.

61–62: The poet's pure love for Scotland is his sacrificial offering.

WL9

Text: *The pilgrime's farewell* (1618), sig. G2.

Title: Supplied. Lithgow's couplet is more of a motto.

The poem belongs ostensibly to the genre of love-epistle, but it is characterised by a love of paradox worthy of the Metaphysical poets, with the disruption of the rhetoric of amatory convention extending even into the ambiguous valediction.

10: Lithgow refers to his first, then his second, thought.

WL10

Text: *A Most delectable discourse* (1623), pp. 203–04.

Title: Adopted from Lithgow (1623, p. 202).

1–14: At the end of his book, the poet in a sonnet makes a lists of the impressive worldly sights that he has encountered, but which have ultimately filled him with disgust (cf. Simion Grahame).

13: The pale streams (of worldly vanities) leave little (and no lasting) mark on the poet's eyes, which are watery from disillusion.

15–68: Lithgow is evidently imprisoned in a Charterhouse. The Protestant poet passes sardonic comments on the Italian and Spanish Catholics who are responsible for his physical sufferings. Ironically, the renowned frugality of the Carthusians (cf. the 'feast' in line 20) prepares the poet for a glimpse of heaven. This leads to a *faux-naif* stoical frame of mind in which the poet, hoping for heaven, affects to contemplate death with equanimity.

23–24: These words are Lithgow's ironic address to his Carthusian captors, whom he views as misguided in their lifestyle.

25: The poet confesses and boasts that the founder of his 'order' is none other than Christ.

27–28: The belief that good deeds help in salvation leads to the forging of the record of merits.

58: The humble commit minor sins through human nature, but the mighty through culpable neglect.

67: 'Learn to die' [*disce mori*] is a traditional maxim of Christian philosophy.

Robert Allen

RAL1

Text: *Mausoleum, or the Choisest Flowres of the Epitaphes, written on the Death of the never-too-much lamented Prince Henrie* (Edinburgh, 1613), sig. π4v.

Allen's epitaph is no. 13 of 16 in this little volume. The motto on the title-page is a famous line from a sonnet by Petrarch: *Cosa bella mortal passa, e non dura* [A beautiful and mortal thing passes away, and does not last.] (*Canzoniere*, 248).

RAL2

Text: *Teares of Joy* (1613), sig. B2.

The title-page indicates the author only by the initials 'R.A.', but 'Robert Allyne' signs [A3v] the dedicatory poem to Sir Thomas Erskine.

The motto, *Iam redit et virgo, redeunt Saturnia regna* [Now a virgin comes back, the reign of Saturn returns], is from Virgil's famous Eclogue IV, containing a prophecy of a future reign of religious peace and prosperity.

1: In 1610, on the death of his father, the convinced Calvinist Frederick V (1596–1632) became the Elector-Palatine within the Holy Roman Empire. His maternal grandfather was William the Silent, the leader of the Protestant Dutch Revolt against Spanish Habsburg rule.

2: Unlike James's daughter Princess Elizabeth, Frederick was by birth princely, not royal. In 1618, however, he would be chosen king of Bohemia – a step which triggered the Thirty Years War. The difference in respective ranks was also noted by John Donne, who in his Epithalamion on the Palatine marriage, compared Frederick to the moon, and Elizabeth to the sun.

3: Whose – referring to Frederick.

5–6: Frederick was noted for his intellectual talent and his spirituality.

13–14: The Palatinate supplied one of the seven eminences entitled to elect the Emperor [*Cæsar*]. The main part of the territory lay on the Rhine, with its capital at Heidelberg; there were also further exclaves, including some in what is now Bavaria.

16: James would have found enticing the prospect of being grandfather to a future Emperor.

20: The Elector Palatine was the hereditary *Erztruchses* or 'Arch-sewer' (i.e. chief steward) at the Imperial court. The coincidence of designation would doubtless have pleased King James Stewart.

RAL3

Text: In *Lithgow, A Most delectable discourse* (1614), sig. A3v.

Title: This indicates real affection between Allen and Lithgow. The uncommon term 'Condisciple' suggests that they may have been fellow-pupils at school in Lanark. According to the poem, Lithgow's travels offer great benefit to the stay-at-home noble spirits.

9: Allen would seem to have known Lithgow since his early years.

17–18: The poet is clearly aware of the demands of rhetoric and composition.

RAL4

Text: In Hannay, *The Nightingale* [etc.] (1622), sig. A4v.

Title: The 'image' in the title refers to a small engraving of Hannay's face, which, as one detail on the title-page of the 1622 collection, appears below a list of his works.

3, 10: Philomela is the main figure in Hannay's *The Nightingale* (based on Ovid). She is raped by her brother-in-law Tereus, king of Thrace – who cuts out her tongue to prevent disclosure of the deed. Philomela weaves a cloth with scenes depicting her tragic fate, and sends it to her sister Progne. In a mad fit, Progne kills her young son and cooks his flesh, which is served up in a banquet of honour to her husband, Tereus. Finally, all three are metamorphosed into birds, and it is as a nightingale that Philomela tells her story to the narrator.

4: 'Marian' is the heroine in Hannay's romance, *Sheretine and Mariana*. In Vienna, she falls in love with the hopeful youth John Sheretine, who unfortunately has to depart to war. Meanwhile, the rich Nicholas Turian arrives and pays court to her. The heroine is put under great pressure, and at length reluctantly consents to marriage. On his return, Sheretine is distraught, and dies of grief. Mariana commits suicide (as does Turian), but her soul is denied entry to the Elysian Fields before her ghost, in a dream, has completed telling her story to the narrator, who is enjoined to be true to his own mistress, one Cælia.

4: In *A happy Husband*, Hannay gives a witty description of the character of the male, and then of the female, partner in a marriage.

4: On *Elegies*, see PH1 and notes.

11–14: A tantalising hint of Hannay's literary talents.

RAL5

Text: EUL MS Laing.III.436, pp. 65–66.

1: It is possible that Allen has in mind the ford at Crossford, downstream from Lanark.

4: None can tell where the sword ended up.

9: Learned Sisters – the Muses.

12: *ars* [art] in book-titles denotes a book containing theoretical analysis and advice on application.

13: Ratcliffe was a suburb east of London, and a centre of shipbuilding; the Strand runs from the City towards Westminster.

16: Cheapside, a street in the City, is near London Bridge, and was a centre of financial activity; the Royal Exchange is located in the centre of the City, and was a focal point for official proclamations and for finance.

19: States – the authorities in the Dutch provinces, since 1572 in rebellion against Spain.

21: Lombard – money-lenders, or the pawn-shop.

28: 'hingers' are usually short swords, but here the poet seems to refer to the belt from which such short swords were suspended. At Court, and if the decoration of the hinger is sufficiently ornate in its decoration, the blade is left untested as to its true quality.

31: Agenor of Tyre sent his son Cadmus to retrieve Europa, who had been ravished by Zeus. Towards the end of his life, Cadmus was transformed into a snake. Through the allusion, Allen suggests that he has been sent abroad to fight for James's daughter, who with her husband, after being expelled by the Emperor from Bohemia and the Palatinate, had taken refuge in the Netherlands.

38: As the snake annually sheds its skin, so servants at court receive new livery at New Year – thus becoming turn-coats. In this literal sense, Allen comes to resemble the mythical Cadmus.

RAL6

Text: EUL MS Laing.III.436, pp. 51–52.

Title: A jerkin was made either of leather or of grogram.

The message of the poem would seem to turn on Allen's sense of not being appropriately rewarded for his (military?) service of almost two years. The never changed coat would thereby become an ironic symbol of the poet's unchanging loyalty – contrasting with the fickle turn-coats rewarded at Court.

12: The poet puns on 'freeze' and 'frieze' (a coarse woollen cloth). The contrast of temperatures may be an ironic evocation of the typical condition of the fire and ice torments of the Petrarchan lover. It is not inconceivable that there is a further pun on Friesland, as synecdoche for the Netherlands.

31: Owercomer – unrecorded in *DSL*. The poet ironically evokes the custom of burying the armour (spoils) of a dead hero in his tomb (cf. RAL5/22).

32: two* – emended from *tuo tuo*, for metrical reasons; the second word could, however, be the intensifying adverb 'too'.

RAL7

Text: EUL MS Laing.III.436, p. 77.

On James's efforts to bring about religious peace see Patterson (1997). This epitaph is ostensibly, and may well be genuinely, positive, but the laconic style of the genre makes it impossible to ascertain the poet's actual attitude to his subject.

Robert Kerr

RK1

Text: *Correspondence of Sir Robert Kerr, First Earl of Ancram*, ed. David Laing, Bannatyne Club, 2 vols. (Edinburgh, 1875), ii, 4888–89. From a letter, dated 24 April 1624, sent to Kerr's son William, then in Paris. Title: Kerr adds as subtitle: 'Out of Buchanan, to be sung to the French tune'.

13–18: Kerr has expanded on the psalm-text.

RK2

Text: *Correspondence of Sir Robert Kerr*, ed. Laing, ii, 521–22.

Title: In a letter sent to Drummond from Cambridge, dated 16 December 1624, Kerr sent this sonnet and records that it was written in the 'very Bed-Chamber' [i.e. of the King].

1: Where and how to find tranquillity of the soul was a popular topic for those of a neo-Stoic persuasion (cf. Allan 2000; MacDonald 2009b) – cf. Drummond's sonnet WD16.

2–3: Kerr adapts the Latin adage, *Felix quem faciunt aliena pericula cautum* [Happy is he whom the perils of others make circumspect] – cf. Robert Henryson, *Fables* (1033) – but rejects the thereby implied attitude of prudential *Schadenfreude*.

5: The poet, in his own note to this line, explains that, when the sun rises in the morning, it shines on dwellers in the country, and passes over those residing at Court.

George Lauder

GL1

Text: Edinburgh, NLS MS 1806 (Newhailes MS), fol. 1r-v.

Title: Supplied. Lauder's original header runs in the MS: '*Georgius Lauderus, ex antiquissima LAUDERORUM familia de HALTON Oriundus, Scotia descedens, Kalend*[is] *August*[i] *Patriæ, Parentibus, et amicis valedicit.*' [George Lauder, stemming from the most ancient family of the Lauders of Haltoun, on leaving Scotland on the first day of August says farewell to country, kin and friends.]

This poem, in the genre of the dier (cf. Verweij 2013), was written on or shortly after leaving Edinburgh for London. The poem begins on a neo-Stoical note, with Lauder accepting his fate, before it becomes a series of *adieux* to the members of his family circle. In the MS, the poem is followed by 'Laudero / Edenborough, 1622. / London', which suggests that the poem, even if begun in Scotland, was finished at London, and sent from there back to Lauder's family (cf. MacDonald 2018: 23–25).

1: shore – the Firth of Forth, by Edinburgh.

9: Like Simion Grahame and William Lithgow, the poet sets off on international travels.

14: Crœsus – king of Lydia, famous for his huge wealth.

18: The River Tagus (Portugal) was known to bear golden ore.

20: Bearing the ruler's stamp on coins.

22: The idea of *arete* [virtue, excellence] runs all through Lauder's writing.

23: Midas, king of Lydia, turned all he touched into gold.

24: An echo of the English poem, 'My mind to me a kingdom is', often attributed to Sir Edward Dyer (d. 1607).

33: cf. Matthew 6:19–21.

40: The fertile province of Lothian. Haltoun, the house where the poet was born, is not far from Edinburgh, the capital of the province.

41: Sir Alexander Lauder, 10th laird of Haltoun (d. 1627).

42: The achievements of the grandson (Sir Alexander) outshine those of the grandfather (George), killed at Flodden.

43: Nestor, in Homer, was the old and wise king of Pylos.

45: Annabel Bellenden, Lauder's father's second wife.

49: Lauder addresses the children of his father's two marriages.

51: When the time comes to accept death.

54: The poet had two half-sisters; presumably one was still unmarried.

63: The identity of Lauder's *inamorata* is unknown.

70: Lauder echoes the motto of Simion Grahame's 1604 collection.

71: 'Time trieth truth' – proverb.

GL2

Text: *Anatomie* (1623), sig. D4.

Title: Pope Alexander VI (ruled 1492–1503); sixth – emended from *third*.
   The Neapolitan humanist Jacopo Sannazaro (1458–1530) wrote prose

and poetry in Italian and Latin; his satire on this corrupt Borgia Pope was famous, and Lauder here quotes the first line. [Stay, traveller; perhaps you do not know of whom this monument is made.]

3: Philip of Macedon, father of Alexander the Great.

10: Lucrezia Borgia (1480–1519), Pope Alexander's daughter and – reputedly – concubine.

14: Caligula and Heliogabalus – two notoriously wicked Roman Emperors.

GL3

Text: *Anatomie* (1623), sig. C2v–C3v.

Title: Lauder's own addition to his translation and adaptation of *Cento ex Virgilio de vita monachorum* [Virgilian cento on the life of monks] by Lelio Capilupi (1497–1560). Capilupi was secretary to Isabella d'Este (1474–1539), Marchioness of Mantua and a leading figure of the Italian Renaissance. The very popular cento consisted of recombined phrases taken from the Roman poet Virgil.

1: Lauder here refers to the Pope.

16: The power of the keys, given to St Peter (cf. Matthew 16:19); emblem of the Popes.

18: The *triregnum* with which Popes were crowned.

20: Visitors to the Vatican kissed the Pope's slipper, as a gesture of their humility.

22: The East and West Indies, under the control of Catholic rulers. Lauder puns on *potent* (powerful) and *putent* (stinking [Latin: *putens*]).

29: An insulting reference to the Pope.

30: The Conclave, convened to elect a new Pope.

35–39: The scandalous legend of Pope Joan necessitated a check of the sex of any new Pope.

37: †*Platina, de vitis Pontific*[um] *Roman*[orum], *etc.*†

53: †*Witnesse the two last kings of France.*†.

55–56: An anticipation of the assassinations of William of Orange (1584) and Henry IV (1610).

60: †*Witnes the tapestry hangings in his parlour at Rome, wherein the description of the massacre at Paris is gorgeously set out.*†

GL4

Text: Newhailes MS: Edinburgh, NLS MS 1806, fol. 3v.

Title: The MS adds that this poem written in Paris in 1624.

Brackets in the MS (cf. MacDonald 2018: 223–25, 371) make it clear that, in each stanza, the first two lines, and also the fourth, are to be repeated, presumably for the purpose of singing; such features have precedents in the work of Alexander Scott and other poets in the Bannatyne MS. In its flippant style and wholly male-centred perspective, the poem is also reminiscent of Ayton (cf. RAY3, 7, 8).

35–36: To wear the willow was, traditionally, to mourn a lost lover; horns symbolise the cuckold.

37: The rose, by metonymy, stands for the beloved.

41: cf. Donne, Elegie VIII.

BIBLIOGRAPHY

Primary Sources

Craigie, Sir William A., ed., *The Maitland Folio Manuscript*, STS, 2 vols. (Edinburgh and London, 1919–27).

Craigie, James, ed., *The Poems of James VI of Scotland*, STS, 2 vols. (Edinburgh and London, 1955–58).

Drummond, William, *The Works of William Drummond of Hawthornden* (Edinburgh, 1711).

Echlin, David, *L'adieu au monde de David Echlin* (London, 1627).

Echlin, David, *Echlin par la grace de Dieu resuscité* (London, 1628).

Flood, John, ed., *The Works of Walter Quin: An Irishman at the Stuart Courts* (Dublin, 2014).

Gullans, Charles B., ed., *The English and Latin Poems of Sir Robert Ayton*, STS (Edinburgh and London, 1963).

Irving, David, ed., Thomas Dempster, *Historia ecclesiastica gentis Scotorum*, Bannatyne Club, 2 vols. (Edinburgh, 1829).

Jack, R. D. S. and R. J. Lyall, eds, Sir Thomas Urquhart, *The Jewel* (Edinburgh, 1983).

Jameson, Robert, ed., Sir David Murray, of Gorthy, *Poems*, Bannatyne Club (Edinburgh, 1823).

Jameson, Robert, ed., Simion Grahame, *The Anatomie of Humors, and the Passionate Sparke of a Relenting Minde*, Bannatyne Club (Edinburgh, 1830).

Kastner, L. E., ed., *The Poetical Works of William Drummond of Hawthornden*, STS, 2 vols. (Edinburgh and London, 1913).

Kastner, L. E. and H. B. Charlton, eds, *The Poetical Works of Sir William Alexander*, STS, 2 vols. (Edinburgh and London, 1921–29).

Kinnear, Thomas, ed., *Poems by Sir David Murray of Gorthy*, Bannatyne Club (Edinburgh, 1823).

Laing, David, ed., *Various Pieces of Fugitive Scotish Poetry; principally of the seventeenth century* (First Series) (Edinburgh, 1825).

Laing, David, ed., *The Poetical Works of Alexander Craig*, Hunterian Club (Glasgow, 1873).

Laing, David, ed., *The Poetical Works of Patrick Hannay*, Hunterian Club (Glasgow, 1875).

Laing, David, ed., *Correspondence of Sir Robert Kerr, First Earl of Ancram* [etc.], Bannatyne Club, 2 vols. (Edinburgh, 1875).

Laing, David, ed., *A Theatre of Scottish Worthies: and The Lyf, Doings, and Deathe of William Elphinston Bishop of Aberdeen, by Alexander Garden*, Hunterian Club (Glasgow, 1878).

Lawson, Alexander, ed., *The Poems of Alexander Hume (?1557–1609)*, STS (Edinburgh and London, 1902).

Legg, J. Wickham, ed., *The Sarum Missal* (Oxford, 1916).

Lodge, Thomas, trans., *The Famous and Memorable Workes of Josephus* [etc.] (London, 1602).

Loxley, James, Anna Groundwater and Julie Sanders, eds, *Ben Jonson's Walk to Scotland: An Annotated Edition of the 'Foot Voyage'* (Cambridge, 2015).

MacDonald, Alasdair A., ed., *The Gude and Godlie Ballatis*, STS (Edinburgh, 2015).

MacDonald, Alasdair A., *George Lauder (1603–1670): Life and Writings* (Cambridge, 2018).

MacDonald, Robert H., ed., *William Drummond of Hawthornden, Poems and Prose* (Edinburgh, 1976).

Meikle, Henry, James Craigie and John Purves, eds, *The Works of William Fowler*, STS, 3 vols. (Edinburgh and London, 1914–40).

The Muses' Welcome [etc.] (Edinburgh, 1618).

Nostodia in serenissimi, potentissimi, et invictissimi monarchae, Jacobi [etc.] (Edinburgh, 1617).

Parkinson, David J., ed., *Alexander Montgomerie, Poems*, STS, 2 vols. (Edinburgh, 2000).

Proctor, F. and C. Wordsworth, eds, *Breviarium ad usum insignis ecclesiae Sarum*, 3 vols. (Cambridge, 1882–89).

Reid, Steven J. and David McOmish, eds, *Corona Borealis: Scottish Neo-Latin Poets on King James VI and his Reign: 1566–1603* (Glasgow, 2020).

Reid-Baxter, Jamie, ed., *Poems of Elizabeth Melville, Lady Culross* (Edinburgh, 2010).

Scott, Hew, ed., *Fasti Ecclesiæ Scoticanæ*, 11 vols. (Edinburgh, 1915–).

Tough, William, ed., *The Works of Sir William Mure of Rowallan*, STS, 2 vols. (Edinburgh and London, 1898).

Secondary Sources

Aldis, Harry G., *A List of Books printed in Scotland before 1700*, 2nd edition (Edinburgh, 1970); now updated online by NLS.

Allan, David, *Philosophy and Politics in Later Stuart Scotland: Neo-Stoicism, Culture and Ideology in an Age of Crisis, c. 1540–1690* (East Linton, 2000).

Atkin, Tamara and Jaclyn Rajsic, eds, *Manuscript and Print in Late Medieval and Early Modern Britain: Essays in Honour of Professor Julia Boffey* (Cambridge, 2019).

Barroll, J. Leeds, *Anna of Denmark, Queen of England: A cultural biography* (Philadelphia, 2001).

Bawcutt, Priscilla, 'The Commonplace Book of John Maxwell', in Gardner-Medwin and Williams, eds, 1990: 59–68.

Bawcutt, Priscilla, *Dunbar the Makar* (Oxford, 1992).

Bawcutt, Priscilla, 'James VI's Castalian Band: A Modern Myth', *SHR* 80 (2001), 251–59.

Bawcutt, Priscilla, 'Scottish Manuscript Miscellanies from the Fifteenth to the Seventeenth Century', *English Manuscript Studies* 12 (2005), 46–73.

Bawcutt, Priscilla, 'Gavin Douglas's *Eneados*: The 1553 Edition and its early Owners and Readers', in Atkin and Rajsic, eds, 2019: 73–85.

Bell, S., 'Simion Grahame', *ODNB*.

Borthwick, Alan R., 'Hamilton family', *ODNB*.

Bosworth, Clifford Edmond, *An Intrepid Scot: William Lithgow of Lanark's Travels in the Ottoman Lands, North Africa and Central Europe, 1609–21* (Aldershot, 2006).

Brammall, Sheldon, *The English Aeneid: translations of Virgil, 1555–1646* (Edinburgh, 2015).

Brown, Ian, Thomas Clancy, Susan Manning and Murray Pittock, eds, *The Edinburgh History of Scottish Literature, vol. 1: From Columba to the Union* (Edinburgh, 2007).

Burgess, Glenn, Rowland Wymer and Jason Lawrence, eds, *The Accession of James I: Historical and Cultural Consequences* (Basingstoke, 2006).

Cockburn, Sir Robert and Harry A. Cockburn, *The Records of the Cockburn Family* (London and Edinburgh, 1913).

Crawford, Robert, *Scotland's Books* (London, 2007).

Dickson, Robert and John Ph. Edmond, *Annals of Scottish Printing* (Cambridge, 1890).

Dorleijn, Gillis J. and Herman L. J. Vanstiphout, eds, *Cultural Repertoires: Structure, Function and Dynamics* (Leuven, 2003).

Duffin, Ross W., ed., *Shakespeare's Songbook* (New York, 2004).

Dunnigan, Sarah, *Eros and Poetry at the Courts of Mary Queen of Scots and James VI* (Basingstoke, 2002).

Dunnigan, S. M., 'Sir David Murray of Gorthy', *ODNB*.

Dunnigan, S. M., 'Elizabeth Melville, Lady Culross', *ODNB*.

Fleming, Morna, 'The Translation of James VI to the Throne of England in 1603', in van Heijnsbergen and Royan, eds, 2002: 90–110.

Gardner-Medwin, Alisoun and Janet Hadley Williams, eds, *A Day Estivall: Essays … in honour of Helena Mennie Shire* (Aberdeen, 1990).

Garrett, Martin, 'William Lithgow', *ODNB*.

Graham, Michael F., *The Uses of Reform: 'Godly Discipline' and Popular Behavior in Scotland and Beyond, 1560–1610* (Leiden, 1996).

Greig, Elaine Finnie, 'Hamilton, James, first earl of Arran', *ODNB*.

Green, Roger P. H., 'The King Returns: *The Muses' Welcome* (1618)', in Reid and McOmish, eds, 2017: 126–62.

Gullans, Charles B., 'New Poems by Sir Robert Ayton', *MLR* 55 (1960), 161–68.

van Heijnsbergen, Theo, 'The Interaction between Literature and History in Queen Mary's Edinburgh: the Bannatyne Manuscript and its Prosopographical Context', in MacDonald et al., eds, 1994: 183–225.

van Heijnsbergen, Theo, 'William Lithgow's "Fierce Castalian Veine": Travel Writing and the Re-location of Identity', in McGinley and Royan, eds, 2010: 223–40.

van Heijnsbergen, Theo, 'Coteries, Commendatory Verse and Jacobean Poetics: William Fowler's *Triumphs of Petrarke* and its Castalian Circles', in Parkinson, ed., 2013: 45–63.

van Heijnsbergen, Theo and Nicola Royan, eds, *Literature, Letters and the Canonical in Early Modern Scotland* (East Linton, 2002).

Henderson, T. F., *Scottish Vernacular Literature: A Succinct History* (Edinburgh, 1898).

Houwen, L. A. J. R., A. A. MacDonald and S. L. Mapstone, eds, *A Palace in the Wild* (Leuven, 2000).

Hume Brown, P., *Early Travellers in Scotland* (Edinburgh, 1891).

Jack, R. D. S., 'The Poetry of Alexander Craig: A study in imitation and originality', *Forum for Modern Language Studies* 5 (1969), 377–84.

Jack, R. D. S., ed., *The History of Scottish Literature. Volume I: Origins to 1660* (Aberdeen, 1988).

Jack, R. D. S., 'Poetry under King James VI', in Jack, ed., 1988: 125–39.

Jack, R. D. S., *The Italian Influence on Scottish Literature* (Edinburgh, 1972).

Kerr-Peterson, Miles, *A Protestant Lord in James VI's Scotland* (Woodbridge, 2019).

Kerrigan, John, *Archipelagic English: Literature, History and Politics 1603–1707* (Oxford, 2008).

Kewes, Paulina and Andrew McRae, eds, *Stuart Succession Literature: Moments and Transformations* (Oxford, 2019).

Lewalski, Barbara K., 'Lucy Countess of Bedford: Images of a Jacobean Courtier and Patroness', in Sharpe and Zwicker, eds, 1987: 52–77.

Lyall, Roderick J., *Alexander Montgomerie: Poetry, Politics and Cultural Change in Jacobean Scotland* (Tempe, AZ, 2005).

Lyall, Roderick J., 'London or the World? The Paradox of Culture in (post-) Jacobean Scotland', in Burgess et al., eds, 2006: 88–100.

Lynch, Michael, *Edinburgh and the Reformation* (Edinburgh, 1981).

MacDonald, Alasdair A., 'The Sense of Place in early Scottish Verse', *ES* 72 (1991), 12–27.

MacDonald, Alasdair A., 'The Cultural Repertory of Middle Scots Lyric Verse', in Dorleijn and Vanstiphout, eds, 2003: 59–86.

MacDonald, Alasdair A., 'Allegorical (Dream-) Vision Poetry in Medieval and Early Modern Scotland', in Suntrup and Veenstra, eds, 2009a: 167–76.

MacDonald, Alasdair A., 'Florentius Volusenus and Tranquillity of Mind: Some Applications of an Ancient Ideal', in MacDonald et al., eds, 2009b: 119–38.

MacDonald, Alasdair A., 'Poetry, Propaganda and Political Culture: *The Whole Prophesie of Scotland* (1603)', in Parkinson, ed., 2013: 209–31.

MacDonald, Alasdair A., 'The Scottish Renaissance: A rough beast slouching to be born?', *European Journal of English Studies* 18 (2014), 11–20.

MacDonald, Alasdair A, Michael Lynch and Ian B. Cowan, eds, *The Renaissance in Scotland* (Leiden, 1994).

MacDonald, Alasdair A. and Kees Dekker, eds, *Rhetoric, Royalty, and Reality: Essays on the Literary Culture of Medieval and Early Modern Scotland* (Leuven, 2005).

MacDonald, A. A., Zweder von Martels and Jan R. Veenstra, eds, *Christian Humanism: Essays in Honour of Arjo Vanderjagt* (Leiden, 2009).

MacDonald, Robert H., *The Library of William Drummond of Hawthornden* (Edinburgh, 1971).

MacLeod, Catharine, R. Malcolm Smuts, Timothy Wilks and Rab MacGibbon, *The Lost Prince: The Life and Death of Henry Stuart* (London, 2012).

Mason, Roger A., ed., *Scots and Britons: Scottish political thought and the union of 1603* (Cambridge, 1994).

Masson, David, *Drummond of Hawthornden: The Story of his Life and Writings* (Edinburgh, 1873).

May, Stephen W., *Sir Walter Ralegh* (Boston, 1989).

McCabe, Richard A., 'Panegyric and its Discontents', in Kewes and McRae, eds, 2019: 19–36.

McCrie, Thomas, *Life of Andrew Melville* (Edinburgh and London, 1856).

McGinley, Kevin J. and Nicola Royan, eds, *The Apparrelling of Truth: Literature and Literary Culture in the Reign of James VI.* (Newcastle, 2010).

McGrail, T. H., *William Alexander, first earl of Stirling* (Edinburgh, 1940).

Merriman, Magnus, 'Hamilton, James, second earl of Arran', *ODNB*.

Morét, Ulrike, 'An Early Scottish National Biography: Thomas Dempster's *Historia ecclesiastica gentis Scotorum*', in Houwen et al., eds, 2000: 249–69.

Munro, Gordon, et al., eds, *Notis musycall: Essays on Music and Scottish Culture in Honour of Kenneth Elliott* (Glasgow, 2005).

Parkinson, David J., ed., *James VI and I, Literature and Scotland: Tides of Change, 1567–1625* (Leuven, 2013).

Patterson, W. B., *King James VI and I and the Reunion of Christendom* (Cambridge, 1997).

Patrick, Millar, *Four Centuries of Scottish Psalmody* (London, 1949).

Petrina, Alessandra and Ian Johnson, eds, *The Impact of Latin Culture on Medieval and Early Modern Scottish Writing* (Kalamazoo, 2018).

Quitslund, Beth, *The Reformation in Rhyme: Sternhold, Hopkins and the English Metrical Psalter, 1547–1603* (Aldershot, 2008).

Reid, David, 'Alexander, William, first earl of Stirling', *ODNB*.

Reid, David, 'Patrick Hannay', *ODNB*.

Reid, Steven J., '"Quasi Sibyllae folia dispersa": The anatomy of the *Delitiae Poetarum Scotorum* (1637)', in Williams and McClure, eds, 2013: 395–412.

Reid, Steven J., 'A Latin Renaissance in Reformation Scotland? Print Trends in Scottish Latin Literature, c. 1480–1700', *SHR* 95 (2016), 1–29.

Reid, Steven J. and David McOmish, eds, *Neo-Latin Literature and Literary Culture in Early Modern Scotland* (Leiden, 2017).

Reid-Baxter, Jamie, '*The Nyne Muses*, An Unknown Renaissance Sonnet Sequence: John Dykes and the Gowrie Conspiracy', in MacDonald and Dekker, eds, 2005: 197–218.

Reid-Baxter, Jamie, 'The Songs of Lady Culross', in Gordon Munro et al., eds, 2005: 143–63.

Reid-Baxter, Jamie, 'Liminary Verse: the paratextual poetry of Renaissance Scotland', *JEBS* 3 (2008), 70–94.

Reid-Baxter, Jamie, 'The Apocalyptic Muse of Francis Hamilton of Silvertonhill (c. 1585–1645)', *JNR* 2 (2012) = *Natio Scota* [online].

Reid-Baxter, Jamie, 'Elizabeth Melville, Calvinism and the Lyric Voice', in Parkinson, ed., 2013: 151–72.

Reid-Baxter, Jamie, 'Elizabeth Melville, Lady Culross: New Light from Fife', *IR* 68 (2017), 38–77.

Ross, Sarah C. E., 'Peripatetic Poems: Sites of Production and Routes of Exchange in Elizabeth Melville's Scotland', *Women's Writing* 26 (2019), 53–78.

Royan, Nicola, ed., *Langage Cleir Illumynate: Scottish Poetry from Barbour to Drummond, 1375–1630* (Amsterdam, 2007).

Saunders, J. W., 'The Stigma of Print: A Note on the Social Bases of Tudor Poetry', *Essays in Criticism* 1 (1951), 139–64.

Sharpe, Kevin and Steven N. Zwicker, eds, *Politics of Discourse* (Berkeley and Los Angeles, 1987).

Shire, Helena Mennie, *Song, Dance and Poetry of the Court of Scotland under King James VI* (Cambridge, 1969).

Shire, Helena Mennie, 'A Scots Poet of 1618 Rediscovered? R. Allane', *SLJ* 1/2 (1974), 5–14.

Smith, Jeremy J., *Older Scots: A Linguistic Reader*, STS (Edinburgh, 2012).

Speirs, John, *The Scots Literary Tradition* (London, 1962).

Spiller, Michael, 'Poetry after the Union 1603–1660', in Jack, ed., 1988: 141–62.

Spiller, Michael, *The development of the Sonnet: an Introduction* (London, 1992).

Spiller, Michael, 'Craig [Craige], Alexander, of Rosecraig', *ODNB*.

Spiller, Michael, '"Quintessencing in the Finest Substance": the Sonnets of William Drummond', in Royan, ed., 2007: 193–205.

Spiller, Michael, 'Found in the forest: the missing leaves of Alexander Craig's *The Pilgrime and Heremite*', in Williams and McClure, eds, 2013: 379–94.

Stevenson, Jane, 'Adulation and Admonition in *The Muses' Welcome*', in Parkinson, ed., 2013: 267–81.

Stevenson, David, 'Gordon, Patrick, of Ruthven', *ODNB*.

Suntrup, Rudolf and Jan R. Veenstra, eds, *Himmel auf Erden / Heaven on Earth* (Frankfurt am Main, 2009).

Verweij, Sebastiaan, 'Ten Sonnets from Scotland: Text, Context and Coterie Writing in Cambridge University Library, MS Kk.5.30', *English Manuscript Studies 1100–1700* 16 (2011), 141–69.

Verweij, Sebastiaan, 'Poulter's Measure: Sir Edward Dyer and the Dier in Jacobean Scotland', in Parkinson, ed., 2013: 299–321.

Verweij, Sebastiaan, *The Literary Culture of Early Modern Scotland* (Oxford, 2016).

Williams, Janet Hadley and J. Derrick McClure, eds, *Fresche Fontanis: Studies in the Culture of Medieval and Early Modern Scotland* (Newcastle, 2013).

Wittig, Kurt, *The Scottish Tradition in Literature* (Edinburgh, 1958).

Wormald, Jenny, 'The union of 1603', in Mason, ed., 1994: 17–40.

INDEX OF FIRST LINES

(NB: Extracted passages are marked with *.)

THE ASSOCIATION FOR SCOTTISH LITERATURE
ANNUAL VOLUMES

Volumes marked * are, at the time of publication, still available.

2012*   *A Song of Glasgow Town: The Collected Poems of Marion Bernstein*,
         eds Edward H. Cohen, Anne R. Fertig and Linda Fleming
2013*   *From the Line: Scottish War Poems 1914–1945*, eds David Goldie and Roderick Watson
2014*   David Pae, *Mary Paterson, or, The Fatal Error*, ed. Caroline McCracken-Flesher
2015*   *Poets of the People's Journal: Newspaper Poetry in Victorian Scotland*, ed. Kirstie Blair
2016*   *A Kist o Skinklan Things: an anthology of Scots poetry from the first and second waves
         of the Scottish renaissance*, ed. J. Derrick McClure
2017*   Susan Ferrier, *Marriage: A Novel*, ed. Dorothy McMillan
2018*   *Edwin Morgan: In Touch With Language*, eds John Coyle and James McGonigal
2019*   *Corona Borealis: Scottish Neo-Latin Poets on King James VI and his Reign, 1566–1603*,
         eds Steven J. Reid and David McOmish
2020*   *Dràma na Gàidhlig: Ceud Bliadhna air an Àrd-ùrlar (A Century of Gaelic Drama)*,
         ed. Michelle Macleod
2021*   *Jacobean Parnassus: Scottish Poetry from the Reign of James I*,
         ed. Alasdair A. MacDonald